MAJOR TRENDS IN MEXICAN PHILOSOPHY

MAJOR TRENDS IN

MEXICAN PHILOSOPHY

Mario de la Cueva

Miguel León-Portilla

Edmundo O'Gorman

José M. Gallagos Rocafull

Rafael Moreno

Luis Villoro

Leopoldo Zea

Fernando Salmerón

Translated by

A. Robert Caponigri

Mexico (City) Universidad Nacional,

NOTRE DAME & LONDON
UNIVERSITY OF NOTRE DAME PRESS

Grateful acknowledgment is made to the Latin American Translation Program of the Association of American University Presses for having provided the means for translation and preparation of the manuscript for this book.

PREFACE

Thinkers of all the peoples and nations of our planet gathered in September 1963 in Mexico City to engage in dialogue on the problems of philosophy. The Organizing Committee of the Thirteenth International Congress of Philosophy selected two themes: Man and The Criticism of Our Own Times. The first is the perennial question of philosophy, which was born with man himself and which will only die with him. The second is identical with the theme of man, analyzed with relation to the circumstances of the century in which we live: a stormy time with which destiny visits us, a sign of the alienation of man, who no longer finds himself in the world which past generations have bequeathed to us; an artificial society in which man lives alienated, a stranger to himself, bent under the weight of economic necessity and state power. A certain portion of the responsibility for this condition belongs to positivism, a conception of the world which pretended to separate men from the fundamental theme of their origin, essence, and destiny, bidding them trust in science, nature, and techniques.

Fortunately for the history of culture, "l'homme revolté" of the twentieth century has returned to philosophy; we find ourselves before a new awakening of the spirit, another "illumination" to forge a new world for the new generations.

The Thirteenth International Congress of Philosophy, which will address the themes of man and whose task will be to mark out the new paths of thought, takes on a singular stature because it is the first time that an event of universal importance in the world of philosophy will be celebrated in a Latin American country, and precisely in one of the countries of the New World which knew how to make history in the lands of Anáhuac and Yucatan and to construct a culture; Mexico can offer its illustrious guests not the ruins and the remains of an extinguished civilization, but the most ancient monuments and manuscripts of the American continent, integrating elements of the unchangeable foundations on which the particular philosophy of the Mexican is built. The visiting philosophers will also find themselves surrounded by the flood of the Spanish Golden Age, the second, equally unchangeable base, of our special style of life, of which Golden Age this National University, now in its fourth century, and the colleges which preceded it, Tlaltelolco and Tiripitio, are manifestations. The two cultures, that of this continent, which had not yet been baptized, and the Spanish, have become fused into a synthesis, which is the soul and the life of Mexican man.

The Consejo Técnico de Humanidades asked some of the more illustrious teachers and friends of the Casa de Estudios to prepare historical studies about our philosophy, as an offering of sympathy and of the highest and most disinterested love of knowledge. This Consejo brought together the schools and institutes which are devoted to the cultivation of the great manifestations and expressions of the spirit: social life, history, art, justice, and philosophy. Its invitation was inspired by the great interest attaching to the event. Those invited were Miguel León-Portilla, Edmundo O'Gorman, José M. Gallegos Rocafull—whose last essay, written a few days before his death, is published here—Rafael Moreno, Luis Villoro, Leopoldo Zea, and Fernando Salmerón.

The essays brought together in the present volume are all concerned with the history of philosophy in Mexico. They comprise seven essays that review some of the principal movements of the spirit, those upon which Mexican philosophical thought is founded. They do not, however, form a history, or, even less, a complete history. To achieve a complete history, it would have been necessary to indicate all currents, even those of lesser importance, as well as to pass judgment on all the philosophical writers. Lacking are studies of some movements which possess singular interest, both in themselves and in relation to the period of Spanish domination, e.g., the thought of Gamarra and of the scientific thinkers of the eighteenth century, such as Alzate and Bartolache. However, the reader will find herein indications that will make it possible for him to follow the progress of their ideas on his own. The already classical work of Samuel Ramos, *Historia de la filosofía en México* (The History of Philosophy in Mexico), though it has been superseded by the many special studies of the last twenty years, remains a valuable source to be consulted. An essay on the thought of liberalism, which assumed very special characteristics in Mexico, characteristics which had a determining effect on the political history of the nation during half of the past century, will also be missed. However, the equally classical work of Jesús Reyes Heroles, *El liberalismo mexicano* (Mexican Liberalism), may be consulted to fill this gap. With these limitations, the volume may be said to offer a true image of what ought, with justice, to be called Mexican philosophy.

The first of these essays, from the pen of Dr. Miguel León-Portilla, studies pre-Hispanic philosophy, offering some idea of the mind of the Indian who once inhabited the valleys where this very Congress was celebrated. The article by Edmundo O'Gorman sets in relief the idea of America in the years following the conquest, as well as the correct formulation and solution of the questions concerning the reality, meaning, and history of the New World. José M. Gallegos Rocafull and Rafael Moreno review the thought of the sixteenth, seventeenth, and eighteenth centuries, so closely bound to Catholic doctrine and to Spanish thought, though given new life, especially in the eighteenth century, by the awakening self-consciousness of the New World.

Luis Villoro makes a contribution to the definition of the characteristics of the generation of Independence, pointing out its inquietudes and aspirations. Leopoldo Zea describes the positivist philosophy, which in Gabino Barreda and in his contemporaries and disciples took on an original aspect, becoming the official doctrine of the triumphant bourgeoisie.

The volume closes with the exposition of the ideas of the Mexican philosophers of the twentieth century, presented by the Rector of the University of Veracruz, Fernando Salmerón, with genuine affection.

The Consejo Técnica de Humanidades expresses its gratitude to the persons who have made the publication of this volume possible.

Mario de la Cueva
Coordinator of the Humanities

CONTENTS

        TWENTIETH CENTURY   246
        Fernando Salmerón

        NOTES   289

        BIBLIOGRAPHY   319

        INDEX   325

MAJOR TRENDS IN MEXICAN PHILOSOPHY

Miguel León-Portilla

to Dr. Justino Fernández,
philosopher of pre-Hispanic art

I. PRE-HISPANIC THOUGHT

Introduction

The thought of the ancient Mexicans, their particular vision of the world and of man, can be learned through the symbolism of their art and, more directly, in the content of inscriptions, codices, and texts of pre-Hispanic origin. As a matter of fact, this has become possible thanks to the discovery and study, undertaken in a humanistic spirit during the last decades, of the rich literary heritage of what is called Nahuatl culture, which flourished at least from the time of the Toltecs (ninth century after Christ) to the final splendor of the Aztecs. Of this ancient culture of the high central plateau of Mexico there are preserved—even more than in the case of the Mayas—numerous texts in the indigenous idiom, the expression of ancient forms of thought.

It will not be out of place to recall that when this Nahuatl literature began to be studied and translated into the European languages, there were not lacking persons who called into question its origin and authenticity. Now the numerous works of Dr. Ángel Ma. Garibay K., based on the most rigorous documentary

3

and historical criticism, have forever dissipated all of these doubts.[1]

The study and translation of many of these documents have placed in evidence the diversity of themes treated in them; there are chronicles, myths, and legends; sacred hymns, canticles, and poems; laws and ritual ordinances; discourses and dialogues of the ancient sages as well as expositions of their religious doctrines, of their doubts and problems, and of what may be called their particular vision of the world.

We ourselves have been especially interested in the study of the texts which discuss this last point: the Nahuatl vision of the world. Among them are the accounts of myths of the ancient ages of the world, or "suns," which have existed; the doctrines concerning the courses, directions, or paths of the universe; the "cemanáhuac," that is, the earth surrounded or encircled by the immense waters with the thirteen heavens or superior crossbeams and the nine lower levels with the paths of the subterranean world which lead to the region of the dead. Of equal interest are those texts which contain the most elaborate doctrines about the "Ometéotl"—the supreme god of the duality, which is also "Tloque Nahuaque," lord of the enclosure and the union—as well as the more personal ideas of the ancient pre-Hispanic teachers, those called "tlamatinime," "those who know something," who speak of man as the possible "lord of a face and of a heart" and of his existence on earth as "perhaps as a dream." There are also texts concerning the various meanings of "flower and song," the discovery of the symbol which might lead to the utterance of "words with root" and to teaching what lacks life to lie: the stone and the clay in order to transform them into the image of what the heart itself has perceived.

Having studied and translated some of these texts, we have been able to find in them the forms and structure proper to the ancient pre-Hispanic vision of the world and of man. The trajectory of Nahuatl thought appears in them, already elaborating on the ancient myths and transforming them into religious doctrines, beginning especially with the lucubrations attributed to the priest and wise man, Quetzalcóatl. Later texts reflect in their turn new forms of the evolution of this religious thought beginning with the fourteenth century in the Aztec world and in the world of the neighboring states which had the same language and culture. Finally and, as it would seem, as a continuation of this initial process of rationalization, we encounter in the ancient documents the appearance of certain doubts and problems concerning the commonly accepted religious doctrines. Thinking in terms of their own categories, such as "flower and song," "face and heart," "dream and root," the "suitable," "the right" and many others, the tlamatinime appear, "those who know something," who try to reach different conceptions which might give meaning to their existence in a world constantly menaced by forces which could put an end to the present age, the actual "sun of movement." We also encounter words spoken by men like Nezahualcóyotl, tormented because he sees that everything in the world itself is like the plumage of a bird that rends itself, conscious of change and death, and of the necessity of speaking words with root about Tloque Nahuaque, the lord of the enclosure and the union. And we equally find the expression of the thought, at times antagonistic, of other tlamatinime who came to exercise great and powerful influence upon the life and ideals of the Aztec world. On more than one occasion the Nahuan wise men appear gathered together to discuss their different points of view, as in the case of the celebrated "dialogue of flower and song" which took place at the end of the fifteenth century in the house of Lord Tecayehuatzin, prince of Huexotzinco.

The discovery of this rich mine of documentation—all of pre-Hispanic origin, as will be shown when we come to treat of sources—has made it possible for us to affirm in earlier publications the existence not only of an ancient Nahuatl vision of the world and of elaborated religious doctrines but also of a special form of pre-Hispanic philosophy as well.[2]

This earlier affirmation—that is, the application of the concept of philosophy, of Greek-Western origin, to this more elaborated form of pre-Hispanic thought—has aroused criticisms and objec-

tions. These have been directed not only toward the authenticity
of the texts but also toward the legitimacy of applying the concept of philosophy to their content and even more toward the very
possibility of finding an adequate method for comprehending
historically the forms peculiar to ancient Nahuatl thought.[3]

We have tried to reply in a direct manner to the objections
and criticisms mentioned above. Concretely, we shall try to show
why we call "philosophy" certain determined forms of Nahuatl
thought and in what sense we think it possible to learn historically
the modes and categories proper, and sometimes exclusive, to it.
As it seems to us, to show this implies an answer to a problem
which has ever-wider implications. This problem is very closely
related to the theme of historical and anthropological knowledge.

I
APPLICATION OF THE CONCEPT OF "PHILOSOPHY"
AND THE POSSIBILITY OF DETERMINING THE
INTRINSIC CHARACTER OF NAHUATL THOUGHT

There exist in Western thought concepts which, like that of
"philosophy," have at various times been employed to describe
cultural phenomena of other peoples who have lived at different
times and in different places. Among such concepts are those of
art, law, religion, literature, history, etc. These concepts originally
possess a specific content. They refer, as is obvious, to that which
in the Western world is held to be art, law, religion, literature, etc.

From the time of Herodotus in the Greek world, Marco Polo
in the Middle Ages, and the relations and chronicles of the
Spanish and Portuguese navigators and "conquistadores," we find
the application of concepts like art and religion to the cultural
creations and institutions of entirely different peoples and civilizations. Even later, the founders of modern ethnology, among whom
are to be numbered such figures as Fray Bernardino de Sahagún
in the sixteenth century, used these key concepts in the effort to
understand different cultures. In their works, and even more in
those of modern anthropologists, we will find the concepts of

society, law, justice and right, religion, art, literature, economy, and so on, as points of reference for approaching the institutions proper to other cultures.

In the new context these key concepts seem to have extended beyond their original connotation, acquiring a new sense of universal comprehension or applicability. At the present time, to cite but a single example, one speaks of Chinese or of Hindustani art, of the art of the peoples of Africa or of the art of pre-Columbian America. Such universalization of the connotation of such fundamental ideas is a clear index that Western culture, itself under the influence of numerous contacts and relations, is in process of transforming itself into universal culture.

As a matter of fact, the culture of the West has been the only one which has entered into contact with other human cultures. It is also the only one which, in trying to understand those other cultures, has invented sciences such as anthropology and ethnology with all their subordinate branches. These sciences would find it difficult to exist if they had not expanded the capacity of connotation of their own concepts and fundamental categories which before had been restricted and applied solely to the cultural institutions of the West.

Nevertheless, this process of universalization has in its turn engendered new problems, epistemological in character. From the first, those who enter into contact with other cultures frequently describe in a confused manner the institutions and facts proper to other cultures by making use of clearly inadequate concepts. To give an example, the concept "empire" is applied to what was, perhaps, a conglomeration of confederation of tribes. In a word, there takes place a spontaneous projection, more or less ingenuous, of one's own ideas to explain foreign realities, whose peculiar physiognomy one is not successful in understanding.

As a remedy for this first kind of ingenuity, different scientific attitudes have arisen, sometimes "scientistic" rather than scientific. To arrive at what might be considered undeniable facts, to describe them, measure and classify them, would seem an ideal solution. To this is added a more rigorous historical and philological criticism, with the purpose of reaching and adequately comprehending every cultural phenomenon.

However, this "scientistic" point of view proves to be, many times, equally and even more ingenuous. It would presuppose that in trying to approach an historical fact of another culture, it would be possible to prescind from one's own proper and inalienable mentality, rooted, as is obvious, in the models of Western thought, according to which it must inevitably contemplate things.

It would seem that every process of understanding historical facts, or a different culture, implies in reality a peculiar form of internal dialectic. On the one hand, there is the effort to make contact, which involves prescinding from what is properly one's own. On the other hand, however, this very effort to understand would not be able to be effective if he who investigates could really prescind from the categories and attitudes of his own cultural context. Inevitably, his own mentality, with its own categories, must be present and active if anything is to be understood. In a way similar to the relativism inherent in nuclear physics, and in the world of history and anthropology too, the observer necessarily modifies and alters, in order to understand, the historical fact or the other culture whose image he hopes to reach.

No matter how great may be the knowledge of the sources and the documents, this modification and alteration inevitably gives rise to a special kind of knowledge in the historical and anthropological field. When the investigator enters into contact with what we call historical or anthropological entities, there arises a process of knowledge directed to making those entities comprehensible to him in order to give them a determinate meaning. Inevitably, too, the process begins by projecting concept and mental categories which the observer already possesses in his own intellectual equipment.

It frequently happens, however, that the historical or anthropological entity seems to reject the application of ideas taken indiscriminately from the equipment of the investigator. These ideas are ineffective for the constructing of an adequate mental image that might be able to give meaning to that which has been rendered present. The cognitive process which seeks the image or the historical being of these facts takes then a different slant. One goes on to the creation or the "invention" of a new idea which might be capable of explaining and giving a meaning to the facts in question.

There is no question here of postulating a renewed form of the idealist conception, but rather of emphasizing, by making it our own, a fundamental idea of Edmundo O'Gorman, about what seems to constitute the specific root of historical and anthropological knowledge.[4] The effort is to make precise the function of thought which gives a meaning to these facts or ideas historically distant or, if one wishes, give them an "essence" which makes them comprehensible to the investigator in a different historical context.

It is precisely this concept of invention in the field of historical and anthropological knowledge which permits us to answer the question. In what sense is it possible to speak of a pre-Hispanic philosophy and how may the understanding of its specific categories and modulations be carried out?

We have already insisted on the existence of manuscripts and historical sources in which are expressed the myths and religious doctrines and in which there appears the slow process of rationalization which led the tlamatinime to doubt and to devise new forms of thought. We have approached this historical phenomenon, studying the codices and texts and preparing the most faithful translation of them in our power. To try to understand them in their proper context, we have studied pre-Hispanic culture, within which the doubts arose and the problems took root. Our express purpose was to find the categories proper to this peculiar form of thought. However, it is necessary to repeat, in all this study, we have not been able to prescind from our own mentality, from our own concepts obviously rooted in Western culture.

As a matter of fact, it was this mentality and these concepts which moved us to undertake the study of these forms of an alien thought. However, precisely that which moved us to study them prevented us from describing fully what must have been in themselves the preoccupations and attitudes of peoples separated in time and culture. In order to describe, with an ostensibly scientific criterion, what this thought was in itself we would have to cease being what we are. There had to begin in us, however, the dialectical process to which we have referred. In order to find in those sources the testimony to a process and an attitude parallel in some degree to that of the Greek philosophers and of the Western world, we apply to the concerns, doubts and problems of the tlamatinime the qualification "philosophy." In this way we proceed exactly like those who used the concept of art, or of philosophy, with regard to phenomena proper to other cultures. Thus, some speak specifically of the philosophy of China or of Hindustani because they find in those cultures realities analogous to those to which the concept "philosophy" is applied in the Western context.

However, once the concept philosophy has been applied to the specific phenomenon of the pre-Hispanic world, the same dialectical process led us, rather than to the description of an unattainable being-in-itself of this thought, to the invention of an historical image of it. The invented image of this thought is necessarily accompanied by an awareness of the specific and inescapable limitations of every form of historical and anthropological knowledge. It supposed, indeed, an approach based on sources and historical criticism to the thought of the tlamatinime. But as this approach was achieved by way of a mentality which could not be the pre-Hispanic mentality, there could not be either the discovery of something uncontaminated or any absolute comprehension of what that pre-Hispanic mentality was. It is only an effort to approximate different categories, to rethink and rediscover them, and to perceive, in a functional relation to them, a content comprehensible to man as he is today.

In this sense we believe that it is possible to speak of a pre-

Hispanic philosophy and, what is more important, to be able to learn to a certain degree its specific and distinctive content.

Our final understanding will thus be the result of historical invention, just as any possible approach to other philosophies must be understood and thought in such different ways, including Greek thought itself, as, for example, has been the "invention" of Aristotle made, among many others, by St. Thomas Aquinas, Franz Brentano, or, more recently, Werner Jaeger.

In presenting in what follows—the sources in the Nahuatl language and the forms of thought we perceive in them—we may understand the fecund richness of pre-Hispanic philosophy from the point of view of historical invention. We will be able to see how many of these ancient texts may be turned into occasions of thought. It ought not to escape us that only those texts which were at one time genuine expressions of intuition or thought can succeed in becoming occasions or evocations of new forms of thought and sensibility. These texts, whatever might be their origin, are "the legacy of the classics" in the world of culture. To understand them it is necessary to reinvent them. The pages which follow are an effort in a very small way to rethink the legacy of pre-Hispanic thought.

II
Sources for the Knowledge of Pre-Hispanic Thought

For the general study of pre-Hispanic thought in Mexico we have at our disposal four categories of sources: (a) archeological discoveries of every kind, including monuments and sculptures, ceramics, pictures and inscriptions preserved in a script which is principally ideographic but also, in part phonetic; [5] (b) the few indigenous codices and manuscripts which escaped destruction during the conquest, as well as a few copies of them made in the sixteenth century; [6] (c) other texts in the native tongue but written in the Latin alphabet close to the time of the conquest; in these texts are contained both the transcriptions of

ancient codices as well as written versions of ancient oral traditions, especially of the commentaries, chronicles, poems, and songs
which were systematically memorized in the pre-Hispanic centers
of education; [7] and (d) the histories and chronicles of the sixteenth century, left principally by Spanish missionaries and also
by certain native historians, sometimes in their own language,
at other times in Castilian.[8]

Such are the principal categories into which the sources for
the study of the ancient cultures of Mexico may be distributed.
We must now indicate more precisely the sources which are
available for the study of pre-Hispanic philosophy. First of all
we will note that the present work voluntarily limits itself to
philosophical thought in the Nahuatl idiom, for which there exists
a more abundant and secure documentation. The Nahuatl language, known also as Aztec or Mexican, was, as will be shown
further on, an adequate medium for the expression of the thought
of a culture which was certainly a thousand years old. The first
flowering of this culture probably dates from Teotihuacanos times
(first to seventh century A.D.); it continues through the Toltec
period (ninth to eleventh centuries A.D.) and, after passing
through other intermediary stages, culminates in the Aztec
splendor which ended with the conquest of Mexico in 1521.

About the most ancient period, that is the Teotihuacan, there
are preserved sculptures, paintings, and calendary inscriptions
in the great ceremonial center,[9] while in the texts as well are to
be found myths and traditions which are more or less legendary.
From this period would seem to date the deepest roots of the
later Nahuatl religious vision of the world. This vision bears a
considerable similarity to the religious thought of the Mayans,
due probably to the fact that the two cultures had received a
common legacy from an older civilization, earlier even than the
Christian era.

The historical testimonies about the Toltec epoch are much
more abundant. They enable us to get much closer to its institutions and forms of life. Due to this fact it is possible to get an
insight into the theological conception of the priest and sage

Quetzalcóatl, who had so much influence on the following periods. About him and his religious ideas there exist various texts in the Nahuatl tongue. These are transcriptions of ancient codices and manuscripts as well as traditions systematically taught in the pre-Hispanic centers of education. The principal texts are the following:

Toltec-Chichimeca History (transcription of codices, edited in the Nahuatl idiom). The work of unknown authors, it was compiled about 1545. It preserves a number of poems which express the ancient Toltec vision of the godhead and the world.[10]

The *Annals of Cuauhtitlán* (part of the *Codex Chimalpopoca*) constitute another compilation of texts in the Nahuatl language, a transcription of the content of pre-Hispanic manuscripts. The collection was made by native historians of the sixteenth century, disciples of Sahagún. It contains, among other things, sections of capital importance for the study of the religious thought of Quetzalcóatl and for that of the Toltec period.[11]

Finally, there are the *Codices Matritenses* of the National Palace and of the Academy of History, as well as the *Florentine Codex* of the Biblioteca Laurentiana. These contain the compendium of the texts of the native reporter of Fray Bernardino de Sahagún. Taken together they comprise about a thousand folios in the Nahuatl idiom with information about the principal cultural institutions of the pre-Hispanic Nahuatl world. They contain transcriptions of ancient manuscripts and of oral traditions systematically preserved in the centers of education. Entire sections refer especially to the religious vision of the Toltecs.[12]

These are the principal, first-hand native sources for the knowledge of the theological and mythological thought of Quetzalcóatl and of the Toltec period in general. Their interest lies in the fact that pre-Hispanic philosophical thought arose precisely within this tradition and cultural context.

The special forms of what we have called pre-Hispanic philosophy are expressed and preserved principally in the texts proceeding from the Aztec world and from the other neighboring states which had the same language and culture. In speaking of

the tlamatinime, "those who know something," these sources
transcribe their elaborations of problems, their doubts, and their
particular doctrines. Here are to be found the specific categories
of pre-Hispanic philosophical thought as well as the peculiar
ideas and conceptions of certain tlamatinime. Among the latter
are Nezahualcóyotl (1402–1472), poet and philosopher, lord of
Tezcoco, who was preoccupied constantly with the problems of
becoming, time, and the divinity; Tlacaélel (1398–1476?), statesman extraordinary, counselor to a number of Aztec governors,
and fashioner of a new vision of the world; Tecayehuatzin, lord
of Huexotzinco about 1501, interested in finding the form of
saying true words on earth; and, finally, Ayocuan Cuetzpaltzin
(about 1395–1441), who found in pleasure and art the only
palliative that might make him forget the fleetingness of life
and the constant threat of death.

The thought of these and other tlamatinime can be studied in
three sources which are absolutely firsthand. All of the following
are of native origin, transcriptions of ancient ideographic and
partially phonetic manuscripts or a reduction to writing of traditions systematically preserved.

There is the so-called *Collection of Mexican Song,* texts collected by the native disciples of Sagahún. The original manuscript
is preserved in the National Library of Mexico. Even now there
exist only partial translations of it.[13]

There are manuscripts known as *Romances de los señores de
la Nueva España,* also in Nahuatl, with texts summarized or
abridged by the Tezcocan Juan Bautista Pomar in the sixteenth
century. It is at present preserved in the Latin-American Collection of the library of the University of Texas.[14]

Finally, there are also the various "huehuetlatolli," or "discourses of the ancients," all of them collected after the beginning
of the sixteenth century, a very important source for the study
of the moral and philosophical thought of the ancient Mexicans.
In many of these huehuetlatolli there are also to be found many
ideas clearly of Toltec origin.[15]

In addition to these sources there may also be mentioned as secondary sources other works by native writers of the sixteenth century and also of chroniclers and historians, missionaries for the most part. A selection of these is given in the bibliography at the end of the present chapter.

We will only add that in bringing to completion this study of the ancient pre-Hispanic philosophy found in the Nahuatl tongue, we have submitted these sources, and others which are not mentioned here, to an historical and philological examination, the most rigorous in our power. Precisely because these texts offered the possibility of reaching different forms of thought, every caution seemed insufficient. From the point of view of the theory of historical and anthropological "invention" we have tried to rethink and make our own the meaning and the profoundly human message of the tlamatinime, the philosophers of ancient Mexico.[16]

III
The Thought of Quetzalcóatl and the Toltec Cosmovision

The tlamatinime of the thirteenth to the sixteenth centuries were aware of their cultural legacy from the ancient Toltec world. In order to understand their thought it is an indispensable condition that one know the idea which they entertained, as the fruit of their own historical invention, of the Toltec vision of the world. Their own view and peculiar forms of thought must be conceived precisely in function of that idea. For them the ancient vision of the world, which gave root and meaning to their life, appeared to be the supreme creation of the sage and priest Quetzalcóatl.

Nahuatl histories and myths speak of Quetzalcóatl (ninth century? A.D.), also known in the texts as *Ce Ácatl Topiltzin*, "he who was born in the day 1—Cana, Our Prince." While still a young man, Quetzalcóatl sought a solitary life in the region of

Tulancingo in order to meditate and study. When he was in his twenties, he was sought out by the people of Tula and asked to become their ruler and guide.[17]

Quetzalcóatl built four great palaces in Tula. From them he began to govern the Toltecs and to teach them the arts which he himself had learned and above all the religious doctrines at which he had arrived in his meditations. His thought, such as we are able to know it, gave a new meaning to a more ancient vision of the world, preserved in the symbolism and in various myths common to different peoples of Central America.

In these myths the world appeared as an immense island divided horizontally into four great quadrants or courses, beyond which existed only the immense waters. These four paths converged at the center, the navel, of the earth, and each of them implied a group of symbols. That which we call the east is the region of light, of fertility, and of life, symbolized by the color white; the north is the black quarter of the universe, where the dead lie buried; in the west is the house of the sun, the land of the color red; finally, the south is the region of sowings, and its color is blue.[18]

Vertically, the universe has a series of levels, or superimposed divisions, above the earth and beneath it. Above are the heavens, which, joining the waters that surround all parts of the world, form a kind of blue vault furrowed by paths, along which move the moon, the stars, the sun, the morning star, and the comets. Come then the heavens of various colors and, finally, the most removed metaphysical region, the realm of the gods. Beneath the earth are to be found the lower levels, the paths which must be traversed by those who die until they reach the deepest level, where lies "Mictlan," the region of the dead.

This world, full of gods and invisible forces, has existed as an intermittent reality at various consecutive times. Through unnumbered and innumerable years the great creator gods have carried on among themselves the great cosmic struggles which are described in the myths. The period of the predominance of each of these gods constituted an age of the world, or a "sol," a sun, as the pre-Hispanic peoples called it. In each case destruction in the form of a cataclysm, and then a new age arose. Four suns have existed and have been brought to an end by the work of the gods, the ages of earth, air, fire, and water. The present epoch is the sun of movement, the fifth of the series, which had its beginning when as yet all was night, thanks to a mysterious sacrifice of the gods, who with their blood had created it and turned it over to be populated.[19]

This was the ancient Toltec vision of the universe. Among the cosmological categories more or less latent in it are the necessity of a universal explanation, the periodification of the world into ages or cycles, the spatialization of the world through dimensions or quadrants, and the concept of struggle as the model for thinking the coming to be of the cosmos. Into this world, where the gods create and destroy, had men been born under the threat of death and of a cataclysm which might put an end to the present age, the present sun of movement.

This image of the world was exactly the object of Quetzalcóatl's reflection and meditation. What in it he could not understand perhaps became a motive which led him to invent a new doctrine about a supreme god and an "earth black and red in color" (Tlilan, Tlapalan), the place of wisdom, beyond death and beyond the destruction of the suns and the worlds.

By rethinking the popular beliefs, Quetzalcóatl was able to express his message. It is stated in a text that Quetzalcóatl in his meditation sought to draw near the mystery of the divinity "moteotía," "he sought a god for himself." Quetzalcóatl found him in the end. He conceived the divinity, recalling perhaps even older traditions, as a being one and dual at the same time, which, conceiving and engendering, had given origin and reality to everything that existed.

The supreme principle is "Ometéotl," god of the duality, the dual god. He is metaphorically conceived with a masculine countenance, "Ometecuhtli," lord of the duality, and with features which are at the same time feminine, "Omecíhuatl," lady of the duality. The divinity is also Tloque Nahuaque, which

means the owner of what is near and what is far, that which
makes its action felt in every quarter. The following text speaks
precisely of this doctrine conceived by Quetzalcóatl. In addition it mentions some of the attributes which the wise priest
believed he had discovered in the supreme dual godhead:

> And it is stated and said that
> Quetzalcóatl called upon, as his
> proper god, one who dwells in the
> interior of the heaven.
>
> He invoked her, surrounded by a skirt of stars,
> him who gives light to all things;
> Mistress of our flesh, lord of our flesh,
> She who clothes herself in black,
> He who clothes himself in red,
> She who established the earth firmly,
> He who gives activity to the earth.
>
> Thither did he direct his words,
> thus did he know himself,
> toward the place of the duality
> and of the nine crossbeams
> in which the heaven consists.
> And as he knew,
> He called on him who dwelled there,
> directed supplications to him,
> living in meditation and in retirement.[20]

The dual god, Ometéotl—who in the night covers his feminine
aspect with a skirt of stars, while during the day he is the star
which is resplendent and gives light—appears also as the lord
and mistress of our flesh, as he who vests himself in black and
red, the colors which symbolize wisdom, and is, at the same
time, the one who gives stability to the earth and is the origin
of all activity in it. However, this god who dwells in the
place of duality, beyond the nine celestial crossbeams, was also
invoked by the title of "precious twin," which, as Seler and
Garibay among others have shown, is the meaning of the word
"Quetzalcóatl" in addition to "feather of the bird." Probably

the wise man and priest had derived his own name from this title of the supreme deity. The priest thus taught the Toltecs the form of drawing near to Ometéotl-Quetzalcóatl:

> They were solicitous of the things of god,
> they had but one god,
> they held him to be the only god,
> they invoked him,
> they made supplications to him,
> his name was Quetzalcóatl.
>
> The guardian of their god,
> their priest,
> his name was also Quetzalcóatl.
>
> And they were so respectful of the things of god
> that everything which the priest Quetzalcóatl told them
> they did, and did not depart from it.
> He persuaded them, he taught them:
> This only god,
> Quetzalcóatl is his name.
> He demands nothing
> except serpents, except butterflies,
> which you must offer to him
> which you must sacrifice to him.[21]

The Toltec people understood the doctrine of Quetzalcóatl. Under his guidance they were able in this way to relate the idea of the dual god with the ancient image of the world and the destiny of man on earth:

> And the Toltecs knew that the heavens are many;
> they said that there are twelve divisions one upon the other.
> There abides,
> there lives the true god and his partner.
> The heavenly god is called lord of the duality,
> And his partner is called mistress of the duality, heavenly lady.
> Which means:
> he is king, he is lord over the twelve heavens.
> From thence we receive our life,
> we men.

From thence falls our destiny
when he is conceived,
when the child issues from the womb.
From thence comes his being and his destiny,
within him is placed
the commandment of the lord of the duality.[22]

The wise priest insisted that the supreme dual god was the
creator of all that exists and the one responsible for the destinies
of man. It was necessary to approach the divinity, striving to
reach the most elevated principle in it, its wisdom. Sacrifices
and abstinence were only a means to achieve this end. More
important was meditation, directed to the quest of the true
meaning of man and of the world: to become master of the
red and the black, the colors which gave form to the symbols
and the pictures of the codices. Quetzalcóatl knew that in the
orient, in the region of light, beyond the immense waters, there
was precisely the land of the color black and red, Tlilan,
Tlapalan, the region of wisdom. By escaping into the land of
light perhaps the world of the transitory might be overcome,
the world always menaced by death and destruction. Quetzalcóatl and some of the Toltecs would one day depart for that
region of wisdom, to Tlilan, Tlapalan.

However, in order that man might reach the land of light,
he had to imitate the wisdom of the dual god and consecrate
himself on earth to the creation of the "Toltecáyotl," that is,
the complex of the arts and institutions of the Toltecs. To
dedicate oneself to the Toltecáyotl was fundamentally to repeat
in a small way the action which engenders and conceives, that
is, the supreme attribute of the god of the duality, who is also
Tolque Nahuaque, lord of nearness and proximity.

Exactly the image which the later Nahuan wise men will
invent of Quetzalcóatl and of the Toltecáyotl is offered in the
most vivid colors, as though it were an ancient epic poem, by
the recountal of the discoveries and creations of Quetzalcóatl.

The Toltecs were wise men,
the Toltecáyotl, the complex of their arts,
their wisdom,

all proceeded from Quetzalcóatl . . .
the Toltecs were very rich,
they were very happy,
they were never poor or sad. . . .
The Toltecs were very experienced;
it was their custom to converse with their own hearts. . . .
They were expert in the knowledge of the stars;
they imposed names upon them.
They knew their influence;
they knew well the movements of the heaven,
how it moves to and fro. . . .[23]

The marvelous picture of the Toltec world in which every-thing was abundance and artistic creation, thanks to the wisdom of the priest Quetzalcóatl, was not to be confused, nevertheless, with the most elevated ideal of the ancient wise man and hero of culture. The greatness of the Toltecáyotl continued to be, despite all, but a creation in time, in a world menaced by a final destruction. The true ideal was wisdom, which could be reached only by overcoming the present reality, beyond the immense waters which surrounded the world, Tlilan, Tlapalan, the land of the color black and red.

After the great priest had already been transformed into a myth, the Nahuatl historical invention of Quetzalcóatl con-cludes by going on to narrate his escape from Tula, his abandon-ment of the Toltecáyotl, and his final journey to Tlilan, Tlapalan. Quetzalcóatl had to depart, forced by wizards come from afar with the purpose of introducing into Tula the rite of human sacrifices. The priest experienced a moment of weakness. He broke his life of abstinence and chastity. However, repenting immediately, he rose up again to affirm anew the ideas to which he had consecrated his life. Quetzalcóatl then gave himself wholly to his own religious conception, and he decided to make a reality the quest for Tlilan, Tlapalan.

It is said that when Quetzalcóatl lived there,
the wizards many times sought to ensnare him
so that he would offer human sacrifices,
so that he would sacrifice men.

But he never conceded, for he loved his people very much,
his people, who were the Toltecs. . . .

And it is said, it is recounted,
that this vexed the wizards,
so that they began to mock him,
and to scoff at him.
The wizards and the magicians said that
they wanted to afflict Quetzalcóatl
so that he would finally go away,
as indeed it came to pass.

In the year I-Caña Quetzalcóatl died
it is truly recounted
that on dying he went thither,
to the Land of the Color Black and Red.[24]

These are the principal traits of the image which, it would
seem, the tlamatinime formed for themselves about Quetzalcóatl and of the ancient Toltec vision of the world. Summing
up, we may distinguish four fundamental points of this image.

First, the conception of the world, with its quadrants, its
celestial and infernal levels, and its intermittent existence in
the various ages or suns, with the ever-present threat of a
violent end. And the peculiar character of the Toltec vision of
the cosmic cycles ought to be noted, for, different from other
forms of fatalistic thought, it opens the doors to a number of
possibilities. Every age or sun may come to a sudden end; however, it is also possible that it may continue to exist, since in
reality its being depends on the gods, and the will of the gods
remains unknown to men.

Second, the affirmation of a supreme, dual-divinity principle
which generates and conceives (Ometéotl), lord of the near
and proximate (Tloque Nahuaque), with respect to which the
numerous pairs of gods seem to be but mere manifestations,
the symbol of his omnipresence.

Third, the discovery of the meaning and mission of man on
earth, following the thought of Quetzalcóatl: to take part in
the creation of the Toltecáyotl, the complex of the arts of the

Toltecs, imitating in this way the activity of god, so that he finds, in what today we call art, the first meaning of the existence of man on earth.

Fourth, the conviction that to find more profound meaning it is necessary to overcome the Toltecáyotl itself, in quest of Tlilan, Tlapalan, the region of the color black and red, the world of wisdom. This is the idea, transformed into a myth, that it is necessary to put aside, by means of meditation which seeks wisdom, the present reality, in which all is like the plumage of the bird which rends itself in order to achieve a kind of personal salvation through approaching the dual god whose being is found beyond the immense waters, in the mysterious Tlilan, Tlapalan.

These ideas, attributed to the Toltecs, were the inheritance of the later Nahuan peoples. Incorporated with the religious thought of the different groups descended from the plains of the north, they were to survive because they were rethought and even lived out in their fullness by some of the tlamatinime. In this way the Toltec vision of the world became present again. The study of that same vision in traditions and codices permitted the Nahuan wise men to make their own the ancient mental categories, probably enriched with other new nuances or modes of thought, rooted in their turn, almost without exception, in the cultural legacy of the Toltecs. These categories, expressed in an unmistakable manner in the Nahuatl language itself, would determine to a great extent the direction and the meaning of later elaborations: the problems and doubts, the doctrines and the solutions of the tlamatinime.

IV
The Specific Categories of Nahuatl Thought

The question whether or not the languages of the ancient American peoples were capable of expressing abstract and universal concepts has frequently been discussed. In the case of Nahuatl the answer is clear, as acute investigators—from Clavijero and Boturini, to Seler and, most recently, Garibay

—have already noted. The Nahuatl, like the Greek and the German, is a language which offers no resistance to the formation of extensive compounds. By means of the juxtaposition of radicals or semantic elements, of prefixes, suffixes, or infixes, words are able to express complex conceptual relations. Many times these conceptual relations are of an abstract and universal character, and the words frequently prove to be true prodigies of "linguistic engineering."

By the use of the rich capital of abstract and universal terms the tlamatinime were able to express the specific nuances of their thought. However, they also made their own other forms of expression, with metaphorical meaning, some probably already minted from Toltec times, others conceived by themselves. Of these stylistic forms of expression, the most frequent and characteristic in the Nahuatl language is the juxtaposition of two words which—because they are synonyms, adjacent, or even contraries—complement each other in meaning so as to evoke one single idea. By way of metaphor the two juxtaposed terms point to specific or essential traits of the being which they connote, introducing a peculiar mode of poetry as an almost habitual form of expression. The metaphor, many times confronted in the thought of the tlamatinime with strictly abstract and universal ideas, frequently becomes the point of departure toward new forms of understanding.

The analysis of some of these metaphorical expressions and of some abstract and universal terms will permit us, therefore, to describe the specific categories and nuances of Nahuatl thought. The further conceptual elaborations of the tlamatinime, their structuralization of problems and their formulation of resolutions, will be worked out precisely from the point of view of these categories. Only by approaching them, by making them familiar to ourselves, so far as this is possible, will we be able to see the specific and peculiar meanings of the Nahuatl philosophy.

We will begin this analysis by trying to understand those terms which connote different aspects of the Nahuatl vision of the world. The ancient image, received as an inheritance from Toltec culture, implied, as we have seen, the existence of three different planes in the universe. Horizontally, there is the earth with its five directions, the center and the four dimensions, or quadrants, of colors. Above and beneath the earth are the immense transverse beams, or superior and inferior levels: above, the stars and the gods; below, the region of the dead. That which is "upon the earth" (in "tlaltícpac") can be seen, is tangible, changes, and is perishable. That which is "above us in the celestial planes" ("Topan") and that which is below us "in the region of the dead" ("Mictlan") is invisible and impalpable; no one may say that he knows them.

From this point of view, for Nahuatl thought to say Topan, Mictlan (that which is above us and the region of the dead) is equivalent to speaking of that which surpasses direct experience, that which is beyond what human words can express. To speak, on the other hand, of tlaltícpac is possible up to a certain point. At least it is known that in tlaltícpac everything is like the plumage of a bird that rends itself, everything is like a dream. Men have flourished on the face of the earth. On the earth they live and must earn merits in their character of "macehualtin" (made worthy by the blood and the sacrifice of the gods).

The earth, in its intermittent existence, has already ceased to be four times. The present age is the age of the sun of movement (Ollin Tonatiuh). Man personally, as well as everything which is upon the earth, tends to come to an end. Man by death will go to Topan or to Mictlan, perhaps to the region of the dead or, again, perhaps to that region which is above us, the mysterious world of the gods. The earth with its sun of movement will also have a violent end. In order to postpone the final cataclysm, various kinds of rites and sacrifices are practiced. Men come to believe that they can collaborate with the gods in their work of preserving the life of the sun and of tlaltícpac with all that exists on the earth.

In order to speak of man who lives in tlaltícpac, between

Topan and Mictlan (that which is above us and the region of the dead), Nahuatl thought conceived a metaphorical expression: man is "the possible master of a face and a heart." In addressing themselves to other persons in the language of the wise man it was said that they spoke to their "ixtil," their "yólotl," their face or their heart. The face seems to connote the moral physiognomy of the human being. The "yólotl" means his mobility, the dynamic nucleus of human beings. (Yólotl was derived from the same root as "ollin"; however, the abstract form was "óllotl," and "y-óllotl" referred to an individual.) When the child is born, neither his face nor his heart is well defined. For this reason it is said of the teacher that he is the one "who makes one acquire a face," "who makes it develop," teixcuitia-niteixtomani." [25] It is also said of him that he is the one who gives to hearts a basis or root as firm as a rock or as the trunk of a tree. The concept itself of education, "neixlamachiliztli," means "the action of giving wisdom to the faces." Finally, the ideal of the adult man is eloquent from this point of view:

> The mature man:
> heart as firm as a rock,
> a heart resistant like the trunk of a tree;
> a wise face,
> master of a face, master of a heart,
> able and understanding. [26]

However, one ought not to forget that the face and the heart, once acquired, may be lost; they can change, go back and forth, as one reads expressively in one text; they may go without a trace on the earth. What is it that man, situated in tlaltícpac (upon the earth) can and must do before the enigma of Topan, Mictlan (that which surpasses us and the region of the dead)? Knowingly or unknowingly, a man can be lost.

> Where has your heart gone?
> Thus do you give your heart to everything,
> without a course you carry it:
> you are destroying your heart.
> Upon the earth
> can you by any chance go in pursuit of something? [27]

Perhaps remembering the lesson left by Quetzalcóatl, the creator of the Toltec arts, Nahuatl thought harbors expressions which indicate various possible attitudes of the heart or mobility of each of the faces. One is that of "moyolnonotzani," that of one who engages constantly and intensely in dialogue ("nonotzani") with his own heart ("móyol"), the man who recollects himself interiorly in order to remember the ancient traditions and the wisdom preserved in the codices. By this path one may succeed in becoming a "yoltéotl" (a deified heart), at once a kind of soothsayer and creator. Indeed, this is precisely what is said of artists: that with a deified heart they seek to introduce into the stove, the clay, or the fig paper of their codices what today we would call the symbolism of the divine, the personal version of the meaning of the ancient myths, beliefs, and traditions.[28] However, just as the heart may become a creator and, by dialogue with itself, approach the mystery of Topan, Mictlan, it can also be lost, become an "enshrouded heart" ("yolloquimilli"), a heart which turns about and goes back and forth in vain.

Consequently, in their dialogue with themselves, face and heart in tlaltícpac must take into account the huehuetlamaniliztli, "that which remains established from ancient times": fundamentally, the principal "in qualli, in yectli," "that which is assimilable by the individual himself, that which is suited" ("qualli"); however, only that is the right and the just, follows the just path, which is suitable and which can be assimilated, precisely because it is "yectli." [29]

However, the truly wise face and the heart planted as firmly as the rock can find in tlaltícpac that which is perhaps most valuable: the world of "flower and song" ("in xóchitl, in cuícatl"). Flower and song are equivalent in a certain way to our concept of poetry, of art and of symbol in general. Before the vision of this "world of movement," in which even gold and jade come in pieces, in which everything is like a dream, Nahuatl thought discovers in flower and song a personal manner of finding roots and even of approaching the mystery of Topan, Mictlan (that which is above us and the region of the dead).

As we shall see in treating the particular thought of various tlamatinime, the theme of flower and song appears continuously in the texts in which their doctrines are preserved. Sometimes they speak of the heart which holds dialogue with itself and suddenly discovers the reality of flower and song. At other times, instead, there appears the anguish of one who affirms that he has not been able to find flowers and songs in tlaltícpac. Particularly interesting is the expression of the wise man Tecayehuatzin, who states that flower and song is perhaps the only way of saying "true words" on earth.

The Nahuatl notion of truth, as the tlamatinime conceived it, is entirely different from our own. Truth, in Nahuatl "neltiliztli," is a term, abstract in character, derived from the thematic syllable "nel-," which originatively connotes the idea of "solid establishment, profound rootedness." Taking this into account, it will not seem strange to find in many texts questions such as the following: Do men perhaps have roots, are they rooted? What is it that perhaps stands on its feet? What is it that makes tlaltícpac endure, that gives it roots?

In his sense "to speak true words on the earth" seems to point to the idea of saying words which can give root to the heart and, if this be possible, which can point to the hidden root of Topan, Mictlan.

The myths and beliefs had placed the dwelling place of the gods exactly in Topan, Mictlan. In the highest of the celestial planes, as Quetzalcóatl had said, dwells the god of duality, Ometéotl. Subordinated to him, the other gods—perhaps his sons, or perhaps so many other manifestations of himself— also exist in the different dimensions of the world. In the very region of the dead, in Mictlan, there also dwells a divine pair, the lord and mistress of the region of the dead (Mictlantecuhtli, Mectecacíhuatl).

However, though the reality of these gods is found in Topan, Mictlan, one must not forget the constant affirmation of Nahuatl thought about the dual god in so far as it is Tolque Nahuaque, lord of the enclosure, of proximity. The divine thus appears remote and near at hand at the same time. But despite his nearness and his proximity, he does not cease to be "yehualli, ehécutl," "invisible as the night and as impalpable as the wind."

The ancient myths speak of the action of the gods, of their presence and their disappearance in the various dimensions of the world, of their struggles among themselves, of their intervention, so very important, in the affairs of men—rain, wind, fire, agriculture, illness, birth, and death. However, once again—despite these ancient beliefs and the numberless rites, feasts, and sacrifices—the face and the heart of the tlamatinime were fully aware as will be seen below, that the reality of the gods belongs to the order Topan, Mictlan, that which is above us, the region of the dead. The divinity is before all else yohualli, ehécutl, impalpable as the night and invisible as the wind.

Before the enigma of the gods, with the experience of tlaltícpac; in the age or sun of movement, in which everything changes; before the menace of the death of the sun and the more proximate and inescapable death of the individual—the wise faces and the hearts which hold dialogue formulate different questions and offer answers to them in the light of the principle of flower and song. In what follows, we shall see the flowers and songs as conceived by three of the tlamatinime, whose thought is both original and different: the wise king Nezahual-cóyotl, the counselor Tlacaélel, and the Lord Tecahyhuatzin, prince of Huexotzinco.

V
THE FIGURE OF THE "TLAMATINI"

In the pre-Hispanic world so familiar and well known must have been the figure and the function of those who received the title "those who know something," the tlamatinime, that there is preserved in an old folio of the *Códice matritense* the ideal image of these ancient wise men and philosophers. The Castilian version of the text which describes the make-up and the concerns of the "tlamatini" will serve as an introduction to the study of the specific thought of the thinkers already mentioned, about whose ideas we shall concern ourselves presently:

The tlamatini: a light, a torch,
an ample torch which does not smoke.
A mirror pierced through,
A mirror full of holes on both sides.
His is the ink black and red,
his are the codices,
he is the master of the books of paintings.
He is himself the scripture and the wisdom.
He is the way, the true guide for others.
He leads persons and things,
he is the guide in human affairs.

The good tlamatini is careful (like a doctor)
and guards the tradition.
His is the wisdom handed down,
he is the one who teaches it,
he follows the truth
and he does not desist from counseling.
he makes strange faces wise,
he makes others take a visage,
he makes them develop it.
He opens their ears, he illuminates them.
He is the master of guides,
he gives them their path,
and one depends on him.

He puts a mirror before the others,
he makes them prudent, and careful;
he makes them acquire a face.
He establishes things,
regulates their path,
disposes and orders.
He turns his light upon the world.
He knows that which is above us (Topan)
and the region of the dead (Mictlan).

He is a thoughtful man;
everyone is comforted by him,
is corrected, is taught.
Thanks to him, the people humanizes its desire
and received a strict instruction.

Comforter of the heart,
comforter of the people,
help and remedy,
he brings healing to all.[30]

By making a brief résumé of the text, its meaning may better be understood. In its first seven lines the figure of the tlamatini is described symbolically, and his chief traits are evoked by metaphors. The tlamatini illuminates the world and man, as "a full torch which does not smoke." He is also a kind of organ of contemplation, like the pierced mirrors which formed part of the attributes proper to some gods and served them in contemplating the world and human affairs. The tlamatini is, in imitation of Quetzalcóatl, master of the black and red, the symbol of wisdom. Finally he also has under his charge the ancient books of paintings, in which he reads and to which he consigns his thought.

The following lines show the tlamatini in his function as teacher. It is said of him that he is the way, that he knows the tradition, that he follows the truth, that which can give root in tlaltícpac where all appears as the plumage of a bird which rends itself. His concern is to help humans to develop their proper face, guiding them and placing a mirror before them so that they "become prudent and careful."

Referring to his desire to know, both that which is in tlaltícpac, as well as the mystery of Topan, Mictlan, it is said of the tlamatini that "he shows forth his light over the world and knows that which is above us and the region of the dead." Finally, summarizing his attributes and his principal mission, it is stated that "thanks to him men humanize their desires, fortify their hearts, and receive a strict instruction."

This is the ideal figure of the tlamatini. Let us now consider the thought proper to various men who historically made their own this special vocation of "knowers of something."

VI
THE THOUGHT OF NEZAHUALCÓYOTL

Among all the tlamatinime of the Nahuatl world, the best known, without doubt, is Nezahualcóyotl. Born in Tezcoco in 1402, son of King Ixtlilxóchitl, Nezahualcóyotl passed the first years of his youth in the midst of persecutions and was forced to confront innumerable difficulties. While still a boy, he saw his father die, assassinated, and saw the ruin of Tezcoco, made subject to the power of the neighboring state of Azcapotzalco. Various indigenous chronicles refer to his unfortunate life, until the moment in which, allied with the Aztecs, he achieved the independence of Tezcoco, the state which by his own right he returned to govern. His long reign appears in the texts as a period of splendor, in which culture and the arts flourished in an extraordinary manner. Nezahualcóyotl built palaces, temples, and zoological and botanical gardens, and he was counselor to the Aztec kings. As architect extraordinary, he directed the construction of causeways, the works which brought water to Mexico, and the construction of the dikes and barricades which isolated the salty waters from the lakes and prevented future inundations.

As legislator, he promulgated a series of laws, many of which are preserved in ancient transcriptions and which permit us to glimpse his wisdom and his profound sense of justice. However, the most notable trait of Nezahualcóyotl's face and heart is probably the profundity of his thought, which has come down to us in the testimony of indigenous historians and, more directly, in his poetic compositions and discourses. Thoroughly cognizant with the ancient thought of the Toltecs, and despite the fact that he was under the political pressure of the mystical-warrior ideology of his neighbors and allies, the Aztecs, he gave a personal and independent slant to his thought. The version of some of the texts which can, with reason, be attributed to him will help us to understand some of his principal ideas.[31] Among these is his statement, often repeated, about change and time—expressed in Nahuatl by the word "cáhuitl," "that which is about to leave us"—and, in sum, of the fugitiveness of everything that exists. The consequence of this experience is his almost obsessive concern with the theme of death and the possibility of overcoming it in some way by finding a root and a stay beyond time and change.

Knowing the traditions of the Toltecs, in his personal life he took no part in the cult of the gods and the official religion, opposing, so far as he could, human sacrifices. As a visible testimony of his more intimate persuasion, opposite the temple of the god Huitzilopochtli erected in Tezcoco as a sign of the Aztec dominance, Nezahualcóyotl built, in honor of Tloque Nahuaque, lord of the nearness and of proximity, another temple with an elevated tower composed of various bodies to symbolize the crossbeams or levels of heaven without any image. In order in some way to overcome death and change, Nezahualcóyotl sought root in this unique god of whom Quetzalcóatl had spoken. He did not, however, accept the ancient religious doctrine of the Toltecs passively. Nezahualcóyotl devoted long meditations to the clarification of the enigma of the human faces and hearts before the god Tloque Nahuaque. The texts in which he expresses his ideas about the possibility of knowing and approaching "Moyocoyatzin," "that which is inventing itself," may, without exaggeration, be numbered among the classical works of the philosophical thought of all times. Preserved to the present, the version of some of the compositions of Nezahualcóyotl will permit us, better than anything else, to come near to his thought.

As we have said, Nezahualcóyotl's point of departure seems to have been his profound experience of change and of time, cáhuitl, "that which is about to leave us." Everything in tlaltícpac —that is, upon the earth—is transitory, appears for a short time here, only soon to rend itself and to vanish forever. Here is Nezahualcóyotl's own expression:

> Perhaps one with root truly lives upon the earth?
> Not forever on the earth;
> Only for a short time here.
> Even if it be of jade it will be broken,
> even if it be of gold it will be shattered,
> even if it be the plumage of a bird that rends itself.
> Not forever on the earth;
> only for a short time here.[32]

If jade and gold shatter and break, faces and hearts, more
fragile than they the more noble they have been, dry up and
vanish as flowers:

> Only for an instant does the meeting endure,
> for a brief time there is glory. . . .
> None of your friends has root,
> only for a short time are we given here as loans,
> your lovely flowers . . .
> are only dried flowers.
> Everything which flourishes in your mat or in your chair,
> nobility on the field of battle,
> on which depends lordship and command,
> your flowers of war . . .
> are only dried flowers.[33]

The persuasion that in tlaltícpac the union or meeting of
faces and hearts endures but for a short time is the root not only
of sadness but also of new forms of thought in the soul of
Nezahualcóyotl:

> I am inebriated, I weep, I am afflicted,
> I think, I say,
> within myself I find it;
> if I would never die,
> if I would never disappear.
> There where there is no death,
> there where death is conquered,
> there will I go.
> If I would never die,
> if I would never disappear.[34]

Already the object of doubt in the thought of not a few of
the tlamatinime were the religious doctrines, accepted by the
state and by the people, about the immortality of the
warriors as companions of the sun, or about a happy life in
the gardens of Tláloc, or which held that dangers and proofs
must be faced in the lower realms of Mictlan, the region of
the dead. Nezahualcóyotl, remembering ancient concepts, perhaps of Toltec origin, expresses his doubt by asking where one

must go or what wisdom must one find in order to reach "Quenonamican," "where in some manner one lives," or "can on ayac micohua," "where death does not exist":

> Whither shall we go
> where death does not exist?
> But for this will I live weeping?
> Let your heart be set straight:
> here no one will live forever.
> Even the princes are doomed to die;
> there is the cremation of people.
> Let your heart be set straight:
> here no one will live forever.[35]

Nezahualcóyotl himself will set his heart straight, which is equivalent to saying, when we understand the Nahuatl connotation of yóllotl (heart), that he gave a meaning to his mobility, to his dynamic nucleus. His heart fortified, Nezahualcóyotl says that he has discovered the profound meaning of "flower and song," the Nahuatl expression for art and symbol, so that he might approach, thanks to it, from tlaltícpac the reality of Topan, Mictlan, "that which is above us and the region of the gods and the dead." Four masterful lines give testimony of this discovery:

> Finally, my heart understands it:
> I hear a song,
> I see a flower,
> Behold, they will not wither! [36]

The heart which has finally understood what must be its way desires then to find songs and flowers which do not wither. Nezahualcóyotl will not fall again into doubt. His heart must find flowers and songs with life and root. Probably for this reason he said:

> They will not end, my flowers,
> they will not cease, my songs.

> I, the singer, lift them up,
> they divide, they spread abroad.
> Even when the flowers
> wither and grow yellow,
> they will be carried thither,
> to the interior of the house
> of the bird with the golden plumes.[37]

The truth is, as Nezahualcóyotl adds, that the heart of the one who has discovered flowers and songs has been born to sing, has his dwelling in the springtime which never ends, can finally reach the mystery of Topan, Mictlan. The wise Lord of Tezcoco, who knew the doctrines of the Toltecs, made the object of his meditation the theme of Tloque Nahuaque, lord of the enclosure and of proximity, who is also Moyocoyatzin, the one who is inventing himself. By the paths of flower and song he expressed his thought about the one who is like the night and the wind, the giver of life, who in his book of paintings has made the sketch of our faces and hearts, the arbitrary inventor who also writes and draws with flowers and songs:

> With flowers you write, giver of life,
> with songs you give color,
> with songs you overshadow
> those who must live in tlaltícpac.
> Afterwards you will destroy eagles and tigers,
> only in your book of paintings do we live,
> here upon the earth.
> With black ink you will strike out
> that which was brotherhood,
> community, nobility.
> You will overshadow those who must live in
>   tlaltícpac.[38]

The face and heart of the man in tlaltícpac is near and far from Moyocoyatzin, the inventor of himself. It is certain that eagles and tigers, brotherhood and nobility, exist in the book of paintings of the lord of the near and the union. But despite this fact, the supreme giver of life, like the night and the wind that he is for man, remains hidden and unattainable. The thought of Nezahualcóyotl, plunging deeper into the mystery, expresses precisely this impossibility of drawing close to him:

> Only there in the interior of heaven
> you invent your word,
> giver of life!
> What will you determine?
> Will you give weariness here?
> Will you hide your fame and your glory
>   in tlaltícpac?
> What will you determine?
> No one can be the friend
> of the giver of life. . . .
> Whither then shall we go . . . ?
> Set yourself right, because all of us
> will have to go to the place of mystery. . . .[39]

Despite having stated that "no one can call himself the friend of the giver of life," Nezahualcóyotl continues his quest tenaciously. Many are the flowers and the songs of his text about the divinity which we might quote here. But since this is impossible in the space available, we will offer only two more testimonies. The first is an expression of questions, we might almost say doubts, about the reality and root of the one who in himself invents his word and gives being in his mysterious book of paintings:

> Are you true (do you have root)?
> Only he who dominates all things,
> the giver of life.
> Is this true?
> Perhaps it is not, as they say?
> Let our hearts
> not be tormented!
>
> All that is true
> (that which has root),
> they say that it is not true

(that it has no root).
Only the giver of life
shows himself arbitrary.

Let our hearts
not be tormented!
For he is the giver of life.[40]

In spite of the doubts and the mystery which surround the
giver of life, it is necessary to accept his reality. This is the
only thing which, as a matter of fact, gives peace and root to
the heart. Such seems to be the conclusion to which Nezahualcóyotl comes in his effort to draw near the mystery of Topan,
Mictlan. If Tolque Nahuaque is absolute and incomprehensible,
he is also the giver of life in whose book of paintings we exist.
Human faces must accept the mystery. They must invoke and
praise Tolque Nahauque. Thus may one live in tlaltícpac.

The flowers and songs, art, the most human creation of man,
are the path of approach. It would seem that the giver of life
himself wished to make us drunk here with his own flowers and
songs. The following text of Nezahualcóyotl seems, from this
point of view, to be the final synthesis of his thought:

The house of the inventor of himself can
    be in no part.
God, our lord, is invoked on every hand.
In all places he is also venerated.
His glory, his fame are sought on earth.
He is who invents things,
he is who invents himself: god.
On every hand he is invoked,
in all places he is also venerated.
His glory, his fame is sought on the earth.
No one may here,
no one may be the friend
of the giver of life;
he alone is invoked,
at his side,
joined to him,
one can live on the earth.

He who finds him
knows only this: he is invoked,
at his side, joined to him,
it is possible to live upon the earth.

No one in truth
is your friend
O giver of life!
Only as we seek someone
among the flowers,
thus do we seek thee,
we who live upon the earth,
while we are at your side.

Your heart will be sated,
only for a brief time
will we be joined close at your side.

He makes us mad, the giver of life,
he intoxicates us here.
Perhaps no one can stand at his side,
or be successful, or reign on the earth.

Only you change things
as our heart knows:
perhaps no one can stand at his side,
or know success, or reign on the earth.[41]

To someone the conclusion to which Nezahualcóyotl comes may seem pessimistic. He ought to keep in view what may be described as the internal dialectic of the thought of Nezahualcóyotl: he states that no one can be the friend of the giver of life, that perhaps no one can be at his side on earth; at the same time, however, he holds that it is human destiny to seek him, as one seeks after someone amid flowers. He who invokes him, he who seeks him, may live upon the earth. It may also be said that he finds himself at his side, joined to him, exactly because he is lord of the nearness and of proximity. Pure thought probably leads to doubt: "are you true, do you have root?" Because "all that is true, they say is not true."

But this idea, the impossibility of understanding the root of the only being which shows himself in an arbitrary way makes the heart suffer. Instead, to invoke Tolque Nahuaque seems already to have found him, gives peace, and makes it possible to live upon the earth. Nezahualcóyotl, persuaded that his flowers and songs will not perish, trusts and reposes in this further conclusion: the giver of life makes us drunk here on earth, and, seeking, we follow him "as though we were seeking someone among the flowers."

The ideas expressed, supported by the texts basically ascribed to Prince Nezahualcóyotl, the wise man, constitute a first effort at the historical invention of his thought.

He certainly deserves a much more ample study, in which would finally be included all those compositions and discourses which, after careful documentary cirticism, may be held to be his. Possibly then one might achieve a more exact and just understanding of the ideas of this extraordinary tlamantini, in whose praise a pre-Hispanic poet ventured to say:

> You speak with flowers,
> you live within yourself,
> you write within yourself,
> you find the giver of life
> who is god,
> Oh prince chichimeca, Nezahualcóyotl! [42]

VII
The Thought of Tlacaélel

If Nezahualcóyotl represents the attempt to rethink and to give a new meaning of personal salvation to the intellectual heritage of the Toltecs, the figure of Tlacaélel is, by contrast, the symbol of an entirely different attitude: that of the man who discovered and endowed the Aztecs with the most profound root of their warrior-mysticism.

Despite the fact that Tlacaélel, as counselor to various rulers, was the founder of Aztec greatness, his figure has remained for a long time in oblivion. Indeed, some historians, like Torquemada, have gone to the point of denying his existence.[43] This last fact justifies our referring, however briefly, to the historical sources which treat of his activity and thought.

The *Crónica mexicáyotl,* written in Nahuatl by the native historian Tezozómoc, gives us the genealogy of Tlacaélel. He was the son of Huitzilíhuitl, second Lord of Mexico-Tenochtitlan. His mother was called Cacamacihuatzin and was a native of Teocalhuiycan. Among his several brothers was Moctezuma Ilhuicamina, whose counselor Tlacaélel was later to become. The same *Crónica* gives us the name of Tlacaélel's wife, his sons, and his descendants down to the time of the conquest.[44]

Chimalpain, another entirely independent, native historian, gives us in his *Séptima relación* the exact date of Tlacaélel's birth. This event took place in the year 10-Conejo; in our calendar, 1398.[45]

The *Anales de México-Azcapotzalco* and three related works which have certain common elements among them—that is, the *Códice Ramírez,* the *Crónica mexicana,* and the *Historia* of Durán—make numerous references to the activity of Tlacaélel and, in a special manner, to his thought.[46] Finally, a number of Mexican songs of pre-Hispanic origin allude to his triumphs, while the *Códice Cozcatzin* refers to a distribution of lands made by Tlacaélel and the codices *Xólotl* and *Azcatitlan* preserve pictographic representations of him.[47] For his part, the celebrated scientist and historian, Henrico Martínez, conscious of the extraordinary importance of Tlacaélel in the Aztec world, wrote at the beginning of the seventeenth century that Tlacaélel was the man "to whom almost all the glory of the Mexican empire was due." [48]

The first public action of Tlacaélel took place at the moment in which the Aztecs, about the year 1427, were confronted by the alternative of slavishly accepting the tyranny of Azcapotzalco or of reacting against it by declaring war. In alliance with Nezahualcóyotl, who was also being persecuted by the same tyrant, the Aztecs, after various armed encounters and contrary to all expectations, were victorious against the people of

Azcapotzalco.[49] The texts then go on to mention the new measures which Tlacaélel, who had become counselor to Lord Itzcóatl, ruler of Mexico-Tenochtitlan, put into effect.

The first step which Tlacaélel undertook was a dual reform: to distribute titles and lands to the Aztecs who had distinguished themselves in the contest, thus consolidating a recently established nobility, and to give to the Aztec people a new warrior-mystic vision of the world and of man, the root of the future greatness of the people of the sun.[50] This last point—from which were to flow substantial changes in the religious, economic, sociopolitical, educative, and military organization of Aztec society—constitutes the very marrow of Tlacaélel's ideological undertaking.

Tlacaélel, like Nezahualcóyotl, spent the days of his youth in the "calmécac," or center of higher education, and studied the ancient religious doctrines deriving from the Toltecs. However, his thought had also become centered on the importance which the tribal gods of the Aztec's—especially the supreme warrior-god, Huitzilopochtli—ought to have among the Aztecs.

He knew the myths which spoke of this god, from his portentous birth on the Mountain of the Serpent as the son of Coatlicue, who had conceived him virginally without man, to the victory which Huitzilopochtli himself had won over his brothers, the four hundred of the south. Huitzilopochtli had been the guide of the Aztecs from their place of origin in the great plains of the north. He had freed them from dangers without number. Huitzilopochtli had led them ("the people of unknown face") to the region of lakes. Thanks to him, the Aztecs had contemplated the eagle devouring the serpent in Mexico-Tenochtitlan, the end of their long peregrinations.

Despite all this, up to that time the other peoples of the same culture and language had given scarce importance to Huitzilopochtli and his mother, Coatlicue. In the ancient codices of Azcapotzalco and of the other states the power of the titular god of the Aztecs was unknown. But in reality, as Tlacaélel saw the matter, the victories of Huitzilopochtli narrated in the myths, and his words which had guided the Aztecs to Mexico-Tenoch-titlan, were the legacy of his people, that which distinguished them from the others and which gave them their special root.

With these ideas Tlacaélel gave a new meaning to the vision of the world and to Aztec history. Beginning with the victory over Azcapotzalco, "his continuous purpose," as Chimalpain re-counts, "was to persuade the Mexicans that their god was Huitzilopochtli." [51]

In order to make efficacious his effort to increase the symbolic stature of the power and force of Huitzilopochtli, Tlacaélel ad-vised the Lord Itzcóatl (of whom the *Códice Ramírez* states categorically that "he did nothing more than Tlacaélel advised him to do") [52] to collect both the books of pictures of the con-quered people of Azcapotzalco and those of the Aztecs themselves and to destroy them so that it might be possible then to compose the true history of the Aztec nation. This fact, which shows the importance which Tlacaélel placed on the knowledge of history, is recorded in Nahuatl in the *Códice matritense:*

> Their history was preserved.
> But then it was burned.
> When Itzcóatl reigned in Mexico.
> A resolution was taken,
> The lords of the Mexicans said:
> it is not fitting that all the people
> should know these pictures.
> Those who are subject, the people,
> will be spoiled
> and the land will be twisted,
> because many lies are preserved in
>   those books
> and many in them have been held as gods. [53]

When the ancient books of pictures had been burned, Tlacaélel announced his vision of history. The texts of Aztec origin that are preserved today are proof of this. They were conceived to become the root of a new greatness. In them there stands out the im-portance of the Aztec people through their relation, in various

ways, with the Toltecs and other powerful peoples. Huitzilopochtli and Coatlicue are placed on the same plane as the
divinities of Toltec times.

The ancient doctrine of the various stages or suns which had
existed and passed away, due to the struggles and death of the
gods, receives a new interpretation, or, if one prefers, a new
historical invention. In it, Huitzilopochtli is the one who presides
over the present stage, the sun of movement. The young warrior-
god is also identified with the sun itself in various sacred hymns.
The Aztecs, the elect people of Huitzilopochtli, have as their
mission to collaborate with him to prevent the end of the age
of movement.

According to the ancient myths this age had begun to exist
through the self-sacrifice of the gods, who with their blood had
made life possible again. That blood is the precious water
("chalchíhuatl") in which is enclosed the vital energy which
keeps men alive. It was therefore necessary to return or compensate the sacrifice of the gods by offering up to them the same
precious liquid which gives strength and which holds off death.
By increasing the number of human sacrifices, whose heart and
blood were offered to Huitzilopochtli, the life of the sun could
be indefinitely strengthened and preserved.

In order to carry out these blood-offerings more easily Tlacaélel
introduced among the Aztecs the practice of the "wars of flowers."
These were periodic struggles with the neighboring states of
Tlaxcala and Huexotzinco, undertaken for the sole purpose of
securing victims for the sacrifices. The Aztec people, thanks to
the "wars of flowers" and those of conquest, then seemed in the
thought of Tlacaélel to be fulfilling an extraordinary mission of
cosmic consequences: that of holding off the cataclysm which
might put an end to the present age in which we live.

From this idea there derived, in turn, a deeper meaning of the
Aztec vision of the world. The Aztecs stood at the side of the
sun-god Huitzilopochtli; they therefore considered that they were
on the side of the good in a war without truce against the powers
of death and of night. However, from another utilitarian point

of view the Aztec alliance with sun-god Huitzilopochtli brought with it the justification of all their conquests, the persuasion that by subjecting other peoples and making them tributaries they were realizing a supreme mission. For, as Tlacaélel expressed the matter in a short discourse,

> This is the mission of Huitzilopochtli,
> our god,
> for this was he come:
> to collect
> and thus to bring to his service
> all nations,
> with the power of his breast and of his head. . . .[54]

Such is the core of the mystical-warrior conception thought out by Tlacaélel in order to make possible the greatness of the Aztecs. Proclaimed and transmitted by means of his books and pictures, of hymns and poems, what might be called "the philosophy of the people of the sun" succeeded in becoming the root of Mexico-Tenochtitlan. The sacred hymn of Huitzilopochtli, preserved in the *Códice matritense*, is eloquent in this sense:

> Huitzilopochtli, the young warrior-god,
> who works above, pursues his course!
> "Not in vain did I put on the robe of
>   yellow plumage,
> For I am the one who causes the sun to
>   rise."
> The portentous one,
> he who dwells in the region of wings,
> Your hand opened! . . .[55]

Once the ideological reform had been cemented, thanks to the mystical-warrior concept, Tlacaélel became a kind of political and social thinker, dedicating his attention to a number of points of fundamental importance. The *Códice Ramírez* gives us a résumé of the arrangements put into practice as a consequence of Tlacaélel's thought when Motecuhzoma Ilhuicamina already reigned in Mexico-Tenochtitlan:

Tlacaélel was then a man of great experience and wisdom. With the aid of his counsel and effort king Motecuhzoma, the first of that name, brought order and harmony to all his subject nations.[56]

The dispositions of Tlacaélel refer to three basic matters: modifications in the religious organization by placing the cult and the sacrifices to Huitzilopochtli above all others; the construction of a new and greater temple, extraordinarily rich and sumptuous, in honor of Huitzilopochtli and of Tláloc, the god of rain; strengthening and restructuring of the army, conceived as the arm of Huitzilopochtli for bringing into his service all the peoples of tlaltícpac. And, finally, there were substantial reforms in the political, economic, and juridical organization which guaranteed the development and aggrandizement of Mexico-Tenochtitlan, now become a metropolis to which the tributes from conquered regions flowed.

This is the manner in which Tlacaélel consolidated the greatness of the Aztecs. While never accepting the dignity of supreme ruler, which was offered to him again and again, he remained the one who always inspired the designs of the People of the Sun. When after the death of Motecuhzoma the Aztecs tried once more to make him their king, or "tlatoani," the words which he pronounced are significant. The following discourse clearly shows the attitude of the great counselor of the Aztec rulers:

> Certainly, my sons, I thank you
> and the king of Tezcuco.
> However, come hither:
> I ask you to tell me,
> during the eighty or ninety years
> that have passed since the war of Azcaputzalco,
> what have I been? In what place have I stood?
>
> Have I then been nothing?
> Have I ever put a crown upon my head?
> Or have I ever used the royal insignia which the
>   kings use?
> Then is it good for nothing, all that I have judged
>   and commanded?

Have I unjustly condemned the delinquent to death
or pardoned the innocent?
Then have I not been able to make lords
and unmake lords as I have determined and decided? . . .

Evil have I done in vesting myself with the vestments
and the semblances of the gods,
and shown myself with their likenesses,
and like those gods taken the knife
to kill and sacrifice men;
and if I have been able to do it
and have done it for these eighty or ninety years,
then King I am and such have you held me to be;
then what more of a king do you wish me to be? . . .[57]

The best comment on this very expressive discourse of Tlacaélel
is offered by the *Códice Ramírez:*

And he did not lack reason (it is stated there), for by his effort, though
not king, he did more than he might have done had he been king . . .
for nothing was done in the whole reign save what he had commanded.[58]

The texts adduced have made clear the importance of the
thought and activity of Tlacaélel as the creator of the mystic-
warrior vision of the Aztecs. A thinker with great political and
social effects, his ideas differed radically from those of most of
the tlamatinime. Although taking his stand, as they did, on the
ancient Toltec inheritance, his attention was directed not only
to the clarification, from a personal point of view, of the enigmas
of Topan, Mictlan but also to providing his people with a philosophy of action. This philosophy was based on the concept and
reality of struggle, to give to the heretofore unknown Aztecs a
definite "face" and a power which made it possible to extend
their dominions from one ocean to another and to regions so far
apart as those which are today known as Chiapas and Guatemala.

As witness to the splendor they achieved, the Aztecs, who
were probably the most extraordinary sculptors of ancient Mexico,
left various works in which they bequeathed an enduring plastic

reflection of their mystic-warrior vision of the world. If the great sculpture of Huitzilopochtli, which Tlacaélel commanded to be made, has been lost, there are preserved, instead, the Sun Stone, a marvelous synthesis of their thought about the world and time, and the imposing statue of Coatlicue, the divine mother of Huitzilopochtli.

Doctor Justino Fernández studied the esthetics of the ancient, native art in his already classic work on Coatlicue. He has shown how in the intricate pattern of symbols and forms which are peculiar to that colossal statue there is expressed plastically not only the Aztec conception of cosmic space but also their integral and dynamic vision of the world and of man as well. The analysis which Justino Fernández has made of Coatlicue's statue in order to determine the specific meaning of Aztec art has led him to rethink the ancient ideas which, transformed into symbols, can be "read" in that expression of the Aztec vision of the world which the statue of the divine mother really is. The following paragraph, taken from the work mentioned, illustrates better than anything else, what has been said. Anyone who has contemplated, even in a photograph, the statue of Coatlicue will understand how in it the thought of Tlacaélel, which gave a new meaning to the Toltec doctrines about the divinity and about the world, was incorporated in stone by the work of the genius of the sculptors of ancient Mexico:

Finally, or in the first place, on the highest level we come to "Omeyocan," the place where dwelt the divine duality, "Ometecuhtli" and "Omecíhuatl," creator par excellence, origin of the generation of gods and of men. If this dual-faced mass takes the place of the head and seems to rise out of the very entrails of the whole, it also has a meaning of decapitation which alludes to Coyolxauhqui, the Moon, with which the astral system is completed.

There must also be added the four cardinal directions that are expressed in the form of a cross, and the fifth direction, up and down, in the center of which stands "Xiuhtecuhtli," "the old lord," the god of fire. And finally, the pyramidal form, of ascent and descent, which goes from the depth of the earth, the world of the dead, up to the highest place, "Omeyocan." Thus the sculpture is not only conceived from without, in an exterior manner, but the bodies of the serpents, whose heads become visible at the highest point, arise from its entrails; and it must be remembered that beneath its levels there extends the world of the dead. All of it, therefore, lives and vibrates; within and without all of it is alive and dead; its meanings embrace all directions and extend out into them. In summary, "Coatlicue" is, *in nuce*, the cosmic-dynamic force which gives life and which maintains itself by death in a struggle of contraries, so necessary that its ultimate and radical meaning is war. . . .[59]

The vision of the world, whose ultimate and radical meaning is war, was the supreme creation of Tlacaélel. Thanks to him, this vision, based on the concept and the reality of struggle, came to be identified as the specific attitude of the Aztecs. Two short Mexican songs which state that the root and basis of Mexico-Tenochtitlan resided in struggle, symbolized by spears and shields, are perhaps the happiest synthesis of the mystical-warrior thought begun by Tlacaélel:

> With our spears,
> with our shields,
> the city has existence.[60]

> There where the spears are dyed,
> where the shields are dyed,
> and the white perfumed flowers,
> the flowers of the heart:
> the flowers of him who gives life open
>   their buds,
> whose perfume the princes breathe in in the
>   world:
> There is Tenochtitlan.[61]

VIII
TECAYEHUATZIN AND THE DIALOGUE OF "FLOWER AND SONG"

The existence in ancient Mexico of forms of thought not only different from each other but actually opposed has been made

clear, though we have only touched on some of the principal
ideas of men like Nezahualcóyotl and Tlacaélel. This variety of
positions, barely indicated here with regard to two bodies of
thought which may be considered extremes, though both have
their roots in the same cultural tradition, might be more fully
studied in the case of the numerous different and personal points
of view of the various other pre-Hispanic tlamatinime. The necessary brevity of the present work permits us to offer only a single
example, that of the Lord Tecayehuatzin, prince of Huexotzinco
about 1501.[62]

The texts which are known to be from the hand of Tecayehuatzin and which permit us to glimpse his principal preoccupation
are numerous and varied. His concern is to find the form of
thought and to speak true words on the earth, words capable of
giving root. Cognizant of the possibilities of expression open
to man, Tecayehuatzin elaborated his own version of the meaning, achievements, and origin of "flower and song." Like the rest
of the tlamatinime, he knew that "flower and song" was the
expression which connotes the world of art and symbol. Without
escaping from doubt, Tecayehuatzin wished to confront his
thought with other possible answers. Nothing could serve this
end better than to hear the words of those others who also frequently referred to "flower and song." The manuscript of *Cantares
méxicanos,* preserved in the National Library of Mexico, includes
the dialogue, real or imaginary, which took place in Huexotzinco.
In this dialogue there appeared as participants Tecayehuatzin
and various other tlamatinime, his friends. In it are expressed,
in a literary language, the various opinions of the many pre-
Hispanic wise men about poetry, art, and symbol: "flower and
song."

The conversation begins with a salutation by Tecayehuatzin,
followed by a eulogy of "flower and song." Tecayehuatzin then
asks himself whether "flower and song" is perhaps the only truth
which can give root to man on earth:

> Is this perhaps the only thing on the earth . . . ?
> Only with flowers do I surround the nobles,

with my songs I join them
in the place of the timbrels.
Here in Huexotzinco I have called a gathering.
I, the Lord Tecayehuatzin,
have brought together the princes:
precious stones, plumes of the bird.
Only with flowers do I surround the nobles.[63]

Tecayehuatzin is further interested to know the origin of flower and song. He desires to know whether it is possible to find flowers and songs with root, or whether perhaps it is the destiny of man to undertake searches without end, to think that he has found what he desires and at the end to have to depart, leaving here only the memory of his fugitive life.

The questions of Tecayehuatzin receive many different answers. One by one the various invited guests present these answers. The first to speak was Ayocuan Cuetzpaltzin, lord of Tecmachalco, whom we knew through various other texts, among them a particularly interesting one depicting him as repeating on every hand and all occasions the following words:

That the earth may abide!
That the mountains stand firmly rooted!
This has Ayocuan Cuetzpaltzin gone about
    speaking
in Tlaxcala, in Huexotzinco.
In vain are the aromatic flowers of cacao
    scattered about ...
That the earth may abide! [64]

The answer of Ayocuan in the dialogue has reference to the origins and possible permanence of "flower and song." For him, art and symbol are a gift of the gods. And it is also possible that flowers and songs may be at least a remembrance of man on the earth:

From the interior of heaven come
the beautiful flowers, the beautiful songs.
Our desire deforms them,
our inventiveness mars them. ...

Must I depart like the flowers that perished?
Will nothing of my fame remain here on the earth?
At least my flowers, at least my songs.

Here on earth is the realm of the fugitive moment.
Perhaps it is also thus in Quenonamicah,
the place where, in some manner, there is life?
Is there joy there, is there friendship?

Or only here on the earth
have we come to know our faces? [65]

For his part, Aquiauhtzin, wise man of Ayapanco, gives a
different meaning to art and symbol. For him flowers and songs
are the form of invoking the supreme giver of life. The giver of
life may perhaps become present by way of the world of symbol.
Perhaps it may be said that we seek him like one who, among
flowers, goes in quest of a friend.

Another of the participants, Cuauhtencoztli, answers with a
deeper insight, with the expression of his doubt about the truth
of flower and song because he himself doubts about the possible
root that man may have on the earth:

I, Cuauhtencoztli—he exclaims—am here suffering.
Do man have root, truth?
Will our song still have root and truth tomorrow?
Who by chance will remain afoot?
What is it that will turn out well?
Here we live, here we are,
but we are indigent,
O our friends. [66]

Tecayehuatzin himself and another tlamatini, his friend, reply
to Cuauhtencoztli. They want with their words to dispel what
they consider a pessimistic attitude. Flower and song are the
only things which can alleviate sorrow; they are the joy and
wealth of man on earth.

The dialogue about art and symbol, already described as a
gift of the gods, as a possible memorial of man on earth, as a
way to find the divinity and the wealth of man, then takes a

different direction. A new participant, Xayacámach, states that flower and song are, like hallucinating drugs, the best means of intoxicating the heart and making oneself forgetful of sadness here. When in the sacred gatherings the drugs are consumed, one sees marvelous visions, evanescent forms of different colors, all more real than reality itself. However, afterward this fantastic world vanishes like a dream, leaves man weary, and no longer exists. For Xayácamach this is art and symbol, flowers and songs:

> The flowers which confuse the people
> the flowers which make hearts spin about,
> have come to be scattered.
> Have come to make garlands of flowers
> rain down,
> flowers that intoxicate.
> Who will stand upon the mat of flowers?
> Surely here is your house:
> in the midst of the pictures, says Xayacámach.[67]

Various other opinions are expressed about the same theme. One says that he collects flowers only to bedeck his cabin with them, his cabin which stands close to the house of flowers. The dialogue draws to its end. Shortly before it comes to an end, the host himself, the Lord Tecayehuatzin, again speaks. His heart continues to be open to doubt. His purpose continues to be to learn whether flower and song is perhaps the only way to speak true words on the earth. Very diverse have been the answers offered. He is sure, nevertheless, that if he expresses one idea as the conclusion of the dialogue, all will be in agreement: flower and song at least make possible our friendship:

> Now, O friends!,
> Hear the dream of a word:
> every spring makes us live,
> the golden maize cools us,
> the red maize becomes a necklace.
> At least we know that the hearts of our
> friends
> Are sure! [68]

Perhaps it would be no exaggeration to say that the words of Tecayehuatzin and the other tlamatinime imply fundamentally different conjectures, from the most varied points of view, directed toward understanding the marvelous world of their own pre-Hispanic art. In another sense they are also, as Tecayehuatzin has said, "the dream of a word," the desire to pronounce in tlaltícpac the mysterious reply capable of giving root to hearts and faces.

If it were possible to present here, in a much more ample way, the elaborations reached by way of flower and song, as mentioned by some of the tlamatinime and others, it might be possible to form a much more precise image of the richness and profundity of what we call pre-Hispanic Nahuatl philosophy. Among the many texts which might be adduced, there are innumerable meditations about man and about death; about human faces and Tloque Nahuaque, the lord of nearness and proximity, who is like night and the wind; about the theme of "the assimilable" (the fitting) and "that which follows the right way" (that which is complete), the norm of action which gives wisdom to faces and firmness to hearts. We must be satisfied with saying that hundreds of texts are preserved, as yet unpublished, among them the various collections of Huehuelatolli, "discourses of the ancients" in which is expounded the ancient Toltec wisdom, re-thought later by the priests and the tlamatinime. The little that we have presented here is only an indication of the variety of ideas and doctrine conceived with categories and forms proper to them, which we have tried to approach in order to learn the specific meaning and evolution of pre-Hispanic Nahuatl thought.

IX
CONCLUSION

The translation and study of the texts which we have presented with the support of a sound documentary and philological criticism has probably brought us close to some of the forms of pre-Hispanic philosophical thought. This effort also was probably aided by our adoption, as a method of understanding, of the theory of historical invention, which makes it possible to rethink, up to a certain point, the special character of what is culturally distant and different. We have seen that the tlamatinime certainly did not elaborate great logical or rationalistic systems, in the way that certain philosophers of the West have. We found, instead, testimonies of their inquietudes and doubts, which led them to conduct a dialogue with themselves in order to arrive at conceptions, symbols, and conjectures entirely different, capable of becoming something new when rethought by the modern man of Occidental roots.

In this sense we have said that many of the texts could become pretexts for thinking. Within one's own self, for example, there are thought and relived the different Nahuan conceptions about flower and song, their doctrine about the being of man as the possible possessor of a face and a heart, the ideal of the man who learns to hold dialogue with himself in order to learn to lie to inert matter, to turn the stone, clay, and the fig-bark paper of his codices into symbol.

The world of pre-Hispanic art, conceived by way of flower and song, and also, at times, in relation to the warrior-mysticism of Tlacaélel, arises thus as that which gives meaning to existence, which, in incessant change, seems like the plumage of a bird which rends itself. The remains of this art—discovered by archeologists in ceremonial centers with their pyramids, palaces, and temples covered with pictures—permits us to glimpse something of the cosmic home of Nahuatl man, so laboriously conceived and constructed. The key to enter this world of symbols is in the ancient myths, in the religious doctrines, and in the thought of the tlamatinime.

What has been presented here, it is worth insisting, is only a miniature showing of the richness of pre-Hispanic Nahuatl thought. A more ample approach to the numerous indigenous sources which are preserved, with the aid of an adequate historical method, will permit us to know finally the extraordinary variety of ideas and attitudes entertained by the tlamatinime of pre-Hispanic times. The history of ideas in America and in the world would be enriched then with one chapter more: that of the intellectual legacy of the ancient Mexicans.

Edmundo O'Gorman

*to my friend, the Mexican philosopher
Francisco Larroyo, I dedicate these
reflections on our America*

II. AMERICA

INTRODUCTION

The general purpose of the collection of essays brought together in this book is to present the historical panorama of philosophical thought in Mexico. In order to carry out this project as it should be carried out, it was thought that the collection should have an initial work which would show what the civilization of the ancient Mexicans had achieved in this regard, and the assignment of that study to Dr. León-Portilla could not be improved upon. It is evident, nevertheless, that after this period we encounter a break in the history of Mexican philosophy. The essays which follow, including the present essay, do not refer to the same Mexico, since with the Spanish conquest and colonization there arose a new historico-geographical entity, New Spain, and later, with the political independence of this colony, the modern Mexican State. This observation is not intended to deny influence on Mexican intellectual life proceeding from the modes of thought and speech of the ancient inhabitants of Mexico. The fact, however, that we think of them in this way already shows clearly that after the Europeans took possession of the American continent, we have to deal with an entirely different cultural world.

Awareness of this fact is precisely what motivates the present essay, for from all points of view it seems proper to preface the essays on the various stages of Mexican philosophical thought with a kind of preamble which would try to capture the historical meaning of the New World.

And truly, in order to understand the development of that thought more deeply, it seems to us that a prior question needs to be answered, namely, to what degree and, above all, in what sense the American world is "new," for on this point a very general confusion seems to reign.

Let us examine this very interesting matter more closely. If we review the stages of our intellectual life, it is impossible not to see that, taken as a whole, it reflects the great currents of European philosophy and the course of its mutations, in such wise that without the least doubt the conclusion imposes itself that the American cultural world is but the echo of Western civilization.[1] No sooner, however, has this idea been stated than one is aware that it embraces an equivocation, because then either this world is not as "new" as we are in the habit of saying or its novelty is rooted in something which does not reveal itself immediately. And, as a matter of fact, the very notion of considering American culture as the echo of the European warns us that while linked to the latter, American culture is, unquestionably, something different.

It is different, however, not in the way in which, for example, English and French culture are different, but different when contrasted to Europe considered as a separate historical entity. In this way we come to suspect that the "newness" of American culture sends us back to the peculiar character of its historical constitution, or, if one prefers, to its very *raison d'être* in so far as it constitutes a particular way of life which seeks to realize itself within the range of the possibilities of European culture. In this way it will prove that the "novelty" of American culture resides, paradoxically, in its "Europeanness" in such a way that the latter is a condition which not only qualifies but also actually defines American culture. Its true meaning must be sought, then, not in the habitual comparison with Europe—not in hypotheses and interpretations of filiations more or less naturalistic, based on differences of environment and peculiarities of race [2]—but on the very ontological constitution of America, which was conceived, let us not forget, precisely as the "*New* World."

It seems to us then, that in order to understand the course of Mexican philosophical thought thoroughly, it will not be amiss to review the investigations we have made concerning the being of America, concerning what America is.[3] In this way we will become aware that this philosophical thought reflects the manner whereby the possibility in which this being consists has been realized, and, aware consequently, that in this process one finds the most authentic and definitive meaning of America, its true originality.

I
CRITICISM OF THE TRADITIONAL NOTION OF THE BEING OF AMERICA

We have come to the conclusion that the difference in American culture, its "newness," must be determined by way of an analysis which will show the structure of the being of America as a "New World." If this is to be our immediate object, however, it will easily be admitted that our study must take its point of departure in the examination of the prevailing notion concerning this "being" of America. In this way the analysis will not only profit by the assurance that it has the initial support of an historical reality, but we will also know that its results will permit us to come to a decision as to whether that prevailing idea is acceptable or not.

1. America as a "Discoverable" Entity

When we look about us, in quest of the idea which is now entertained about America, we find ourselves disconcerted by the superficiality of the available notions. Depending on the point of view taken, America proves to be an infinity of things: now simply one of the continents of the earth, again the union, the sum, or more than the sum, of several nations; and another time, land of opportunity and of liberty or perhaps of iniquity and tyranny; now the champion and arsenal of democracy, again the fulcrum of imperialism and exploitation; now a young and striving world, again now a decrepit and deceptive copy of another; and, finally, who knows how many more other views which multiply in the light of prejudices and repugnances, sympathies and hatreds. And to this heap there must be added, in order to make the chaos denser still, national and regional differences, and that very important, perhaps even decisive difference, between the two Americas, the Anglo-Saxon and the Hispano-Latin, which frequently threatens the unity of the general concept because much that is said of the one does not prevail concerning the other. Sometimes this difference is so exaggerated that it seems that one is speaking of two worlds so different that it is impossible to understand how both of them deserve the title "American."

If we wish to come out of this difficulty with some profit, it will be necessary, then, to look for a common denominator underlying all of these pretended characterizations of America, no matter how irreducible they may seem, because none of them recommends itself more than the others and all have an equal justification for being advanced. All contain the grain of sand of their relative value, and we have to take great pains to see whether there is anything which all of them exhibit as a characteristic which they possess unanimously.

All of these notions, ideas, or images of what America is are not arbitrary; nothing is arbitrary in history. All are historical expressions, and it is in history, consequently, that we must look for the common root we are seeking. Let us, then, go back to the origins in order to recall the fact on which everything else depends. As a matter of fact, there was a time when the world was conceived as an entity composed only of Europe, Asia, and

Africa. At the end of the fifteenth and the beginning of the sixteenth centuries, however, there occurred a series of events which ended by placing in crisis that tripartite conception, for it became necessary to admit the existence of an unforeseen and unforeseeable entity, similar to those anciently admitted, the same that was baptized with the name "America." In a word, let us recall the formidable fact of the appearance of America on the stage of history.

However, this appearance has been, and still is, explained as the result of a discovery. America, it is said, appeared on being discovered, and the decisive point for our present undertaking is that since all of the notions which are entertained about it presuppose this explanation, we may expect to find in it that common denominator. What is certain is that however different and contrary these notions may be, all equally refer to this entity of which it is affirmed that it appeared on being discovered. If this be the case, however, it is obvious that the common notion which underlies all the others is that America is a being made in such a way that it was possible to discover it, or, in other words, that we have to do with a "discoverable" entity and that the problem consists, then, in ascertaining what such an idea may suppose ontologically.

2. *America as a Thing-In-Itself*

Since we have to clarify the meaning of the idea of America as a "discoverable" entity, let us begin by taking into consideration the way in which it is said that that discovery took place.

There is no one ignorant of the famous account: on October 12, 1492, Christopher Columbus discovered America when he found an island, today geographically ascribed to this continent. The discovery, nevertheless, was casual, because Columbus did not have the intention of making it, or was he aware that he had done so, for it was his intention to go to Asia, and he always believed that this island belonged to an Asian archipelago.[4]

However, it is easy to notice that the account does not make explicit how the discovery ascribed to Columbus was made, since it is expressly denied that he had the intention or the awareness of revealing the being of the entity which is, nevertheless, said to have been revealed by him. All that is affirmed in this regard, as is obvious, is that the discovery took place in the same moment at which Columbus sighted the island. It is thus, then, that the peculiar problem of this thesis consists in making clear why it is supposed that that sighting affected the revelation of the reality of America, independently of what Columbus thought and believed about his own action.

Moreover, it is clear that the meaning of this thesis consists in presenting these two facts, the sighting of the island and the revelation of the reality of America, as the terms in a relation in which the first is the cause of the second. The difficulty then appears to consist in knowing on what basis such a relation can be established. The reply tolerates no doubt; since the sighting of the island is not thought to be the cause of the discovery because Columbus thought so, it is held to be such in virtue of the fact itself, that is to say, by reason of the purely physical circumstance that someone collided with or perceived the island. Nevertheless, this, far from clarifying matters, seems rather to take them up into the mystery, in such wise that in order to dissipate it we ask what such a strange idea supposes.

It seems beyond doubt that in order to think that the mere physical perception of a thing is a cause enough to reveal what it is, it must be supposed that the reality of that thing must have been given previously, for, on the contrary supposition, the perception of it would have nothing to reveal. And, as a matter of fact, this happens every time we perceive objects which are familiar to us: we know in them the reality which has already been assigned to them, and thus we are able to say what they are. However, in such instances there is no question of discovering the reality of the thing, but simply of recognizing it.

The instance we are analyzing is different. It is a question, not of a thing whose reality was already familiar and, for that reason, able to be recognized, but of a thing unknown and, in the highest degree, unforeseeable. What is it, then, which must further be supposed in order to be able to think that the mere perception is enough to reveal what it is? Manifestly, it will be necessary to suppose not only that its reality had been given it before but also that it possessed it of itself, in its own right. In other words, that its being is essential to it in such wise that it belongs to it inalienably, with complete independence of anything which might be believed in this regard. Only thus, as a matter of fact, is it possible to think that when Columbus perceived this island, in which he thought he recognized the reality of Asia, what he "really" did was to dis-cover America, the reality of America, since what he perceived was then already and forever just that. It is in this way, consequently, that one succeeds in establishing the relation of cause and effect between the purely physical fact of the sighting of the island and the revelation of the American reality which is supposed to be its essence or nature.

We go on to conclude, then, that the ontological supposition of the idea of America as a discoverable entity consists in think- ing that America is an entity which already existed, constituted as such, when Columbus perceived a portion of it. America is a being, then, which was always there, always disposed to be discovered, so that it makes no difference that at the historical moment in which it was perceived, the idea held about the world made it impossible even to conceive it. In a word, the condition of the possibility of the idea which is held about America consists in thinking of this entity as a "thing-in-itself." Such then is the fundamental ontological supposition of the thesis of discovery, and we must now submit its validity to proof and to determine whether or not it is an adequate mode of understanding the historical reality to which reference is made. However, to reach this objective, it will be necessary to take into consideration, first, how it came about that one could think that Columbus discovered America without knowing what he was doing, that is, we must examine the history of this idea.

3. History of the Idea of the Discovery of America

The detailed and documented account of the history of the interpretation of the first voyage of Columbus as the discovery of America is a task which we have already carried out in another place.[5] Here we are going to summarize in a simple and direct manner the results of that work.

A. No one is ignorant of the fact that Columbus believed that his voyage of 1492 was the realization of the very old project of reaching the coasts of Asia from Europe by the western passage.[6] The idea, then, that this voyage meant the discovery of America neither originates with Columbus nor takes into account what contemporary witnesses affirm. It has been, therefore, an historical problem to determine the origin of this idea.

B. Our investigations prove that the idea originates in the general skepticism with which the claims of Columbus, that he had reached the Asiatic coasts, were received. In fact, this lack of credence gave rise to a doubt about what the intentions of Columbus might really have been. Thus, there immediately began to circulate a rumor that held that the enterprise had as its purpose, not to reach Asia, but to verify the existence of some unknown lands of which Columbus had learned from a mysterious sailor who had died in his house.

C. This story, known among specialists as the "legend of the nameless pilot," is objectively false. There has been much discussion about the circumstances and the events which might have provided the pretext for it; however, the important thing is that whatever these may have been, it is to the wide acceptance of the legend that we owe the fact that the voyage of Columbus was conceived in the first instance as an undertaking to discover unknown lands.[7]

D. This alteration in the understanding of the voyage is the first decisive step in the history which we are relating. Not only did it interpret the voyage of Columbus in this new light but it also obscured the true purposes which had animated him.

E. When later, after a prolonged and difficult ideological

struggle (of which we shall give an account in the proper place), the matter finished with the admission that the lands visited by Columbus constituted an unforeseen and unforeseeable "fourth part" of the world, baptized with the name of America, the lands to which that legend referred were identified with this new geographical entity, and in this way there arose the idea that Columbus discovered America.[8]

F. However, this interpretation, of anonymous, popular origin, presented serious difficulties when the historians examined it in order to convert it into an historiographic thesis. In fact, if the intervention of the mysterious sailor be taken as true, the discovery should be attributed to him and not to Columbus. If, on the contrary, it is rejected as false, the problem is to explain how Columbus might have been aware of what these lands were despite their being unknown, since otherwise his act could not be understood as a discovery. The effort to find a solution for such irreducible terms gave rise to a process whose three stages we shall briefly present.

G. *First stage:* the discovery as an intentional act of Columbus. After two fruitless efforts,[9] the solution consisted in affirming:

(a) that the existence of America was completely unknown. Thus is met the condition on the part of the object for conceiving the act as a discovery.

(b) that, nevertheless, Columbus was aware of the existence of America even before sighting it. Thus is met the condition on the part of the subject.

(c) that there is no opposition between these two affirmations because if Columbus knew that America existed, it was not because anyone had told him so, or because he had read it anywhere, but because he inferred it as a scientific hypothesis. Thus, consequently, the voyage was a true discovery and attributable to Columbus and only to him.[10]

H. *Second stage:* the discovery as an intentional act of history. We shall not spend any time in recounting the slow liquidation of the thesis presented above. Since it has been clearly established by present scholarship that the true intentions of Columbus were to reach Asia and that he believed that he had done so, we may pass on to examine the second stage of the process. It is stated:

(a) that the existence of America was entirely unknown. In this way the requirement is met from the part of the object in order that the act be one of discovery.

(b) that Columbus had no further objectives than that of reaching the extreme coasts of Asia by sailing from Europe by way of the western route; that when he found land, he believed that he had achieved this objective; and that, consequently, he had no idea that America existed. Despite these circumstances it is affirmed that thus was America discovered and that the act was not casual, but intentional.

(c) that the justification for this way of thinking consists in believing that history is a process which develops in accordance, not with the personal intentions of men, but with an intention which is immanent in them and rises above their personal intentions. Independently of the purposes which men pursue in the course of their lives, that super-intention of history fulfills itself, employing them as its instruments. And if the discovery of America is considered an event desired by history, it is because it is a matter of a step forward toward the greater scientific knowledge of reality, goal of the teleology of history. In this manner the condition for the act being a discovery on the part of the subject is met.

(d) according to this thesis Columbus' rival is not that mysterious sailor of the earlier stage, but rather history itself. What is certain without doubt is that the act of discovery ends up by being attributed to Columbus because it is held that he was aware of his mission as an instrument of history, since he understood his voyage as a step forward in the progressive march of science and not merely as an undertaking for profit.[11]

I. *Third stage:* the discovery as a fortuitous act. Neither shall we spend time here relating how the idealist explanation of the previous stage came to be abandoned. This fact belongs to the history of the triumph of positivism, which led historians to reject as impossible the notion of teleology in history. The historians, proclaiming their adherence to the positivist mandate of holding only to what is observable, took it as a methodological principle to relate, according to the celebrated formula of Ranke, that which really happened, with rigorous fidelity to the witnesses. One would be led to think that according to this new orientation the idea of conceiving the voyage of 1492 as the discovery of America would be abandoned, since, on the basis of the historical data, it was impossible to meet the conditions of such an act on the part of the subject. What is certain is that, flagrantly violating their principles, the historians insisted on this old idea and, in place of limiting themselves to the information in the sources, affirmed:

(a) that the existence of America was completely unknown. Thus the condition on the part of the object is met, just as in the two earlier theses.

(b) that, consequently, it is necessary to admit that Columbus never was aware of the existence of America. Despite this fact, however, what he really did was to discover it.

(c) it is made clear that the discovery took place when Columbus stumbled on that first island which he sighted on his voyage, with this difference, however, from the earlier thesis; that it is admitted that the act lacked all intentionality and was, therefore, entirely casual or fortuitous.[12]

4. Analysis of the Historical Process of the Idea of the Discovery of America

The critical reader will have noticed that in the casualist thesis of the last stage one cannot see how the condition on the part of the subject for the voyage of Columbus being conceived as a discovery is met or how this fact can be attributed to him. As a matter of fact, with noticeable difference from the two earlier theses, this last would destroy, apparently, the element of intentionality which is postulated in them.

Now clearly, in logical terms this situation is incomprehensible because if a determined meaning is conceded to a certain act, it is necessarily because the correlative intentionality of the act has been postulated. No act is something in itself; its meaning or reality depends on the intention which is attributed to it. Thus, if we see a man leave his house and start toward the neighboring wood, this act will have different meaning according to the purposes we attribute to this man. We will say that he is going for a walk, or that he is fleeing from something, or a thousand things more, according to which intention appears to us to be the true one. If, as a consequence, the same meaning is attributed to Columbus' voyage as in the previous stages, we have to suppose that, despite any affirmation to the contrary, an equal intentionality is postulated in it, except that at the moment one cannot tell to whom it is attributed or where its roots are.

Since in every act the intention which gives it meaning can only be rooted either in the agent, or in the act itself, or, finally, in the object, we can solve the enigma by simple elimination. Effectively, the historical process we have reconstructed tells us that in the first and second stages the intentionality of the act of discovery has its roots in Columbus and in history, respectively; that is to say, in the agent of the act and in the act itself, in such wise that we have to conclude, strange as it may seem, that the intentionality, in the third stage, has its roots in the object of the act, that is to say, in America, for the simple reason that there is no other place to locate it.

We must recognize, then, that in order to be able to affirm that Columbus discovered America when he touched on that island which he thought a part of Asia, it is necessary to suppose that this discovery took place because there was in America the intention of revealing itself to itself. However, this conclusion, though logical, must prove very disconcerting because, in whatever light we consider the matter, America is an entity incapable of entertaining intentions. Let us see, then, how it is supposed that the act of discovery is carried out to meet the conditions of this strange supposition.

Since the personal convictions of Columbus are cancelled out as "erroneous," the only thing which remains meaningful in his act is the fact of his having perceived the island. The scope of the act having been reduced in this way, the most that can be maintained about it is that it made manifest the *existence* of the thing perceived. Nevertheless, since this is not affirmed, but rather this act revealed the actuality or reality of the thing perceived, it is clear that for this thesis the manifestation of the existence of anything implies the revelation of its actuality, or, stated in another way, that the thing itself reveals what it is when anyone makes clear that that thing exists. But what then, in its turn, does such a supposition suppose? It supposes, of course, not only that the thing possesses the reality which it reveals, since otherwise it would have nothing to reveal, but also that it possesses it as a possibility of revealing itself, for under any other condition it would not reveal itself.

In this way we come to realize that the essentialist notion which we encountered as the a priori basis of the idea of America as a thing-in-itself (above pages 63 ff.) implies a kind of intentionality in it, or, better, the attribution of a teleology in virtue of which the thing becomes capable of revealing its reality through its own power by the mere physical fact that someone perceives it.[13] It is in this way, then, that it is possible to understand that in the thesis of the casual discovery of America the intentionality of the act of discovery is rooted in America itself. The actual result, in that case, is that when this thesis assigns the act of discovery to Columbus, it really turns him into a blind and docile instrument of that teleology which it supposes to be immanent to the thing. Thus, in the final analysis a profession of faith is made in a kind of fetishism which ends up by conceiving history, not as a process which depends on decisions taken and carried through by man, but as the result of designs immanent to things, blindly and fatefully carried out by man who is reduced, in this way, to the condition of a slave if he knows not what inexorable finalities of the inanimate world.

From all that has gone before we may conclude:

First, that the effort to explain the manifestation of America as the result of its discovery is unsatisfactory, since this interpretation ends up by reducing itself to the absurd position of denying historical reality as such.

Second, that this logical unraveling is the necessary consequence of the fundamental supposition of this interpretation, that is, of the essentialist idea of America as an entity endowed once and for all, toward all and in every place, with a reality which is predetermined and unalterable.

Third, that, consequently, since it has been proved that this manner of conceiving America yields no adequate reason for its reality, it ought to be rejected.[14]

II
THE "INVENTION" OF AMERICA

We have freely come to the obligation of substituting for the essentialist notion which has traditionally been held about America another which would do justice to its reality. This task implies a method diametrically opposed to that employed up to this point. In fact, instead of starting with a pre-conceived idea about the reality of America and trying to explain how Columbus could have revealed it without being conscious of doing so, it will be necessary to begin with what we know, on the basis of documentation, about what Columbus did in order to explain how he came, eventually, to endow with the "American reality" the lands which he discovered. We have carried out this investigation in a book dedicated to this purpose, and we shall limit ourselves here to presenting a résumé of those results.[15]

1. The History of the "Invention" of America

It has been established beyond all reasonable doubt that when Columbus sighted some land on his first voyage, he believed that he had reached the extreme eastern coasts of Asia. Let us take this belief seriously, and instead of cancelling out as an error the meaning which he conceded to the voyage, let us accept it as the historical reality of the event.

Since it is clear that this meaning is nothing else than his having attributed to these lands the reality of Asia, all temptation to give it a different meaning in virtue of what we now believe these lands to be must be rejected as unauthentic. Manifestly, that opinion of Columbus was not arbitrary; for it is hardly necessary to explain that if he believed that the lands which he had sighted belonged to Asia, it was because he supposed that this continent extended to the place at which he encountered them. His belief had as its basis the geographical image he entertained before sighting them, and to that image he imputed the status of scientific truth. His attribution of the reality of Asia to these lands is nothing else, consequently, than the natural consequence of the effort, on the part of Columbus, to explain them, because this is precisely the necessity under which we lie of adjusting every empirical revelation to the image which we have formed of the reality.

This reflection, banal as it may seem, is important for our purpose because it makes us aware that the connecting thread of history which we are going to reconstruct is that of an explanatory process which will end up by placing in crisis the old image of the world which served Columbus at his point of departure.

A. THE INITIAL EXPLANATION AND THE DOUBT

We have just seen in what consisted the initial explanation which Columbus gave to those new lands. What is peculiar, however, to Columbus' attitude is that he did not propose this idea as an hypothesis but as an evident truth. Columbus not only thought that the lands he had sighted were part of Asia but he also accepted this idea as a belief. In other words, he supposed that these lands could not otherwise be accommodated or adjusted within the image of the world. This explains the extraordinary tenacity with which he adhered to his idea during the course of his life and the titanic efforts which he expended in adjusting to it the new empirical data which later explorations continued to accumulate. This intransigent attitude, however, found no echo either in the official circles which had patronized the undertaking or among the majority of the geographers and map makers who concerned themselves with the event. Independently, then, of the diversity in motives and arguments, what is certain is that Columbus' belief encountered an environment of skepticism which changed that belief into a mere hypothesis needing empirical proof.[16]

B. CRISIS OF THE ANCIENT IMAGE OF THE WORLD

The historical detail of this stage is extremely complex and there is room here only to record the principal vicissitudes through which Columbus' idea passed in the measure in which all the possibilities of proving it were tried.[17]

In the beginning this idea was considered possible but improbable because it was difficult to admit that the Asian continent extended so far. Later, when it was realized that this was a matter, not merely of islands, but of an extensive land of continental dimensions, the hypothesis gained favor to the point of being considered not only probable but quite certain. Nevertheless, for the hypothesis to reach the status of truth it was necessary to establish experimentally the existence of a maritime passage which would connect the waters of the Atlantic with those of the Indian Ocean because it was known that Marco Polo had employed it on his return voyage to Italy from the eastern coasts of China. The discovery of this passage, therefore, became the touchstone which would remove all doubt. The quest for the passage, at the two points at which it was thought that it might exist in accordance with a variation in the idea about the configuration of the Asiatic coasts, motivated the consequent efforts, namely, the so-called third expedition of Americo Vespucci (May 1501–September 1502) and the fourth voyage of Columbus (May 1502–November 1504).

The results of these explorations were decisive not only because the passage was not found but also because the wide sweep which Vespucci made in his quest provided data which could no longer be adjusted to the then current image of the world, and the truth of the latter, consequently, entered into a crisis. It is certain that these data did not make it necessary to discard the Asiatic hypothesis so far as the northern mass of the new lands was concerned, although it permitted it to be supposed that they constituted a geographical entity hitherto unknown. There ensued, consequently, a contest between both possibilities; the truth is, however, that despite this irresolution the idea which projected a vast and unforeseen land-mass running from pole to pole between Europe and Asia was gaining adherents. It soon found its formulation in the celebrated pamphlet entitled *Cosmographiae Introductio,* published by the Academy of St. Dié in 1507, and in the world map of Waldseemüller, of the same year, designed to illustrate this new idea.

These documents express the definitive crisis of the traditional image of the world, and in them, consequently, there takes place the inversion of the process, because now it was a question of offering a new image which would provide the recently discovered lands the accommodation which that other image could not afford them, and, for this reason, the meaning and the proper name which the ancient vision was incapable of giving them.

C. THE NEW IMAGE OF THE WORLD

The pertinent passage of the *Cosmographiae Introductio* is too well known to merit transcription. Let us recall only its essential statements:

(a) that the world—that is, the cosmic domicile of man—has traditionally been conceived as formed of only three parts: Europe, Asia, and Africa;

(b) that recent explorations had revealed the existence of a fourth part;

(c) that, as Americo Vespucci had been the one to conceive

this fourth part,[18] it seemed just to call that land Americo, or, better, America, so that it might fit in with the names of the other parts; and

(d) it is made clear that this "fourth part" is an island and thus different from the other parts which are "continents," that is, lands not separated by the sea, but neighboring and contiguous.

2. The Apparition of America

Considered in its historical authenticity—that is, as the culmination of the process of explaining the new lands—the meaning of these four propositions is transparent.

The first presents, in synthesis, the ancient vision of the world and its tripartite constitution. The decisive point is then that within this image of the reality America was not, according to the accepted way of thinking, something "unknown" but, much more radically, something unforeseeable and, for that reason, *nonexistent*. Under any other supposition one cannot understand, save as pure nonsense, Columbus' faith in the certainty of his convictions concerning the reality of the new lands, the tenacious effort on all parts to prove the hypothesis of the Admiral, and the great difficulty encountered in abandoning it despite the mountain of contrary indications accumulated during the course of the explorations.

The second expresses the crisis of that old tripartite image, induced by its incapacity to explain the new lands as a reality empirically proved, since there is admitted one more "part" of the world in order to provide room for this reality. The decisive points, then, are, first, that not only was the bankruptcy of the traditional way of conceiving the world declared but, even more than that, a different way of understanding it was postulated. Secondly, however, since this change originated in the need to explain the new lands, these became automatically included in the world as its "fourth part." In this manner the new lands were conceded, for the first time, to be a distinct reality, equal in kind to the other three parts which heretofore had constituted the world.

The third assigns a proper name to this new entity and gives it an individual character within the group of other entities of the same species. It was thought justified, and not without reason, to name it America.[19] The decisive point is that this is the way in which America appeared and became visible and not in virtue of any supposed casual discovery which Columbus had achieved by the sole fact of perceiving an island on October 12, 1492.

The fourth and last statement calls attention to the essential difference between the old and the new concepts of the world. As a matter of fact, when it was made clear that the new lands constituted one of the integral parts of the world, despite the fact of being separated from the others by the ocean, it was thought that this fact had made it possible to define the limits between the world and the rest of universal reality. The decisive point is that now, for the first time in history, the world included the entire terraqueous globe, since it already included the ocean, although it was conceived as able to include the universe, since in principle it had no limits.[20]

Such is the extraordinary and incomprehensibly unknown ideological revolution which brought in its wake the invention of America. Not only is its scope greater than the Copernican revolution but it also appears to us to be the historical antecedent of the latter and its condition of spiritual possibility.

III
TOWARD A NEW CONCEPT OF THE REALITY OF AMERICA

We have seen that America appeared when, after a long struggle of ideas, it was conceived, together with the other new lands, as the "fourth part of the world." In this formula, as a consequence, we have the original expression of the American reality. In order to possess it securely, however, it is necessary to make precise the meaning which corresponds to that formula within the new image of the world which that same formula calls forth, since, obviously, it was coined from the terms of the old tripartite conception. Let us begin, then, by considering the meaning of the idea of America as one of the "parts" of the world in order to clarify, thereafter, what is meant by the condition of being, precisely, the "fourth" part, and no other.

1. America as a Natural or Physical Entity

We shall take our point of departure in this initial consideration: if America was recognized, jointly with Europe, Asia, and Africa, as one of the parts of the world, it was so recognized because for some reason it was considered on a par with them; it then becomes a question of determining the motive for thinking it so.

It is clear that there is no question of an assimilation based merely on accidental circumstances, such as the form of the lands, the geographical situation, climate, or other factors of this order; from this point of view America offered novelties so great and extraordinary that they would lead to its being differentiated from, rather than compared to, the other parts of the world. And as we see, the express identification of the most notable accidental difference—namely, that America was separated from the other three parts by the waters of the ocean— did not prevent that assimilation.

If, however, the motive we are seeking is to be found not in this order, it must be rooted in something common and essential to those four parts precisely as parts, that is, components of a whole. When the problem is viewed in this way, the answer is obvious: the motive of this comparison can only be the idea that Europe, Asia, and Africa, together with America, share one and the same nature. This, in turn, can only be the nature which imparts its fundamental unity to the world, with complete independence of the special peculiarities of any of its parts. This conclusion imposes itself logically; moreover, in confirmation there may be recorded here the express affirmation of this view by the chronicler Lopéz de Gomara and, as an instance of much greater weight, the voluminous work of the Jesuit Joseph de Acosta written at the end of the sixteenth century to show that, despite its novelties and strange natural features never before heard of, the American world could be perfectly fitted into the framework of the ideas which were then entertained about the structure of universal reality.[21]

The citation of Acosta's work is, for another reason, very pertinent because it helps us to understand that the comparison between Europe, Asia, Africa, and America belongs to the mere physical aspect; as a result, we can assert that the conception of this last entity, America, as "part" of the world belongs solely to its material constitution, that is to say, its corporeal reality.

In order to express this idea adequately, it was necessary to use a generic term which would include all the parts of the world in as far as they partake of one, same physical nature and which would, at the same time, show that the lack of contiguity of America with the other parts had been cancelled out as of no signification; such lack of contiguity would, in terms of the old tripartite image, have prevented its inclusion in the ambit of the world. We allude, obviously, to the term "continent," which, it should not be forgotten, means in its original acceptance, and rightly so, contiguous, neighboring, or attached.

This, then, is the class of entities to which Europe, Asia, Africa, and America belonged at the time this last being was invented, and such, consequently, was the concept which corresponded to them in the new idea of the world, replacing the archaic concept of "parts" proper to the older image.

We will conclude, therefore, first, that the mode of being under which America was "invented" consists in the conception of the totality of the new lands under the species "geographical continent"; in the second place, however, we conclude that that mode of being belongs wholly and only to its material

being or reality, to its body, something given and already
formed, just as our body is for ourselves.

2. *America as a Moral or Historical Entity*

America was not, however, invented and conceived only as
one of the parts of the world and, therefore, like the others,
but also as the "fourth" part, and hence as different from the
others. In this section we shall try to show in what this difference
consists and what may be its ontological significance.

A. THE CONCEPT OF THE "NEW WORLD"

Let us begin by noting the paradox which is implied by the
fact that America occupies the fourth place among the parts
of the world. From this point of view, it remains undifferentiated
within a numerical series which, in principle, is infinite. From
another point of view, however, this fact singles it out as something unique because to the recognition of a "fourth" part is
due, neither more nor less, the fact that the series, before
closed and limited, now becomes open and infinite. As a consequence, the conception of America as the "fourth" part likens
it to the other parts, both earlier and later. At the same time,
however, this concept sets America apart as the instance which
provoked the crisis and destroyed the old, tripartite image of
the world, and defines its individuality with relationship to
Europe, Asia and Africa considered as a previously constituted unity. Thus, there appears in the midst of the world a
dichotomy whose intrinsic character we shall have to determine
in order to succeed in understanding in what the reality of
America consists.

It is immediately evident that this dualism does not refer
to the idea of the world as a physical entity because we have
already made clear that in the physical order all the parts are
similar. It has its roots, rather, in the idea of the world as a

spiritual reality, understanding this idea, obviously, in accordance with the change involved in the crisis which the admission of America among the parts of the world had provoked. If we recall that this change consists in substituting for the old, static, and providentialistic, the modern, dynamic notion of the world as the work of man, in the degree to which he reduces the universe to the demands of his life, it will not be difficult to see what that dualism rests upon. It rests upon the fact that in the dynamic view of the world its structure is not that of an homogeneous whole (as it is in the material order) but admits of a distinction between that which is already established and that which is in process of establishing itself. The spiritual character of both extremes is the same, and in this sense they are parts of a single, existing world. Their concrete historical reality, however, is different: the one is already fully realized as that world; the other is in possibility to that status. In this sense they are two different "worlds": the one in process, the other already realized; or to express the matter in the received terms, it is a dualism between a new and an old world. We may conclude, then, that in the same way that the concept "continent" translated the original formula of "fourth part"—indicating in this way the similarity of America to the other parts in the order of material reality, the corporeal aspect of its being—so also the concept of "New World" translates or interprets the same formula in order to draw attention to the difference of America with regard to Europe, Asia, and Africa in the sphere of historical reality, that is to say, in the spiritual aspect of its being.[22]

B. THE NEW EUROPE

Up to this point we have succeeded in making clear that America was conceived under its material aspect as one of the geographical continents of the world, and under its spiritual aspect as a possibility of constituting itself as an historical world. In what, then, does this possibility concretely consist? This is the last determination which we must achieve in order to understand the reality of America completely.

Let us take our point of departure in the reflection that if the difference which distinguishes the Old from the New World is that between a portion of the world in possibility of establishing itself as such and another already constituted, this possibility consists in the fact that the as yet unconstituted portion realizes itself according to the model of the part already established, since its structure is in agreement with the whole to which both belong. Thus it is, then, that the spiritual being with which America was originally endowed, consisted in the possibility of actualizing the form of the historical life of the Old World; consequently, we must consider the peculiar structure of the latter if we hope to determine the concrete content of that possibility.

Up to this moment the Old World has presented itself to us as a homogeneous unity because we have only had occasion to consider it from the outside in opposition to the New World. If, however, we examine this unity from within we see that its tripartite division indicates that its internal structure possesses a qualitatively hierarchical organization based on the idea which the culture of the West has entertained of itself. The essential point is that from antiquity the cultural primacy of Europe over the other two parts of the world has been affirmed by example and with ever greater insistency. To be sure, during the course of centuries the geographical definition of Europe has undergone modifications. The high spiritual range, however, which has been accorded it, at least since the time of Herodotus, not only has maintained itself during all these alterations but has also ended up as something very like an incontrovertible historiographical dogma, which was later accorded the theological support of Christianity and the unconditional assent of Renaissance humanism.[23]

The basis of this idea is found in the profound conviction that only in the environment of Western culture is it possible for man to realize himself fully and to reach the goal of his destiny; or, in other words, that this culture represents the single, true historical possibility for mankind. It is a question, then, of a culture which does not think of itself as the exclusive patrimony of one people or one group of peoples. Since, however, it has been the historical task of Europe to be the carrier and the vicar general of this patrimony, this universalism has translated itself into a cultural Europocentrism justified by the sentiment of its historical messianism which expressed itself in a program of colonial expansion. Since this has been the conception of itself entertained by Western culture, it cannot be a matter of surprise that it has conceived the world principally as the cosmic stage of its own existence and the condition for its own development and flowering, in such wise that in the final analysis the idea of the world as a moral entity becomes identified with it in one and the same historical structure. The primacy which Europe assigned itself not only raised it to the apex of civilization but also placed it on the highest step of a hierarchy in which the other parts of the world found places corresponding to the significance given to their forms of historical life in accordance with the norms of the model, Europe. As a matter of fact, and for the reasons noted above, this hierarchy assigned the second place to Asia and the last to Africa. This order became a scientific obligation in the treatment and discussion of the three parts of the Old World to make the structure of its historical unity clear.

In the light of these clarifications, we can now resolve our problem. Since America was conceived as a New World in distinction to the Old World, it is clear that it was not included in that hierarchy; otherwise the distinction would be meaningless. However, since its reality consists in actualizing the historical reality of the Old World, it is no less clear that the concrete content of this possibility lies in becoming the New Europe, since Europe represents that reality. With America, consequently, a second hierarchy is established; while sharing the same vertical axis with the older, it differs from it as the future projection of Western culture in contrast to its projection in the past.

Such is the reality of America: a geographical and historical

being, body and spirit; invented, inevitably, in the image and
likeness of its inventor.

IV
AMERICAN CIVILIZATION

We have reached a precise idea about the reality, the being,
of America; what, then, will be the meaning which must be
conceded to its civilization? In order to reply to this question,
let us first glance at the meaning of its history and in that light
compare the essentialist conception of America which has traditionally been held with that we now hold.

1. The Meaning of American History

If, as the custom is, the reality of America is conceived as an
essence, it is inevitable, in turn, that the history of America be
conceived as a series of events which in no wise affect, nor even
can affect, that being. Thus, only an external relation is established betweeen America and its history, like that between a stone
and the vicissitudes which might befall it. In this case, speaking
strictly, the history attributed to America is not *its* history; for no
matter what meaning is recognized in the events, these events
are always alien to it. In fact, despite all deceiving appearances,
America has and can have no history, and what is considered
such is nothing but a series of events "which happen," while
nothing happens to America. And, as a matter of fact, this is
precisely the meaning which, beginning with a supposed discovery postulated as a casual accident, has been conceded to the
American transaction. All that follows its fortuitous discovery—
its exploration, its colonization, its adventures, and its miseries—
form a long and complex chain of accidental events which leave
America as untouched as it was supposed to have been when
Columbus discovered it. The changes have been many; in the
intimacy of its being, however, America, an impregnable fortress,
is always the same invariable, indifferent, and indestructible

essence which revealed itself on October 12, 1492. "There will always be an America," even though, as is perfectly possible, no living human being remains on the face of the earth. This, then, is the inescapable conclusion: on the one hand, we have America as an entity incapable of a history which is truly its own and, on the other hand, a history attributed to America, but incapable of having meaning as *American* history.

Let us now consider the same problem in the light of the idea which we have succeeded in forming of the reality of America. The panorama changes radically. If this reality of America consists in the possibility of realizing certain cultural values postulated as universal or, to state it more briefly, in becoming a new Europe, these same events referred to America as mere accidents, appear instead as the actualization of that possibility. They take on, in this case, a meaning which makes them inalienably American, since they are referred to her reality in such wise that they not only *affect* her but actually *constitute* her. Between America and its history there is established, not that external relationship between the stone and what befalls it, but a constitutive link such as exists between a man and his biography. It may then be said, with the most exacting rigor, that the history attributed to America is its own, since both fuse into each other and are identified. America, consequently, not only proves capable of having a history but is its history; and this is the reason why we have been able to understand its appearance as the result, precisely, of its own history. And thus all that follows—its exploration, its colonization, the good and the ill that has befallen it—form now, not a chain of accidental happenings, but a meaningful process of the way in which America has realized itself to itself within the limits of its ontological possibility.[24]

2. The Two Americas

Civilization is the product of history, and since the history of America is but the actualization of its being as the possibility of becoming a New Europe, it follows that the concrete result of this process is what we call American civilization. Since this is not a question of the necessary fulfillment of a norm which predetermines history, but rather of a development which permits various efforts, the complete history of this civilization can show variations and modulations, successes and failures, which reveal not only the presence of different circumstances but also the trace of different roads. And, as a matter of fact, this is precisely what is shown us by the existence of the two Americas, the Anglo-Saxon and the Hispano-Latin. Their existence reflects the two ways opened up by the great dissidence which divided Europe in the sixteenth century into two camps, culturally and politically hostile, headed respectively by Spain and England, champions respectively of tradition and of modernity. These two components of American civilization are the result of the actual situation in which America was invented as a possibility of European culture; the division cannot, therefore, be considered arbitrary. Having explained in this way the *raison d'être* and the historical necessity of the two Americas, let us characterize them in their essential traits.

First: since it is a question of two ways which necessarily had to be tried, the one is as authentic as the other. Their necessity justifies their existence, independently of the value to be assigned them according to the degree in which each achieved the reality of America.

Second: since Hispano-Latin America is the historical result of the actualization of the American reality from the traditional point of view of European culture, its manner of establishing the New Europe in America consisted fundamentally in reproducing this model as faithfully as possible through imitation. The reason is obvious, namely, there is no better means of reproducing what is already constituted and done, tried and accepted—that is to say, the traditional—than to imitate it. In general terms, then, the New Europe actualized in Hispano-Latin America was a copy of the old Europe conceived as the fully realized model of the historical or spiritual reality of man.[25] It is impossible not to recognize that this way was destined not to achieve its objective, at least not immediately, because the New Europe, which was actualizing itself in this manner on the soil of America, was "new" only in the sense in which a copy can be new. It is to be noted, then, that in the effort to profit in this manner by the opening offered by the invention of America there lies a negation of the meaning of America as a new possibility of European culture and, for this reason, a paradoxical failure to recognize the very reality of America. It is not an accident, therefore, that the conception of this reality does not belong to Spanish thought despite the fact that this glory should have belonged to it; [26] and there is nothing accidental about the fact that for three centuries Spain stubbornly insisted on employing the archaic and incorrect designation of "the Indies" instead of the name "America."

Third: since Anglo-Saxon America is the result of the way in which the reality of America realized itself by benefiting from the liberty which the invention of America offered to Western culture, it did not have recourse to imitative forms of life already assayed, but permitted itself the creation of other forms which were arising in response to the needs of new circumstances and above all to the desire to satisfy spiritual aspirations impossible to meet in the social environment of the Old World. In this case the New Europe is not set up as a copy of the Old, exalted to the status of eternal and archetypal model of the moral reality of man, but rather as a province of the Old World in which to essay and to develop new promises. If this is the case, it must be admitted that this and only this was the road by which the reality of America found and achieved its full historical actualization. It is no matter of chance, therefore, that the nation which established itself in this way should be America and that its sons, by way of antonomasia, should be called Americans.

We may conclude, then, that Hispano-Latin America actualized in its beginnings an historical reality which still belongs to the conceptual horizon of the ancient tripartite vision of the world, while Anglo-Saxon America belongs to the modern conception of the world as the permanent possibility of the conquest of the

universe by and for man. The New Europe which was founded
in this way was really new, because it was an opening out of
Western culture. In Anglo-Saxon America, consequently, we may
see the first and decisive step in the great process of the
universalization of that culture. If America, however, is the first
fruit of a universalized Europe, the clear and necessary consequence is that the initial dualism between the Old and the New
World disappears, of itself, in the moment at which America
achieves its reality fully; for the difference which separated them
was only the difference which exists between two parts of a
whole, one in a realized, the other in a potential, state. When the
possibility in which the American reality consists is fulfilled, the
New World ceases to exist as such, and necessarily the Old
World as well. There arises the new historical entity, Euro-
america, destined, in its turn, to disappear when the process of
universalization reaches its culmination and fullness on earth.

3. *The Special Problem of Hispano-Latin America*

With the preceding considerations the present work reaches its
goal; however, to complete its concrete proposals a brief reflection on the special problem involved in the history of Hispano-
Latin America since the period of its independence and its reformation into states of the modern type is necessary.

We have seen that the colonizing activity of Spain did not
actualize, in its rigor, the reality of America. This fact can
only mean that while this situation endured, Hispano-Latin
America remained in a state of mere possibility. It still represented the Old Europe in potency to becoming the new. This
clarification is of the utmost importance for understanding completely both the meaning of the Iberian civilizing activities in
the American lands and the peculiar drama of the emergence
of the new nations, so different from the case of the great
Anglo-American Republic. As this theme deserves a detailed
study which far exceeds our actual limits, we shall content
ourselves with the most pressing indications.

That the colonial Hispano-Latin world corresponded to the general undertaking of reproducing the traditional European civilization so tenaciously defended by Spain, is a fact so obvious that it is affirmed and repeated on every hand; and even today profound traces of this fact are readily to be observed. An eloquent indication is the effort made by the crown not only to implant institutions formed on metropolitan models (a very comprehensible measure, as an initial step) but also in maintaining them unchanged in the face of circumstances which were adverse to them; and when these circumstances so imposed themselves that they could no longer be disregarded, the crown had recourse, on the basis of forced analogies, to solutions inspired by the archaic experiences of mediaeval races and even one of races more distant than these. This is what happened, for example, in the implantation of the "encomienda" of the Indians which provoked so many difficulties. This is also what happened, with even more notorious results, in the great debates which accompanied colonization, such as those relative to the legal title of Spain over the new lands, its right to govern the native Indians, and, above all, in the case of the inflamed polemic concerning the human status of the Indians. Everything was Aristotle, patristic and scholastic theology; and while these debates honor the intentions of those who ventilated these issues and the Crown for permitting, and even encouraging, their ventilation, the truth is that they left a sediment which ended by creating in America, in all the orders of colonial life, a strange image of Spain as even more traditionalist and blinder than she really was to the new currents of European culture, from which that other America drew such rapid and such audacious profit.

Time rolled by and insensibly the specious grandeur of the Spanish viceroyalties in America was reduced to impotency before the new historical giant, which without the pomp of titles or rights of primogeniture, had been born to the north. It was in this hour of truth that there shone out in all its crudeness, not to say error, the deviation implied in Spain's commitment to the path of imitation before the possibility offered her by the invention of America. This, stated in our own terms, was what the men who carried to completion the task of founding the nations which have appeared on the ruins and ashes on the colonies obscurely sensed as a great historical deception. They began by calling themselves "Americans," a designation which underlined the desire to define themselves in contrast to the peninsular Spaniards, but above all to realize the historical reality which had been snatched away from them by legerdemain, and very naturally they took those to the north of them as models. Impelled by emulation of these models, they tried to efface, like a bad nightmare, the colonial past, which they perspicaciously referred to as "our Gothic age"; and with a bold leap they imitated the Anglo-Saxon political forms as a panacea which would provide an immediate remedy for all their inherited ills. At the same time, however, love for the customs and veneration for the beliefs in which they had been born and their understandable fear before a strange world, powerful and traditionally hostile, led them to adopt inadequate and confused solutions which formed the nascent nations, in the midst of political disorder, into economic ruin before the tremendous task of liquidating powerful traditional interests.

In another place [27] we have tried to trace the picture of this historical drama as far as it touches on Mexico, endeavoring to discern its positive meaning amid the dense darkness and shadows. We refer the interested reader to those studies so that we may isolate here only the meaning of that drama from the point of view from which we have sought to present American civilization.

If we do not forget the *raison d'être* of the two Americas and the contrast which they offer as the products of the two different ways of understanding the meaning of the invention of America, it will be easy to agree, we hope, that the movement of independence among the Hispano-Latin colonies and the historical processes which derived from it are basically but the delayed actualization (though not too long delayed) of that reality which was ascribed to those lands when they were recognized as the fourth part of the world. The independence of the United States of America was, in the political area, the first unequivocal sign that the New Europe had already emerged in America; that of the South American nations (the designation is historically correct, even though it may not be correct geographically) was, by contrast, the announcement that the Old Europe had disappeared from this continent. This, then, is the difference between the two, though it is, at the same time, the link which unites them. Precisely for this reason, however, the future of those nations is most complex, because they must actualize their reality as American entities, no longer in the original, relatively simple circumstances of a dualism, now vanished, between an Old and a New World, between the old and a renewed Europe, but in the actual circumstances of a world in the process both of establishing itself as a single entity and of carrying out the ancient project of universalizing Western culture.

The great adventure of America which we have tried to understand in the intimacy of its very reality does not fail to be reflected—somewhat shadowy and remotely, but not for that reason unfaithfully—in the mirror of the historical process of philosophical thought in America. In the studies which follow, dedicated to the presentation of this process in New Spain and in Mexico, the reader will be able to discern the image of the old Europe in its scholastic robes. Later, however, he will become aware that the adoption and cultivation of the great European philosophical adventures is, rather than a simple echo, their acclimatization to peculiar and proper circumstances with the purpose of awakening a national consciousness which, in its essence, is the consciousness of the American reality. In the modalities which are thus impressed, in the objective which is thus pursued, and in the new speculations evoked by the gradual realization of this objective resides the historical meaning of philosophy in Mexico and its promises within the wider field of universal philosophy.

José M. Gallagos Rocafull

III. PHILOSOPHY IN MEXICO IN THE SIXTEENTH AND SEVENTEENTH CENTURIES

Introduction

Western philosophy came to Mexico, New Spain as it then began to be called, with the Spanish conquistadores who by the end of February 1517 had reached Yucatan and soon after took control of the entire country. With their arrival there began the contact between two worlds whose historical destiny it was to influence each other mutually so as to create, as soon as possible, another, new world. In the beginning, the efforts which the indigenous cultures had made to decipher the great enigmas which European philosophical reflection had always taken as its proper concern were neither well-known nor justly evaluated. Although the ideas of the natives did not interest the newcomers—there were, of course exceptions, and some very important ones—they were greatly concerned to decipher as completely as possible these lands whose powerful originality created great and intricate problems for them. It was vital for them to know thoroughly both the country and its inhabitants. They quickly became aware that traditional European conceptions would not always guide

them and that they would have to create others under which
the surprising novelty of this new world might fall.

It is an effort which both parties, the indigenes and the
colonizers, will make at the same time in the course of an
eventful war of ideas, a war fatal in the long run for the
autochthonous cultures but which did not leave the invading
culture unscathed. For the latter not only had to amplify its
thematic, opening it to questions unknown in the Old World,
but the whole of it, without ceasing to be fundamentally the
same, would acquire new shadings on being introduced into a
new medium which assimilated it and lived it after its own
fashion. To draw together in summary manner, the chief themes
which arose in those first periods and the results achieved, it is
indispensable to sketch roughly the philosophical panorama of
that time, since philosophy is, in the fullest meaning of the term,
this effort to decipher reality and to find its "logos," or profound
explanatory principle. To this sketch the first part of this study
will be devoted.

The second part, closely bound up with the first, is a review
of the specifically philosophical work achieved, first, by those
from across the sea and, later, by those born in the new world,
Creoles for the most part, although some indigenous thinkers
also take part in the effort. Its principal seat was the religious
houses, prodigally established by the missionaries, and the Royal
and Pontifical University, whose titles clearly reveal the general
orientation of the colonization. In that university the principal
faculty was that of theology, the teaching of which was to be
prepared and served in the Faculty of Arts by a philosophy
faithfully submissive to Christian dogma, that is to say, the
scholastic philosophy in its various schools, especially the
Thomist and, later, the Scotist and Suarezian. The influence of
the Renaisssance also reached here, of which there are outstanding witnesses, nor were there lacking outstanding talents devoted
to the empirical study of nature to the preparation of charts and
maps, to astronomical, geological, and hydrographic observations,
although they were isolated individuals, some simply devoted

amateurs and other technicians especially sent out for this mission, who did not found schools or have continuators of their work.

For the sake of brevity, I shall omit the bibliographical references. Those who want them may find them in my book *El pensamiento mexicano en los siglos XVI y XVII* (Mexican Thought in the Sixteenth and Seventeenth Centuries) published by the Autonomous National University of Mexico in 1951.

I
THE PROBLEMS OF COLONIZATION

St. Thomas Aquinas, citing the authority of Aristotle, says on the very threshold of his *Summa Contra Gentes* that "the usage of the greatest number has commonly established that those persons be called philosophers who order things rightly and govern them well." If credence be given to these words, we will have to accord the great title of philosopher to those colonizers who took upon their shoulders the crushing task of creating order and government in the vast, complex and original continent to which they had come. They were not especially prepared for this exceptional task. Hard necessity, which knows no law, forced them to consecrate themselves arduously to it, without suspecting even remotely the great and beneficial repercussions it would have on their own persons. For no sooner had they set hand to the work than they realized that in order to carry it out, they themselves would have to grow until they attained the height of the work which towered above them; and we must recognize that they truly grew and traversed the limits of time just as, before, they had traversed those of space. Men who in their homeland had not stood out grew to the stature of giants in these lands and set themselves to ordering these lands for good or for ill with a vital frenzy in which there had to be, alongside genial accomplishments, the grossest errors.

The first become more certain, the latter more lamentable, when the great learned men of the time study, analyze, and evaluate them, the men to whom the colonizers—principally the magistrates, missionaries, and agents—had recourse in quest of orientation and support. Before the new Mexico could think for itself, it had already become a problem on the other side of the sea. The most famous of those whose counsel was sought, Fray Francisco de Vitoria, said that his flesh opened up when they sought his opinion on the things that were happening in that strange and distant New World. And it is true that those problems always had a human basis which removed them from the purely intellectual sphere and saturated them with blood, sorrow, and mud.

Those great problems may, in a schematic manner, be reduced to three. The first was the problem of determining the nature of the Indians, which logically led to a new idea of man. Secondly, there was the problem of the incorporation of the Indians into the new culture, whose fundamental element, alike for colonizer and colonized, was the religious element. The third and last was the complex of juridical problems which the conquest and colonization raised, beginning with the problem of the legitimacy of Spanish sovereignty. It will be necessary to attempt a concise synthesis of the three.

1. A New Idea of Man

From the beginning the mode of life of the indigenes, so different from that which they had always seen, disconcerted the newcomers, and when in the course of their enforced association shocks and conflicts arose, some of them came to judge the Indians so harshly that their expressions lead one to believe that they denied them a rational nature. Thus the grave Dávila Padilla wrote in 1596, "there are people, and not unlettered ones, who called into doubt whether the Indians were truly men of the same nature as ourselves." De Remesal reinforces this sentiment when, twenty years later, gathering together the reports of Fray Bartolomé de las Casas, he makes clear that "this diabolical opinion had its beginning in Hispaniola ... many carried it to Mexico and spread it abroad through the territory; principally the soldiers who went there for discovery and conquest, and our province of Guatemala became deeply infected with it."

And this opinion became so widespread that the Bishop of Darien, Fray Juan de Quevedo, testified before Charles V in Barcelona that "according to the information I have about those in the place where I have been and in the territories through which I have traveled, those peoples were savage *by nature.*" Even more extreme, it would appear, is Fray Tomás de Ortiz, who presented to the Council of the Indies an extensive report in which he affirms that "the men of the territory of the Indies seem to grow up with some manners and virtue until the age of ten or twelve years; from that time on they return to the status of brute animals. Finally, I say that God never created a race so far gone in vices and bestiality and without any admixture of goodness or breeding." Approximately the same opinion was expressed by Fray Servando de Mesa, Fray Fernández de Oviedo, one of the sources of Ginés de Sepúlveda, and, in Mexico, Fray Domingo de Betanzos, although in the hour of his death he retracted his statement that the "Indians were beasts."

The opposite opinion, nevertheless, had great and authoritative supporters. The most important were Christopher Columbus and the Catholic Kings, who never doubted the rational nature of the Indians but considered them their vassals, free and equal to those in Spain, although at the moment not prepared to exercise all their rights. In his turn, Alexander VI, in his Bull *Inter Caetera* declared that they were fit to become Christians on an equal basis with other men. In Hispaniola, Fray Antonio de Montesinos in 1511 ardently defended the position that the Indians were men with rational souls. His arguments, carried to Spain by his brother, Fray Reginald, fully convinced the Dominicans of San Estaban in Salamanca where thirteen masters of theology gathered and agreed "against those who held that erroneous opinion (i.e., that the Indians were not capable of receiving the Christian faith) and tenaciously defended it, one ought to proceed with death by fire as one proceeds against heretics."

In Mexico, Hernán Cortés, in his *Segunda carta de relación* wrote "that, considering that this people is barbarous and so removed from the knowledge of God and communication with other rational nations, it is admirable to see what they have achieved in all their affairs." It is the same thesis which the brilliant Fray Bartolomé de las Casas maintained, with copious arguments, all his life. The Franciscans maintained the same point of view, but without his lack of moderation. As early as 1531 they took the part of the Indians in a collective letter sent to Charles V and signed by Fray Juan de Zumárraga, Fray Martín de Valencia, Fray Luis de Fuensalida, and others. Motolinia, in his turn, declared:

He who taught men science, the same provided and endowed these Indians in their natural state with great talent and capacity to learn all the sciences, arts, and duties which have been taught to them.

Fray Bernardino de Sahagún declared with all his authority that "there are among them persons very apt in letters and in theology." No less stinting in praise is the testimony in favor of the Indians given in 1533 by Fray Jacobo de Esteva, Fray Cristóbal de Zamora, and six others of the first twelve Franciscan missionaries to come to Mexico.

It was not the Franciscans, but the Dominicans, who carried the dispute to the Holy Father, at that time Paul III. Before him, Fray Bernardino de Minaya and the first bishop of New Spain, the outstanding Fray Julián Garcés, pleaded the cause of the Indians. The latter sent the Pope a long letter which is, both in content and form, the most beautiful plea ever made in the Indian cause. The outcome of these representations was the Bull *Unigenitus Deus* of Paul III of 1557. In it one reads:

Taking into account that those Indians, as the true men that they are, not only are capable of the Christian faith but seek it with great desire, and seeking to provide the proper remedies in these matters, with apostolic authority, by these letters we determine and declare that . . . the Indians . . . even when they are outside the Faith, are not deprived nor open to be deprived of their liberty, nor of dominion over their goods; even more, they may freely and licitly remain in possession and enjoyment of such dominion and liberty, and they are not to be reduced to slavery.

For the time being, the controversy died down; however, it flared up anew thirteen years later when the famous Cordoban humanist Juan Ginés de Sepúlveda, the royal chronicler, wrote his famous *Democrates alter,* to which Fray Bartolomé de las Casas, even before its publication, advanced the most relentless opposition.

So great was the agitation that it seemed necessary to Prince Philip that their differences should be ventilated before a committee made up of such qualified men as Melchor Cano, Domingo Soto, Gregorio López Bartolomé de Miranda. . . . This was done in Valladolid in two series of sessions which took place in 1550 and 1551.

The controversy maintained itself within the framework of the anthropological and political ideas of Aristotle. Sepúlveda was directly and profoundly conversant with these ideas and on that basis built his argument. He starts from the Aristotelian principle, admitted as undeniable by all of the colonizers, that the less perfect should submit to the perfect, and that, consequently "he who can see with the mind naturally orders and dominates and he who can perform with the body serves and obeys"; the less intelligent must submit to the more intelligent. However, neither Aristotle nor, following him, Sepúlveda limit themselves to postulating that the more worthy should command but, with evident exaggeration, go on to justify the enslavement of the less endowed as a command of nature. As this seemed to be the case of the Indians, Sepúlveda concluded that by natural right, which he identified with the thought of Aristotle, the Indians had to be subject to the Spaniards, and if they did not do so willingly, they should be obliged to it by force of arms.

Against this natural servitude Fray Bartolomé de las Casas brilliantly maintained that every man, no matter what his culture, has in principle all the rights inherent in the human person. And, as St. Thomas Aquinas has said, it is so because he has a reason by which to provide himself with the things he needs by the help of his hands. Reason and hands are the indisputable lot of every man. The Indians possess it, "for all," says Fray Bartolomé de las Casas, "have understanding and will, all five exterior senses and the four interior ones, and are moved by their objects. All enjoy or find satisfaction in the good and are pleased with what is tasty and happy, and all reject and abhor what is evil." (*Historia de las Indias*, vol. II, p. 334) He admits that not all peoples possess the same degree of development, but he denies that any are not capable of receiving culture. On the other hand, those who are today the most retrograde may tomorrow be the most cultivated. He does not openly deny Aristotle's thesis, but he does reduce its application to manifest cases of mental incapacity, which are necessarily few. However, he is not so felicitous when he sketches the different grades of barbarism among peoples.

The contestants did not come to any agreement. Nevertheless, the controversy brought clearly into view the tremendous social and political consequences of the question so bitterly discussed or disputed. And it served to dispel all doubt concerning the human condition of the Indians. Sepúlveda himself recognized that the difference between them and the Spaniards is only that which exists between "children and adults, men and women." In Mexico, as in the whole of Spanish America, the most profound way of recognizing this equality was not to impose such a distinct separation between indigenes and peninsulars, permitting them to mingle neither blood nor culture, but rather, on the contrary, to encourage miscegenation, permitting the Indian to influence freely the Spaniard and to fertilize him with his newness.

2. *The Assimilation of the New Culture*

The spiritual life of New Spain in the first periods of colonization was a continuous struggle to reconcile two undertakings, both essential and both little short of contradictory. On the one hand was the undertaking of making New Spain Spanish, compelling it to assimilate the culture and the way of life of the conquerors; on the other hand, that of permitting the native thought to unfold itself freely, although always within the new ideas. Even with these restrictions the national spirit was forming itself in this struggle, and if its forgers had difficulties, the colonizers also stumbled over grave problems. The first and most important was the problem of the most efficient and adequate way of implanting the imported culture. They took it for granted that inevitably they would have to replace the indigenous cultures; they did not, however, see so clearly what must be the road by which this substitution might be most successfully and most promptly reached. This problem was worsened by the conviction of the colonizers that the most important element of their culture and that which must be assimilated before all others was the religious. To impose the new culture on the Indians was to evangelize them. However, evangelization implied, on the one hand, that the indigenes should renounce their ancestral religion and, on the other, that they would accept Christianity freely and willingly. A double difficulty, which gave the missionaries charged with the Christianization of the natives much to think about.

The first question which they had to resolve was that of determining how to present Christianity with respect to the ancient religions. The dilemma which they found confronting them was this: should they propose Christianity as the perfection, the fulfillment, and fullness of the indigenous religions, or should they present it as something entirely new and incompatible with the old religions? In the first case, could they, in order to make the new religion more acceptable to the natives, utilize some of the elements of their religions, purifying them and adopting them to Christian ideas? In the second case, they had to advocate a total and absolute break with the previous religions, thus eradicating the risk of their amalgamating with the new religion the errors and the pernicious practices in which the natives had been brought up.

It was this second opinion which imposed itself. Upon the missionaries there weighed the Spanish horror of heterodoxy, revitalized and sustained by the condemnation of the Lutheran heresy two years after they had reached Mexico. They were implacable regarding the temples, the idols, and everything which bore the scent of paganism. Monuments, sculptures, and codices disappeared, destroyed with a systematic fury which the mentality of the age fed and even exacerbated. Still, it is a matter of justice to recognize that where there was no clash with religion, the missionaries showed extreme consideration and respect for the native cultures. They studied the languages lovingly, preserved the day-to-day usages and customs, adapted their teaching to the temperament and capacity of the indigenes, and faithfully collected their ideas and traditions.

In this latter effort no one surpassed Fray Bernardino de Sahagún. He lived in New Spain for about sixty years, dedicated to the study of the history, customs, and language of the natives. In his *Historia General de las cosas de Nueva España* he collected the finest fruit of his study and experience. Of this book Robert Ricard says, "it is the effort best fitted in method and most successful in giving the missionary in Mexico an ethnographic formation."

At least in the study of the native languages he was seconded by a substantial group of missionaries. Not for a moment did they think of forcing the natives to learn Spanish; on the contrary, they felt that it was their obligation to study the languages of the country, sparing no effort. Moreover, they realized that these languages must be great and difficult, since in their structure and phonetics they resembled not at all the European languages and, further, since they were divided and subdivided into a multitude of dialects and regional modes of speech. Evidence of their tenacity is provided by the vocabularies, grammars, and other writings by them in several tens of different languages. Of the 1188 titles collected by the Conde de la Viñaza in his *Bibliografía española de lenguas indígenas de América* 141 belong to the sixteenth and 298 belong to the seventeenth centuries.

In this way they contributed to the survival of the old cultures by giving them, by their presence, the opportunity of influencing the new. For the time being, this influence was *nil*, as the instances were very few in which the natives offered reasoned and conscious resistance to the new religion taught them. Moctezuma himself, with great tact, refused to enter into discussion with Cortés upon the value of their idols and limited himself to asking him "not to speak words in their dishonor"; later, some chiefs and native priests entered into polemics with the missionaries, especially in the north. But, in general, the atmosphere was one of frank and open cooperation. The natives opened themselves to Christianity with a fervor which awakened exaggerated hopes in its catechists. With the passage of time they had to realize that if there were many who were sincerely converted, there were not lacking those who continued to practice their old religion secretly and kept their idols hidden in their houses, in the forests, and even behind the crosses and beneath the altars.

Evangelization, however, had another side to it, that of its repercussion on those who practiced it or patronized it, which contributed greatly to giving them a clear consciousness of Christianity as well as of human liberty. The light emerged from a long and sharp controversy in which were disputed points of such transcendence as the following: Must they first submit to the Indians and convert them later, or the contrary? Could we permit idolatry? Should sins against nature be prevented even by recourse to violence? The answers they were given implied a solution to the human problem which, at bottom, transformed itself into the question whether or not the conquerors recognized in the natives all the rights inherent in human personality.

Already in 1523, Charles V confirming the norms established in 1493, gave to Cortés an order that he should abstain from intimidating the natives and forcing them to accept Christianity. Those, however, who lived in the new country and were in close touch with the reality had strong doubts about this "loving treatment" of the natives and, more than once, disobeyed the orders of the Emperor. In Mexico all unanimously agreed that the acceptance of the faith must be voluntary; however, while some, accused as idealists and excessive purists, would not accept even the least sign of coercion, others, who considered them-

selves more levelheaded and prudent, held that in order to preach
Christianity among the Indians effectively it was necessary to
create an atmosphere of submission and security which could
exist only in the presence of armed forces.

These two fundamental tendencies were incarnated in two men
of extraordinary merit, though of differing mentality and character: Fray Toribio de Benevente, or Motolinia, and Fray Bartolomé de las Casas. In his famous treatise *Del único modo de
atraer a todos los pueblos a la verdadera religión* (On the Only
Method of Drawing All Peoples to the True Religion) the latter
maintains, in the light of the whole Christian tradition, that it is
not in the power of men, but in the hands of God, to discern
who, as a matter of fact, are to form part of Christianity. From
this favor "no nation in the entire world has been entirely
excluded." It is the Church which has been charged with calling
the elect of God in time. In order to fulfill this mission she must
call all who have asked to be predestined, that is, all men. And
she must call them in the only way established by Divine
Providence, namely, "the persuasion of the understanding by
means of reasons and the invitation of the uncoerced movement
of the will." They must be given time so that they may be
converted, and all violence must be completely avoided. To
subjugate the Indians and then to preach to them is to unleash
upon them all the evils of war, to deny Christ to follow Mo-
hammed, and to heap up absurdities and blunders. Further, to
say that the Indians are not forced to embrace Christianity but
that the armed forces limit themselves to removing the obstacles
to preaching the faith is to foster an equivocation whose only
result is to create an enduring resentment and to "fake" con-
versions.

Motolinia does not attack these lines of reason. His strong
point was not ideas, but facts. And to these he appealed to refute
Fray Bartolomé. His method was that which was followed in
Cunamá, in Vera Paz, and in Florida; and the results could not
be more discouraging, for some Dominican missionaries went
there, and "as they landed and before they reached the city, in

the port, half of them were killed and the others went back into the boat, and there they had to recount how they had escaped."

The same difficult question arose again in Mexico, that had been so extensively argued in the Middle Ages concerning the baptism of children, the sons of infidels, before they had reached the age of reason, and without the consent of their parents. In fact, what was being discussed was whether the natural dominion which fathers have over their children prevails or not over the divine mandate to baptize all peoples. There prevailed then the opinion of St. Thomas, which assigned priority to the natural right. This was also the opinion which proved victorious in the inflamed debate which broke out over all cultivated Europe when the first information about what was happening in the New World reached there. It was one of many cases in which the hard reality of the New World stimulated European thought, forcing it to revise, rectify, and penetrate more deeply its accepted ideas which, in their turn, found ample resonances in the new lands.

3. Juridical Problems

Many and grave were the problems stirred up by the conquest and colonization of the New World. Goaded by the exigencies of their own situation, those who had the mission of establishing new social, political, and economic structures in those countries tried to solve these problems without a precise rule and in a completely provisional manner. Men of letters, however, principally theologians and jurists, transposed those problems into the intellectual sphere, and, studying them, became aware of the disquieting and enigmatic character of those distant peoples. Not all of them were successful in recognizing its profound message, which, in the final analysis amounted to the necessity of placing the spirit before the letter and that instead of applying the latter whether or not it was adequate, there should be created new ideas, norms, and institutions to meet the new facts. The controversy developed in an atmosphere of the greatest freedom,

and out of it there emerged a generous and humane legislation,
not surpassed by any other colonizing country, and a series of
theories which mark a great juridical progress and incorporated
into the actual situation imperious demands of the law of nations
and the law of the human person. It is not possible to cover
all of its many aspects, but the fundamental problems were those
bearing on the legitimacy of the Spanish sovereignty, with which
was bound up that of the legality of the war carried on against
the natives, and of the form of rule or government which should
be imposed on them.

A. THE LEGITIMACY OF THE SPANISH SOVEREIGNTY

At first glance the legitimacy of the Spanish sovereignty seemed
amply justified by the Bulls of Alexander VI, especially *Inter
Caetera*. Very soon, however, consciences became disturbed, and
the king asked his learned advisers to compose a written opinion
on its validity. The opinions of Dr. Palacios Rubio and of Padre
Matías de la Paz have come down to us, while the others have
been lost, although a good part of the content of that of Martín
Jiménez de Enciso is known. In principle they accept the papal
donation as valid; however, all do not interpret it in the same
way. While Palacios Rubio and Matías de la Paz recognize that
among the Indians there exists a true and legitimate sovereignty
based on natural law, which is not annuled by their infidelity
and still less by their conversion, Jiménez de Enciso maintains
that they had lost that sovereignty by reason of their idolatry
and "that it could be taken by force and those who defended
it be killed or captured and those taken made slaves."

From these discussions emerged the famous "requerimiento,"
or inquiry of Dr. Palacios Rubio, which is a well-intentioned
but impractical effort to reconcile the validity of the papal donation with the natural rights of the Indians. It is neither licit nor
legal, it is stated in that document, to declare war against the
natives without previously explaining to them that the one and
eternal God, creator of heaven and earth, gave to St. Peter "the

whole world for his sovereignty and jurisdiction" and that one of his successors "had made donation of these islands and mainland of the ocean sea to the Catholic Kings of Spain." The latter had sent to them religious men who "would preach to them and teach them our faith," and those "who of their free and pleasing will, without any reward or condition became Christians and are such" the kings of Spain ordered them to be "treated like his other subjects and vassals." All are asked and required to do the same thing, taking "a suitable period of time" to deliberate about it. If they recognize the King of Spain as lord, the latter "will receive you in all love and charity, will give you many privileges and exceptions, and will do you many favors." In the contrary instance, he will make war on them and "the fault will be theirs for the deaths and the losses they will suffer in their persons and their goods."

The "requerimiento" was ineffective, and the discussion, violent and profound, over the validity of the pontifical donation continued; the focus of the dispute, naturally, was the universities and religious houses. The controversy served to overcome definitively the confused political ideas of the Middle Ages and to create modern political law. As the Indies projected their disturbing shadow over the Hispanic peninsula, the Spanish thinkers became aware that they had passed over the political threshold of the Middle Ages to the state organization of modern times, without, however, having a clear awareness of this transcendental transformation. The virgin reality of the New World, enigmatic and wholly original, obliged them to revise their ideas and to carry out a critical, and at the same time creative, work, whose most outstanding representative was Fray Francisco de Vitoria.

In his report *De los indios recientemente desubiertos* (On the Recently Discovered Indies) he holds that the Indians must be recognized as legitimate lords or sovereigns over their lands and that their kings and princes are to be considered as authentic sovereigns of those countries unless they have lost their dominion for any reason which might annul that right. Certainly the supposed papal donation did not annul it, because the Pope as supreme authority of the Church, a religious and spiritual society, holds a spiritual, not a temporal, power. Nor is the Pope "civil or temporal lord of the whole earth," nor "does he hold any power over those Indians" or over the rest of the infidel world. His competence in their regard is limited only to "disposing what may be necessary in order to administer spiritual affairs," as, for example, to send missionaries to them. Even less does Vitoria believe that the moral enormities attributed to the Indians constitute legitimate grounds for depriving the natives of their sovereignty, enormities such as "the eating of human flesh, indifferent concubinage with a mother, sisters, or men, tyranny, human sacrifices . . . because strangers do not have authority over them to punish such offenses."

On the other hand such strangers do have determined rights, as Christians or as men, in virtue of which they may occupy the Indies, inhabit them, have commerce with the natives, make pacts and alliances with them, preach the faith to them, and demand the free exercise of the Christian religion. If the natives respect these rights, there is no reason at all to despoil them of their lordship and goods; however, if they refuse to recognize such rights, the Spaniards might have recourse to force to exercise those rights, including that of making themselves sovereigns of those countries. To define these rights, and especially that of appeal to war, with exactness, was the genial insight of Vitoria, and it was the most important contribution which the Indies made to European thought in the juridical order.

4. The Just Regime to Which the Indians Ought to Submit

Bartolomé de las Casas, the man who held the most humane and generous vision of the political order, first implanted, spread, and imposed this question of the just regime. It is to be regretted that his intellectual endowments did not equal the nobleness of his sentiments. His political ideas are those accepted in the scholastic tradition. These he diluted in a prolix exposition and left in the embryonic condition in which he had found them without developing them in the light of the experience of the New World. Nevertheless, he perceived how clearly the imperative of justice demanded that each nation be left the laws and the rulers it had before the conquest. With all of them there should be formed a kind of federation or empire over which the kings of Spain, like the mediaeval emperors, would exercise a merely protective and honorary supremacy. Obviously, to establish this supremacy, they could employ no other means than persuasion, instruction, and good example.

Vitoria did not expound in an explicit manner the kind of political order which, in his judgment, ought to be established in the Indies. It seems that he was inclined to make of them one or a number of kingdoms subject to Spanish sovereignty, but with the same rights and autonomy enjoyed by Aragon and Catalonia on the peninsula. The point on which he is quite clear is that "it is not permissible to lay upon them a heavier yoke than upon other Christian subjects, whether by imposing greater tributes, by depriving them of liberty, or by other oppressive measures." The kings of Spain "are required to give suitable laws to their republic (that of the Indies) in such wise that they may be preserved and increased and may not be despoiled of their money or their gold." However, "it is not enough that the prince give good laws to the barbarous peoples; he is also obliged to appoint ministers who are able to enforce them, and to the degree to which this is not done, the king is not exempt from blame."

On this last point reason was entirely on his side because, despite so many humanitarian and just laws, great abuses arose in the Indies. The worst of these was the effort to impose slavery. In reality, it was a matter of fact and not of ideology. It is not entirely certain that Juan Ginés de Sepúlveda would defend its licitness, although he returned to the "pure" Aristotle—that

is, Aristotle unsoftened by mediaeval thought—and his consequent justification of natural slavery is at bottom the only argument which, up to our days, has been adduced to justify the
exploitation of man by man, with or without the name of slavery.
For Sepúlveda this norm has the force of law, which he presents as belonging to natural law and the law of nations: "The
persons and the goods of those who have been defeated in a
just war pass to the power of the conquerors," since, although
by nature all men are free, "it is more humane to reduce them
to slavery than to kill them." On the other hand, it is natural,
as Aristotle teaches, that the less well endowed or the imperfect live subject to the perfect. Whence he deduced that it
is not licit to reduce to slavery the Indians who submitted to
the "conquistadores," but only those who offered them resistance.

Slavery, however, was not the most discussed theme; this
was, rather, the "encomienda," the royal land grant. According
to law the Indians subject to such grants were not servants, or
vassals of their holders, but free, and placed under the protection of the crown. By an agreement between the crown and
the grant-holders, the latter could impose tributes and require
personal service of those subject to this arrangement, in exchange for which right the grant-holders promised to keep the
land subject to the sovereignty of the kings and to protect and
to instruct those confided to them. This was the feudal order
which Columbus had established in Hispaniola, and in the beginning it seemed that under this system the profit of the
colonizers and the education and good government of the Indians
coincided so well that Cortés extended it to New Spain as well.
This measure did not please the Court "because God created
the Indians free and not subjects," and the Court prohibited
it. The grant-holders defended themselves, and after many al-
ternatives were reviewed, they concluded that it should be maintained for the duration of two lifetimes.

The grant-holders did not lack able defenders, like Fray
Alonso de Castro and Padre José de Acosta, or opponents of
such weight as Motolinia, Fray Miguel de Salamanca, and the

well-deserving Bartolomé de las Casas. These two groups really could not understand each other because the one group was looking at what the grant-holdings ought to be, while the other was considering them as they were in fact. To the insistence with which the latter defended the liberty of the Indians, the former opposed the necessity of proceeding with prudence on a point so delicate, on which the economic and social regimen of the Indians was based. In the end the opinion of Fray Domingo de Betanzos prevailed; he alleged, on the one hand, that these territories were not secure and that if precautions were not taken, they could be lost; and on the other hand, that it was very dangerous suddenly to change the established laws and customs. The practical men won consequently, and their triumph postponed for a time the victorious march of justice in these lands.

II
Philosophy and Philosophers in Mexico

In the sixteenth and seventeenth centuries there was not, or could there be, in New Spain any other specifically Mexican philosophy than this "ensemble" of problems which winged their way from this land to the other side of the sea, inciting the thought of the "metropolis" and forcing it to make intense and fruitful efforts, the results of which we have reviewed. From beyond the sea there came in exchange a "pleide" of thinkers, writers, and organizers who transplanted to the New World the ideas and the philosophical currents which enjoyed most credit in the Spanish peninsula. In the beginning the selection was not very rigorous, or was the purpose very clear of forging a new culture rooted in the old one, but nevertheless wide open to the pressing necessities of these new lands and peoples. The originality of the New World, nevertheless, is so strong that, knowingly or unknowingly, its message was recognized and its influence made itself apparent in the bias and the shadings the imported doctrine took on. It was the initial sowing from which, with the advance of time, there was to grow a Mexican thought full-blown with its own specific characteristics.

1. The Influence of the Renaissance

The Renaissance arrived in the Indies in an oblique manner, imported by men of letters and religious who, among the ideas of the Old World with which they were imbued, also carried those of the Renaissance. Nevertheless, not even those most profoundly influenced by these latter ideas, such as Cervantes Salazar or Vasco de Quiroga, lived to its depth the great Renaissance journey. Their Renaissance was the same gigantic task, in which they were deeply involved, of incorporating a whole new world into Western culture. They attacked this task with the typical adventurous and heroic spirit of the Renaissance, which made them feel themselves to be other men. They freed themselves from many traditional prejudices, opened themselves to the provocative incitations of a future full of promises, extended their ideas to make them more proportional to the enormous dimensions of these lands, and permitted their imagination to launch forth to create new modes and forms of common life, free of the maculations of the forms of the Old World.

The Spaniards who went to the New World immediately understood that here they could not slavishly reproduce the structures of the peninsula. Still they did not see clearly how to replace them, and so they launched on a series of experiments like the famous experiments of Fray Bartolomé de las Casas in Tierra Firma and in Vera Paz, which turned the Indies into a vast laboratory. The idea which guided them, of clearly Renaissance provenance, is the idea which Fray Domingo de Betanzos expounded before the Council of the Indies:

This, truly, is a matter in which abyss calls to abyss . . . all things in these Indies are an abyss of confusion, filled with a thousand cataracts from which arise a thousand confusions and troublesome problems . . . and there is nothing which is ordered among the Indians from which a thousand troublesome problems do not arise. Although that which is ordered may be good in itself and motivated by a pure intention, when it comes to be applied to the matter in hand it turns out damaging and disordered and redounds in ill and trouble for those to whom we wanted to do good.

As the promoters of the "nuova scienza" postulated, it was a matter of openly distinguishing an a priori knowledge and an a posteriori knowledge which would confirm and support the former.

Neither were there lacking those who felt that almost mystical veneration for nature which the Renaissance had adopted. The exuberance and the majesty with which nature here manifested herself to them attracted many, and although they frequently suffered from her rigors, they felt a very lively interest in studying her and making an inventory of her riches. No one surpassed Dr. Francisco Hernández in this desire to know nature. A "protomedico" of Philip II, he came to Mexico in 1570, and during the seven years he stayed here he described and made sketches of the plants and animals of New Spain with no other help than that of his son, while in the hospitals he tested the effectiveness of the medicinals which the natives used. He was a friend of Arias Montaño, to whom he dedicated a "carmen," in which he recounts his sufferings and hardships. He also wrote about the antiquities of New Spain and composed a series of short philosophical works on problems from the Stoics and from Aristotle which were not known in New Spain.

Many of the first teachers of the Royal and Pontifical University of Mexico and many government officials in the first periods of the colonial age were disciples, colleagues, or readers of the great Spanish humanists of this time. With them came the rich Graeco-Roman inheritance, which was to be one "of the richest and most fertile roots of Mexican thought." Constant reference to Greek and Latin authors and texts marks not only those men who had had a solid preparation in Spain—like the first bishop of Tlaxcala, Fray Julián Garcés; Dr. Bartolomé Frías de Albornós; and Dr. Bartolomé de Melgarejo—but also men of few letters, who were, however, open to the dominant mentality of the era, men like Hernán Cortés and Bernal Díaz del Castillo. Both classes saw to it that "Mexico began to receive the name of 'Athens of the New World.'" From their first arrival in Mexico the Jesuits made a great contribution to this achievement and provided a strong stimulus to humanistic studies. In this work collaborated Padres Bernardino de Llanos, Baltasar López, Francisco Ramíriz, Pedro Salas, and many others.

The first professor of rhetoric in the university was Don Francisco Cervantes de Salazar, Latin secretary to Cardinal Loaysa, president of the Council of the Indies, and friend of Vives. Here he succeeded in becoming rector of the university, chronicler of the city, and "father of an extended generation of orators and professors of 'belles lettres.'" Of the various works he wrote, the most able are the *Dialogues*, saturated with a tranquil humanism, orthodox, completely at one with the "institutions." In them he learnedly expands on the condition of man in a moralizing tone in order to convince man that he ought to reconcile himself to his proper fortune or fate. He continued the *Diálogo de la dignidad del hombre* (Dialogue on the Dignity of Man) of Fernán Pérez de Oliva, while he translated the *Apólogo de la ociosidad y del trabajo* (Apology for Leisure and for Work) of Luis Mexía and the *Introducción y camino de la subiduría* (Introduction and Road of Wisdom) of Juan Luis Vives, to which "I added many additions and clarified much of what the author tried to say in a few words." He also collaborated with Vives in his *Commentaria in Ludovici Vives Exercitationes Linguae Latinae* (Commentaries on the Exercises in the Latin Language of Luis Vives), which he used in his teaching of that language. To the dialogues of Vives he added another seven composed by himself. The last three, written in Mexico, were called *Academia Mexicana, Civitas Mexicus interior,* and *Mexicus exterior,* in which he describes, in pictures filled with animation and life, the environment and the customs of the Mexico of his day.

If the humanism of Cervantes de Salazar is, above all,

moralizing and classical, that of the outstanding Vasco de Quiroga is especially utopian and beneficent. Don Vasco was "auditor of the second audience" and later bishop of Michoacan, and he is, beyond doubt, one of the most outstanding figures among the creators of New Spain. In 1535 he presented to the Council of the Indies an *Información en derecho,* in which he argued that the Indians possessed a soul "naturaliter Christiana" and that in goodness they not only equaled but surpassed the Spaniards. The barefoot Indians, with their long hair and their bare heads, seemed to him to walk "in the way in which the Apostles walked," and he desired to make of them a race of "Christians by right, like the primitive Church." In his *Información* he vigorously attacked slavery, denounced the barbarous procedure of the Spanish slavetraders and slaveholders, and refuted the arguments by which they tried to justify themselves. In this document there flower now and then ideas and sentiments which are like a muted echo of the Renaissance influence.

By contrast, the form of carrying out the colonization is, in his view, itself enslaving; and he acknowledges his debt in this matter to the illustrious humanist Thomas More and his book *De optime republicae statu deque nova insula Utopia.* Taking his inspiration from that author and his work, though in a different spirit, Don Vasco gives a qualitative value to the New World:

For it is not in vain, but rather with great cause and reason, that this is called the New World; not because it has been newly or recently discovered, but because in its people and as a whole it is as the Age of Gold must have been.

The strong realism of Quiroga gave a time and a place to the Renaissance vision, utopian and anachronistic as it was. The age of Gold is in process of being realized *here and now* in the Indies, whose inhabitants are "almost in the same condition, as I have found, that Lucan in his *Saturnalia* ascribes to the servants in those periods of the times of Saturn which are called the age of gold or the golden age." His conviction is so strong that he interprets his mission as bishop and magistrate as that of realizing in New Spain the dream of Thomas More. He has no thought of transplanting to this new country the institutions, customs, and norms of old Europe. Here these norms must be surpassed openly by raising the Indians from their natural simplicity to the heights of a paradisaical way of life.

This was the purpose of the "hospitales-pueblos" (shelter cities), whose creation he proposed in his final report and which later he founded on his own initiative and at his own risk. Their organization was communal; the goods which they acquired were to be common and inalienable; all were to learn two trades so that work in the field could be alternated with work in the city; the products were to be distributed among all according to the needs of each, and what remained was to be given to the sick and the paralyzed "in such a way that no one in the hostel suffered need." Thus, he predicted, they would live "out of danger from the three beasts which destroy and corrupt the entire world, that is, pride, ambition, and covetousness." Never was the spirit of the Renaissance so generously human as in the ideas and the works of Don Vasco de Quiroga.

There are also traces of the Renaissance spirit in the vigorous personality of Fray Juan de Zumárraga, who "for the Cross and martyrdom" agreed to become the first bishop and archbishop of Mexico. To his specifically religious activity he added a constant participation in the numerous and complex problems which the creation of a society born and developed in the shadow of the Church occasioned. Results of this work were the introduction of the press into Mexico and the foundation of its university. It was also he who personified Erasmianism in Mexico.

The Erasmus who influenced him was not the "humanist in the sense we give to the word today, but the interpreter of that more essential and interior Christianity which took possession of consciences in the manner of an interior illumination, the commentator on the divine message. Hence the importance which he assigned, as Marcel Bataillon testifies, to Erasmus' *Paraphrases* of the New Testament and the Psalms, and also, beyond any doubt, to the *Enchiridion,* that intimate and familiar exposition of the *philosophia Christi,* the philosophy of Christ." Its Christian basis and the circumstances of the time more than explain how a book like this, "which bore in itself in seminal form the Reformation and the Counterreformation like twin, but inimical, sisters," would continue to influence, even after it has been condemned repeatedly, not only frontier Catholics of vacillating orthodoxy but also Catholics and religious who always were faithful to the tradition and the authority of the Church.

Among these latter must be counted Fray Juan da Zumárraga, whose *Doctrina breve,* printed in Mexico in 1543, reproduced page after page of the *Enchiridion* and of the *Paraphrases* of Erasmus without mentioning whence he had taken them. From the latter work he takes the paragraph in which Erasmus demands that the Scriptures be translated into the language which the people use, a passage most severely censured in Europe. In the *Doctrina cristiana* (1546), Zumárraga also recast the *Suma* of Dr. Constantine Ponce, "the greatest writing among the Spanish catechisms—in the opinion of Menéndez y Pelayo—although unfortunately not the purest." Not that the doctrine of the book is openly heretical, but after his death its author was condemned as such by the Inquisition. As a result of Zumárraga's efforts, an heretical writer continued to teach the faithful in New Spain, in company with the proscribed Erasmus, without the Inquisition feeling obliged to prohibit his being read in this "free and fortunate land."

2. The Introduction of Scholastic Philosophy

Scholastic philosophy reached Mexico while it was flourishing in Spain through the efforts of such outstanding thinkers as

Francisco de Vitoria, Melchor Cano, Domingo de Soto, Domingo Bañez, Luis de Molina, Francisco de Toledo, Gabriel Vázquez, and Francisco Suárez, all of them also theologians of the first order. It was they who revised its principles, made it more firm and coherent as a system, extended its range of problems; and if, on the one hand, they paid no attention to the new sciences, on the other they made more acute and absorbing its preoccupation with metaphysics, the field in which they achieved their greatest triumphs. Of their many works those which principally were translated and found success in Mexico were those suited for teaching, which was the immediate end assigned to philosophy. This link (with teaching) determined its theme and from the first gave it a rather utilitarian shading. It was almost exclusively a medium for forming minds, disciplining them to logical habits of thought, and preparing them for other studies, such as the theological and juridical sciences, which were considered superior.

The preferred philosopher—indeed, the only one studied—was Aristotle; the whole of his *Organon,* his *Physics* and his *Meteorology* were read in course, as well as the *Generation and Corruption.* The concern for the students of arts was to equip them with a thorough dialectical preparation, a preparation which seemed excessive to many persons, even though it had been considerably pruned. Among these latter persons were Veracruz and Mercado, who had read the harsh diatribes of the estimable Luis Vives in his short work *In pseudo-dialécticos* (Against the Spurious Dialecticians). Fray Alonso de Veracruz did not want his students to waste their time and talents in practice fencing with puerile sophistries. He believes, and he affirms it in the prologue to his *Dialéctica,* that it was time to have done with useless disputes, to restrain swollen scientific pride or vanity, to come to a more intelligent understanding of the Aristotelian texts, no longer to give such unconditional adherence to the authority of the masters, and to renew the whole doctrine by a direct study of the sources.

In the university the first textbooks were the same ones used in the University of Salamanca, that is, the *In Dialecticam Aristotelis* and the *Summula summularum* of Domingo de Soto, which "were not lacking in merit but reflected the decadent influence of the scholastic philosophy of the periods immediately preceding," although the author declares in the preface that his purpose is to restore these disciplines to their proper dignity. In the *Summula summularum* De Soto comments on the famous text of Peter of Spain; and in the *Dialéctica,* on the *Predicables* of Porphory and the *Predicaments* and the *Posterior Analytics* of Aristotle; to which he adds, without commenting on them, the *Perihermenias,* the *Prior Analytics,* the *Topics,* and the *Examples of Sophistry.* The doctrine which he expounds is the traditional one with some original contributions.

There also was studied the *Introductio in Dialecticam Aristotelis* of Master Francisco de Toledo, who was outstanding for his sure or accurate interpretation of Aristotle, for the originality of some of his opinions, and for the excellence of his teaching method. This work faithfully fulfilled its introductory purpose. Without going beyond its depths, it introduces the novice to the technicalities of Aristotle, and clearly and simply defines the words or terms most often employed, maintaining a just mean, equidistant from traditionalists and innovators. It was printed in Mexico in 1578 by the Jesuits of the College of Saints Peter and Paul, probably for use as a text by those who studied the arts in that establishment.

3. Writers and Teachers of Philosophy in the Sixteenth Century

The most outstanding of these figures was the estimable Fray Alonso de la Veracruz, graduate of the universities of Alcalá and Salamanca, doctor of the latter, in which he read a course in the arts. He came to Mexico in 1535, when he was little more than thirty years of age and at the same port of his arrival, Veracruz, entered the Order of St. Augustine, taking at that time the name which he was to make famous as professor, missionary, counselor, and writer. He taught at the colleges of Tiripitío, Tacámbaro, and Atotonilco, where he lectured in the arts, and at the University of Mexico, where he held a chair of Sacred Scripture and a "Chair of St. Thomas with proprietary rights, which would be with the same qualities and pre-eminences as the first." He intervened effectively, and at times decisively, in the most serious problems raised by the evangelization; gave counsel with great discretion to the viceroys; lent authority and prestige to the recently founded university; was a friend of Vasco de Quiroga, Fray Bartolomé de las Casas, Fray Luis de León, whose cause he valiantly defended, and of Ovando, president of the Council of the Indies, to whom he acted as advisor on many occasions. He died in 1584, loved and respected by all in Mexico.

In addition to his copious theological writings, lost for the most part, Fray Alonso de la Veracruz wrote three books in philosophy, entitled *Recognitio summularum, Dialectica resolutio,* and *Physica speculatio,* which form a complete course in the arts as they were then taught. Because of his pedagogical intention he placed simplicity and clarity before originality and profundity. The *Recognitio summularum* was published in Mexico in 1554 and republished several times in Spain, where it served as a text in a number of colleges. In it he rigorously pruned away superfluous questions and useless digressions in order to leave the exposition "chaste and pure," although perhaps he did not achieve this purpose completely. He took his inspiration, as was rigorously required at the time, from the *Summulae Logicales* of Peter of Spain and, by way of an appendix, added a short commentary on the *Topics* and a compendium of the *Refutation of the Sophists.*

The *Dialectica resolutio* dates from the same year, 1554; Veracruz dedicated it to the "famous Mexican University which flourishes in New Spain." In this same dedication he says that he composed it while he was teaching these materials, suppressing everything superfluous and collecting the kernels from among the thorns in order to make the road completely open and accessible. The book is made up of three treatises, in the first of which he comments on the predicables, following the text of the *Isogoge* of Porphory; in the second he examines the categories of Aristotle, whose texts he reproduces and comments upon; in the third he composes a gloss on the text of the *Posterior Analytics* of Aristotle, chapter by chapter, up to the eighth chapter of the first book. Of the remaining chapters of the first book and of the entire second book he gives a brief resumé, since "it is enough," he writes, "to know these matters in order to pass on to other higher sciences."

Also in Mexico there was published, in 1557, the *Physica speculatio*, which contains the doctrine current in his time on physics, astronomy, biology, meteorology, botany, and psychology. Veracruz desires to follow the example of Titleman, and in accordance with his interpretation he expounds the *Physics*, the *On the Heavens and on the World*, the *Generation and Corruption*, the *Meteorology*, and the *On the Soul* of Aristotle. A work of such varied content must of necessity possess a very uneven character. The most valuable treatises are those on the *Physics* and *On the Soul*.

The principal points of the philosophical panorama of Fray Alonso de la Veracruz are then four: How does one think correctly? What is the relation between thought and being? What is nature? What is the soul? Obviously it was an incomplete theme, but ample enough to enable him to implant important philosophical problems and to initiate the studious youth of Mexico into the problems and methods of philosophy.

Not as famous as Veracruz, although in some aspects surpassing him, was Padre Antonio Rubio, who came to Mexico in 1576 and, after spending twenty years here, returned to Spain. A renowned author, he is linked to Mexico by his *Logica mexicana* because he wrote and taught it here. Its exact title is *Logica Mexicana R.P. Antonio Rubio, Rodensis, Doctoris Theologici Societatis Jesu. Hoc est Commentarii breviores et maxime conspicui in Universam Aristotelis Dialecticam una cum Dubiis et Questionibus hac tempestate agitari solitis.* In this book Padre Rubio prescinds from all the material treated by the "summulists" and comments with profundity on the logic of Aristotle. The doctrine is, then, the traditional one, which the author expounds according to the most authoritative opinions of the school, ordinarily adding nothing new. In his manner of treatment, however, he shows to what point the Renaissance criticism of decadent scholasticism was fruitful, for of that decadent scholasticism there is not to be found the least trace in this work, the mature fruit of the same tendency which has been encountered, before its season, in the works of Fray Alonso de la Veracruz. Perhaps the most serious criticism which can be raised is that, instead of presenting the problems as living and urgent he discusses them as though they were problems definitively resolved even while Suárez was already showing at this time, in his *Disputationes Metaphysicae,* the enormous possibilities of development to which the traditional doctrine was susceptible.

Tomás de Mercado, a native of Seville, came to Mexico quite young and in this country took the habit of St. Dominic in 1553. In relation to a treatise of his entitled *Suma de trates y contrates* Fray Louis de León says, "it appears to me that its author is a man of great talent and learning." He wrote two philosophical works, the first of which was entitled *Commentarii lucidissimi in textum Petri Hispani Reverendi Patris Thomae de Mercado, ordinis Praedicatorum Artium ac Sacrae theologiae professoris.* In the prologue, which has a strong Renaissance flavor, he says that it is his purpose "to expound this discipline in such a way that it may be useful and profitable to all and to strip it of all the false decoration of its defects and to return it to its native light and splendor." It is fundamentally a didactic book, in which he gathers his experience as a teacher and tries to accommodate it to the capacity of the student, while saying nothing false, though omitting much that is true. The second work is called *Reverendi Patris Thomae de Mercado, ordinis Praedicatorum Artium et Sacrae Theologiae professoris, in Logicam magnam Aristotelis commentarii cum nova translatione textus ab eodem autore edita.* It was published, as was the first, in Seville in 1571, and its greatest merit is the fidelity of its translation, of which Mercado himself says that it expresses the genuine opinion of Aristotle. In this translation Mercado gives his own interpretation of its sentences in a style at once smooth and polished, as a result of which this text becomes as clear as the others are intricate and obscure.

Padre Antoio Arias, "one of the first and most learned Jesuits who went to New Spain," alternated philosophical with theological and biblical studies. His premature death in 1603 did not prevent him from leaving various philosophical works which are preserved in the Biblioteca Nacional de México. They carry as title *Illustris explanatio commentariorum P.D. Francisci Toleti in octo libros Aristotles de Physica auscultatione per Reverendum ad modum Antonium Arias, ejusdem societatis et Philosophiae in celebri Mexicanorum Academia professorem.* He does not follow chapter by chapter the text of Toledo, but rather gives a compendium of his doctrine and extracts from it the most important questions.

In continuation there follows another work entitled *Aliqua notatu digna super commentaria P.D. Toleti in libros Aristotelis de generatione et corruptione,* in which the same method is followed as in the earlier work. This work is followed, in the manuscript, by another entitled *Tractatus de sphera mundi partim ex veterum astronomorum partim ex recentiorum doctrina et observatione collectus per doctissimum P. Antonium Arias, societatis Jesu,* in which, nevertheless, the doctrine of Aristotle and Euclid prevails. The manuscript ends with another treatise entitled *In libros Aristotelis de Coelo scolia quaedam.* Like the earlier works, these seem to be class notes and prove that Arias was a conscientious professor, very much *au courant* of scientific advances.

Astride the sixteenth and seventeenth centuries, Padre Alfonso Guerrero, also a Jesuit, became famous for the retirement and abstraction in which he always lived. His manuscript work is preserved, like that of Arias, in the Biblioteca Nacional de

México. There are commentaries on Aristotle's doctrine on the soul, on the heavens and the world, and on meteors. The Augustinian Fray José de Herrera was professor of the arts in the University of Mexico, "a man of great literary erudition, eloquent in Latin, Greek, and Hebrew, a great scholar of scripture," who wrote, but did not publish, a *Summa Philosophiae Scholasticae Patris Dominici de Soto ordinis Praedicatorum, in usum Academiae Mexicanae accommodata,* the fate of which is not known. Also an Augustinian was Fray Juan Zapata Alarcón, author of a course of philosophy, read to the students in the religious house of St. Augustine. Professor of the arts since 1578, and also an Augustinian, Fray Juan Contreras, was born in Mexico and left a manuscript entitled *Lectiones Philosophiae studentium captui accommodatae.*

The other professors who, during the sixteenth century, taught philosophy in the university left no works. They were named to their posts by means of competitions which were usually very hotly contested. The candidates were numerous, their talent in no way negligible, and their mental agility even greater. They were completely familiar with the Aristotelian doctrine and were *au courant* of everything being published in Spain. However, because the chairs of arts did not enjoy much esteem, all their concern was to move up to other more important chairs, and only rarely did they devote themselves entirely to philosophical studies. Even so, there were to be found such competent teachers as Doctor Juan García, Fray Pedro de Pravía, the Doctors Juan del la Fuente and Hernando Ortiz de Hinojosa, Fray Juan de San Sebastián, and the bachelor Alonso Muñez, author of a manuscript work entitled *Expositio librorum physicorum Aristotelis.*

Effective auxiliaries of the university in the teaching of philosophy were the religious orders, which from the earliest period established centers of higher learning and studies in which philosophy was earnestly cultivated. Fray Alonso de la Veracruz brought great prestige to the schools of the Augustinians; it is told of him that he took advantage of his living with the students to make them aware of the living problems which the colonization of the country aroused, or those which were being debated in the "metropolis." Among the Dominicans a great promoter of philosophical studies was Fray Domingo de la Cruz, one of their first provincial superiors. The Franciscans, laden down with their apostolic labors, found time to render in their studies fervent cult to the doctrine of Duns Scotus. The Jesuits, who arrived somewhat later, quickly became outstanding with such teachers as the fathers Pedro Sánchez, López de la Parra, Ortigosa, Antonio Rubio and many others who made the College of Saints Peter and Paul one of the major cultural institutions of New Spain.

4. Philosophical Studies in the Seventeenth Century

In philosophy, as in all spheres of life, the general tone of the seventeenth century is one of tradition and repose, like one who, after traversing a difficult road, calls a halt and collects his forces before setting out anew on his peregrinations. The unanimously recognized philosophy continues to be the scholastic, and it is this which was taught in the university and in the convents and colleges of the religious orders. However, notable changes command attention. The imported culture had taken definite root in the country and has already become the connatural expression of the new society in which the Creoles, and not the peninsular Spaniards, were daily achieving a place of greater influence. The creative power of the previous century is lacking, but a continuous increase and consolidation is present. The number of graduates in arts increases, and teaching institutions spread throughout the country. The average cultural level is greatly elevated; yet during the entire century not a single work of philosophy is published, although there continue to be excellent teachers. The gigantic effort which their predecessors had made now made it possible for the men of this century to go at a less accelerated pace. At the same time European thought was decisively departing from

scholasticism and was flowing through other channels, which
were not to the taste which continues to prevail in Spain and
in New Spain. Only at the end of the century, concretely with
Sigüenza y Góngora, do there begin to appear the first signs
of the great change which would bring in the eighteenth century.

In the university the most distinguished teacher was, without
doubt, Dr. Juan Díaz de Arce, of whom Plaza y Jaén, his contemporary, gives the highest eulogies in his *Crónica de la Real
y Pontificia Universidad de México*. He wrote various works
on biblical themes, in which he displayed solid erudition, secure
norms of judgment, a strong bent toward clarity, and excellent
pedagogical qualities. At this time there was established—as
had been done "in the famous and great universities of the
world, Salamanca, Alcalá de Henares, and others in the Realms
of Castille"—the chair "of the subtle doctor, Scotus"; this chair,
though belonging to the Faculty of Theology, greatly influenced
philosophical studies. Also at this time there were determined
the requirements which the candidates for the baccalaureate
in the Faculty of Arts would have to meet; these candidates
numbered, on an average, one hundred and fifty per year. They
had to pass at least two courses in the Summulae, in logic, and
in Philosophy. It was also granted that the graduates of colleges
approved by the university might obtain the grade of bachelor
in the university. According to the chronicler Plaza y Jaén these
colleges, in 1660, were "the old and outstanding College of Our
Lady of All Saints, very near to the university; the Royal College
of St. Ildefonso, of this City; the seminary of the colleges which
are not supported by royal stipend and which offer higher
studies; the Royal College of Christ; that of San Rámon Nonnato,
which was founded by the illustrious don Fray Alonso Enríquez
de Toledo, which is under the patronage of Our Lady of
Merced and was founded in the year 1654; the colleges of St.
Ildefonso and of Saints Peter and John in the city of Los
Angeles."

This report shows the apogée of philosophy in the colleges
conducted by the religious orders. Among their many readers

or lecturers in the arts the first place must be given to the outstanding Fray Diego de Basalenque, "poet, excellent orator, dexterous musician, profound philosopher, eminent theologian, exact historian, and very able astronomer and architect." He left various theological and scriptural manuscripts, as well as some *Summulae* and commentaries on the natural philosophy of Aristotle. Another Augustinian was Fray Diego de Villarrubia, author of the three volumes entitled *Philosophia Scholastico-christiana,* which are to be found in manuscript in the convent at Charo. One of the Franciscan professors of greatest competence at the time was a native of Lima, Fray Bonaventura Salinas, tenacious defender of the rights of the Creoles, who left a *Cursus Philosophicus* prepared for printing but never published. Another famous Franciscan was Fray José Gabalda, author of a *Curso de filosofía,* whose fate is unknown. Neither are there preserved the philosophical works of Fray Juan de Almanza, Fray Martín de Aguirre, and the famous Fray Andrés Borda, who for twenty years held the chair of Scotus in the University of Mexico. Among the Dominicans the most outstanding were Fray Antonio de Hinojosa, author of a *Clypeus thomistarum ex quaestionibus metaphysicis et theologicis affabre compactus,* and Fray José Calderón, who left in manuscript a *Compendium Philosophiae tomisticae,* which was, as a matter of fact, the complete course in arts of de Soto.

However, the Jesuits surpassed all this philosophical production. The most distinguished figures among them during this century were padres Andrés de Valencia, Diego Caballero, Sebastián González, Augustín Sierra, and Marín de Alcázar. Andrés de Valencia was the successor of the famous Padre Juan de Ledesma in the chair of theology in the College of Saints Peter and Paul; earlier, however, he taught philosophy and left treatises in the respective fields of logic, dialectic, and natural philosophy, which it has not proven possible to locate. At the Colegio Mayor de Santa María de Todos los Santos there are preserved some *Controversiae Scholasticae in octo libros Physicorum Aristotelis* of Padre Diego Caballero. In the Biblioteca

Nacional de México there is preserved the manuscript entitled *Institutionum dialecticarum libri tres,* which is a "vademecum" in which the traditional logical doctrine is concisely and clearly expounded and reduced to the points indispensable for passing the examination.

There is also preserved in the Biblioteca Nacional a manuscript, dated 1688, of Padre Augustín Sierra, who was professor, not in Mexico, but in the City of Los Angeles. It includes the following materials: *Tractatus in duos libros Aristotelis de corpore generabili et corruptibili, Tractatus in tres Aristotelis libros de corpore animate, Appendix in Aristotelis libros de Metaphysica, Caelo, Metheoris et Parvis Naturalibus.* These do not seem to be notes taken in class, but the direct composition of Sierra, who had the insight to pass by all the sterile questions and to outline clearly the fundamental elements of the scholastic vision of nature. The eagerness with which he follows Suárez and underlines all the points in which he differs with the Thomists makes him a fascinating witness to the incipient influence in New Spain of the great metaphysician from Granada.

In addition to his abundant theological works, Padre Diego Marín de Alcázar left three philosophical works, and all three are fundamental. They are preserved in the Biblioteca Nacional and bear the titles *Curso trienal de filosofía, Comentarios a los físicos de Aristóteles,* and *Metafísica,* dated respectively 1667, 1668, and 1669. Of the first there are two manuscripts, both incomplete and with differing contents. One of them contains a *Liber unicus summularum,* which is unfinished, and a *Lógica* or *Dialéctica,* much more extensive; the other contains the *Summulae* and the *Dialéctica* in incomplete form as well as *Disputationes in libros Aristotelis de Ortu et interitu* and *Disputationes in libros Aristoteles de Anima,* both with lacunae. In contrast, the second work is complete. Its title page reads *Disputationes in octo Physicorum libros Aristotelis stagyritae sub faustissimis auspiciis tutelaris nostri Angeli Custodis, quam interum atque iterum in Patronum nostrum vocamus. Anno Domini 1688, scribebat P. Didicus Marín.* Comparing these commentaries with other, earlier ones, very significant changes are to be observed. The most notable is the almost complete suppression of the properly physical questions, as though the new developments of the experimental sciences obliged him to limit himself to a strictly metaempirical explanation of nature. Finally, the third manuscript, the *Metafísica,* bears this long title *Disputationes in Universam Philosophiam Scholasticam quam Metaphysicam scientiam universalissimam vocant.* The title does not at all accord with the content of the book since in it are included questions taken from the *Physics* and the third book of *On the Soul.*

The seventeenth century does not offer any other philosophical work so outstanding as that of Marín de Alcázar. It embraces an extensive theme, a solid basis of information, and a resourceful and penetrating argumentation. A polemical tone dominates the entire work, as though the author felt beforehand that his doctrine would be acceptable neither to the Thomists nor to the Scotists. He is entirely convinced that the new theories of Vázquez and of Suárez must be taught and diffused in the schools on an equal basis with the traditional views and that by this addition the schools would become more ample, abundant, and fruitful. Obviously his thought is not completely formed and is far from possessing the profundity and rigor of the work of his masters; nevertheless, the very state, as it were, of fermentation in which he presents his ideas makes them more living and moving. It is regrettable that as yet no work by this fecund author has been published.

Rafael Moreno

IV. MODERN PHILOSOPHY IN NEW SPAIN

In the pages which follow we shall undertake to recount the origin, or introduction, of modern philosophy into Mexico as well as the different stages which had to be traversed before it became firmly established with the thinkers of the second half of the eighteenth century.

In fact, the first indications of the new mentality will be found at the same time in the humanism of the friars, traditionalists, and men of the Renaissance, who created a body of thought which was already Mexican by reason of its object. They still remained in the stream of philosophy which was Spanish in its subjectivity and European in its object, transported from Spanish institutions to those of New Spain by such writers as Alonso de la Veracruz or Rubio, who tried to establish a scholasticism free from logical extravangances and useless questions. It appears, however, once the living themes which the American man provoked had been exhausted, the intellect became involved very quickly in the composition of sterile commentaries or in endless disputes, on the fringes of creative reflection and in supine ignorance of modern science and its vision of the cosmos. The seventeenth century does not yet offer any philosopher who is worthy of being compared with the Renaissance scholastics of the sixteenth. Philosophy declined into the quarrels of the schools. Fray Francisco Naranjo (1580–1655), a Dominican monk born and educated in Mexico, who filled the cloisters with admiration of his prodigious memory, offers us a typical example; he had mastered the *Summa* and was capable of dictating to four secretaries simultaneously on different topics. The decadence of scholasticism, as a consequence, is a fact which all admit. It endured about a century, more or less, from 1625 to 1725. During this period students were confronted with a ready-made philosophy, at least in its fundamental lineaments, possessing the firm coherence of a system and supported by centuries of authorities covered with the aura of sanctity or recommended by the Church. A philosophy, moreover, which was the handmaiden of religion which infected it with its fear of novelties and its preference for what was old. The result of these conditions was that the philosophers clung to the traditional method and ideas, remained ignorant of modern currents, and abused the argument from authority. And as the established philosophy was already an exclusively logical and rational discipline which carried on its back the burden of Aristotelian science, useful and useless questions alike were commented on to the point of satiety. The colonial man lived on the fringe of modernity, and when the ill-understood honor of the religious orders turned philosophy into a battlefield of words, he embroiled himself in sterile dispute, to the point where he thought that the greatest philosopher was the one who shouted and was able to confound his enemies with numberless texts and the hurling of bruising "ergos." Hence we can now understand how impossible it was for the traditionalists to return to the sources, to evaluate their own thought, or to rethink it in relationship to new ideas.

For these reasons the origins of modern Mexican thought are to be found in the earliest writers in whom there exists either an intellectual activity which in some way or other coincides with the modern point of view or in a conjunction of doctrines which clearly indicate the transition from the traditional to the modern. Such are Sor Juana Inés de la Cruz and Don Carlos de Sigüenza y Góngora. After them there comes, inexplicably, an hiatus of half a century until there appears that diffusion and consolidation of modern philosophy which the Jesuits, expelled (from Spain) in 1767, exemplify. By the year 1760 two currents begin to appear which show, in different media of expression, and also with differing implications, the peculiar manner in which New Spain assimilated the modern point of view in the last days of the colonial period. Gammarra, on the one hand, and Bartolache, Alzate, and Hidalgo, on the other, are the representative authors.

Such is the theme of the present work. It may be said to constitute an historical unity: from the moment at which the intellect begins to be no longer scholastic and to become modern to the characteristic expressions of our modernity; from the end of the seventeenth century to the philosophical doctrines of the last quarter of the eighteenth, when ideas became political weapons and when political thought achieved such pre-eminence that the practice of philosophy assumes, in the history of ideas, a secondary place. We should remark that we do not consider here the works of scholasticism, whose decadent cultivators, though devoid of historical meaning, continue active through the century. We seek out, instead, those ideological manifestations which are not expressed in forms ordinarily considered philosophical, such as the *Primero Sueño* of Sor Juana or the periodical journals of Alzate.

I
The Transition from Scholasticism
to the Modern Point of View

1. Sor Juana Inés de la Cruz (1651–1695)

A woman of vast intellectual aspirations, one of the literary glories of Mexico, Sor Juana deserves an important place in the history of ideas. She wrote a number of "Súmulas" in the scholastic manner, which have been lost, and two works in which she expresses with great clarity her vision of the world and her philosophical attitudes: *Primero Sueño* (First Dream) and *Respuesta a Sor Filotea de la Cruz* (Reply to Sor Filotea de la Cruz).[1] In these works there is to be found—with no question of establishing influences of modern doctrines—a body of thought which closely approaches or even coincides with the spirit of the new times. If in the *Reply* she defends the freedom of criticism and indicates the object of the understanding as well as the ancillary role of philosophy with respect to theology, in the *Dream* she develops, by means of poetic images, ideas about reason, the method of knowledge, and the disaster which the quest for truth involves.[2]

According to the literary invention of Sor Juana, night equals the "all." In it the birds sleep, as does the wind, the sea, men, and dogs. "As yet the lover has not unveiled himself." The dreaming poetess dreams that the dream is universal. Nothing escapes from this state. The very activity of the soul within the dream, which consists in the watchfulness of the intellect, becomes changed into dream. While all objects, and even our very body, sleep, only the intellectual activity remains outside the dream and manifests itself in the hunger for knowledge, in the quest for truth, as something belonging to the substance of man. Still, she thinks that the soul, in its very wakefulness and watching, is also a dream. Life is dream, and it is also a dream to dream that life is a dream. Gaos has said, in his interpretation of Sor Juana, ". . . especially and above all is the intellectual life a dream, even to the point that its very nonbeing, save as a dream, is a thing dreamed, a dream."[3]

And it is precisely this assignment of so basic a status to the dream that makes the poem an original philosophical text. Aside from its undeniable literary merits, its content must be recognized as a theme of strict conceptual meaning, since it reduces life to the mere activity of the intellect and, step by step, reflects upon the process of knowledge. In addition, the entire poem revolves about the human aspiration for knowledge, or quest for truth.

Nevertheless, the suspicion may rise that it cannot have this meaning, since it is a question of a literary work, fashioned according to the rules of the period. The form of expression, however, offers no obstacle to this interpretation. The poem comes to be the natural channel through which Sor Juana manifests her ideas, free of the precision demanded in a treatise and, for this very reason, more disposed to utter truths.[4] Thus she is able to present herself to us as a philosopher which speaks persistently of categories, of beings, of universals, of confused concepts, of an ambitious "metaphysical reduction," of "all creation." There is nothing strange, therefore, that there exists in the *Dream* an essay, modern in a certain fashion, on the intellect as well as preoccupations about method and even a thesis on the limits of knowledge.

A. THE INTELLECT

The word "understanding" is, of course, repeated frequently, and its function is that which philosophy has always assigned the understanding "the conceptual comprehension of reality." Waking or sleeping, in the kitchen or in the study, it was animated by a fervent impulse to comprehend, down to their ultimate reality, the things of which the universe is composed.[5] The effort is "to traverse it (the universe) entire." The intellect, therefore, waking within the dream, hastens to "measure the immense quantity of the sphere," with the purpose of "copying images of all things," sublunary and superlunary alike. Attention is drawn to the fact that Sor Juana has, so to say, an active idea of the understanding. It is the understanding which "waking while the universe slumbers" copies "images of all things." It can do so because in the dream it has liberated itself from the body, "from the fleshly chain which grossly weighs it down," and has undertaken the "intellectual flight" toward the knowledge of reality. The insistence upon placing the cognitive activity of the intellect at the apex of existence becomes more surprising. In truth, the nun dreams that with the prison of the body left behind, the intellect is lifted to the summit of a mountain and that the soul finds itself upon a higher plane, "the elevated mental pyramid where the soul sees herself placed." Most important, in our view, are the words of the poem which indicate beyond any doubt how this ultimate elevation is not only verified within the soul itself but actually constitutes a kind of indefinite liberation. The desire for knowledge, she says, "lifted up" the soul in the most eminent part "of its own mind, so high above itself that it believed that it had passed to another, new region." [6]

It is the soul which mounts ever higher and higher. And there only the mind exists; it passes from one part of itself to another, by its own power impelled by the ambitious desire "to know it entire." Thus, freed from its soul, from itself, freed absolutely from the sleeping body and from the universe which slumbers, it sees or seeks to see "the whole of creation." There are now no reasons for fearing or for suffering disillusionments, since with the body have been abandoned those obstacles which cloud the understanding. The doctrine is clear: the soul turns to reality, not considered in the first place, when it is itself, when it alone exists, when it is "wholly converted to its immaterial being and its essence." Then, filled with light, it begins the "intellectual flight" of knowledge, whose reaches will presently be seen.

Sor Juana has an idea of the understanding which already forecasts the positions to be defended in the eighteenth century. Within the dream it abides waking; it reflects, observes, brings to attention the paths of knowledge or its difficulties. In all her work there is to be observed a great concern to try to avoid errors and dangerous deviations. At every step she flies from the "confused concept," from the "confused species," from false appearances. She puts to one side the "useless ministry" of the senses. She seeks the truth but displays diffidence toward the "tortuous intellects," both by reason of the confusion caused by the diversity of objects and by the absence of order in the process of knowledge. She is concerned to shape sound intellects, not in the lecture halls, merely, but in all men. [7] She also exhibits the beginnings of the scientific consciousness, or habit of mind, with the same virtues and limits as the following century. Every day she expresses her wonder before the phenomena of the world which surround her, she records continuous observations, even upon the gyrations of a spinning top or the lard in culinary necessities. And if hers is still the traditional science,[8] the undertaking which she proposes to herself—namely, "to investigate nature"—ceases to be so. In truth, she tries to approach the facts, in order to understand them better, by way of mathematical and geometrical explanations. She was always tracing out the reason of things: why a certain fact, or reaction, or psychological manifestation is brought about, the variety, in a word, of the phenomena of nature and of spirit. Nevertheless, this is not the purpose; the limit or end of knowledge is not here. The soul is called to higher things than "natural effects," as traditionalists held.

On these grounds it is comprehensible why, in her thought, the Renaissance criticism of the scholastic abuses in discussion should recur. The fiery defense of one's own opinion, oversubtlety, the supremacy of words over concepts, stentorian outcries must give way to reason.[9] On the other hand, she defends as legitimate her right to think, even in matters open to conjecture touching directly on doctrines of faith. The "free" intellect does not accept the principle of authority when the truth does not support it or ignorance deceives it.[10] The criterion is in a certain way the modern one. Her works show the longing for knowledge[11] and a boldness in seeking it, which are the characteristics of the new times. Her life consisted—up to the moment when she sold her library, maps, and instruments to devote herself solely to God—in the satisfaction of her anxieties and uneasiness in the realm of knowledge. So much did she scrutinize the things of the universe that her desire to look for and seek explanations might be considered second nature in her. Indeed, this solicitude to investigate everything is an attitude at once new and very old, which, in the case of Sor Juana, shows the modern confidence in reason and in its capacity to understand any object whatsoever. It is true that ultimately she did not place her trust completely in the power of reason and tried to establish its limits beforehand. It remains unquestionable, however, that she not only admired reason but tried on occasion to stimulate it so that it would hurl itself audaciously toward knowledge. Man, she says, "judging it excessive boldness to examine everything, flies from knowledge —coward that he is—because he is afraid to understand it badly, never, or late." [12]

By a curious counterpoint the proposal to "investigate nature" turns reason timid.

Sor Juana also seems quite modern when she teaches that the function of understanding is to order. Order and unity are the two requisites without which a clear idea cannot be formed. The soul is amazed by "so great an object," by "such great diversity," by the "unordered chaos" which it apprehends in reality. However, having collected its attention, it recovers itself in a second act, thanks to the "marvelous discourse" that calms the "dread" of the impressions of all kinds which "flood in upon us without order, separated without order." Objects, however, are recalcitrant to being brought within an order or a "series," and for this reason understanding establishes only a relative disorder which continues to depend on discourse. About impressions she says, "... the more they involve combinations, the more they dissolve into disunities, filled with differences." [13]

B. THE METHOD OF "METAPHYSICAL REDUCTION"

All that has gone before shows how necessary is the existence of a method which would permit "the development of the possibilities of a direct ascent to the truth." Sor Juana, in the first place, essays the path of intuition into the things which constitute the world. But she immediately becomes aware that the understanding fails to understand with "an intuitive act ... the whole of creation," for hardly can there be attained, in this manner, concepts which refer to a single thing, to say nothing of the whole, or which present the confusion of diversity and not the order of certain knowledge. On the other hand, in accordance with the scholastic doctrine, she says that no single act is sufficient for this ideal of knowledge, which requires, rather, various unordered concepts. What is difficult to attribute to tradition is her insistence upon the autonomy and the self-governing activity of the understanding. It is the understanding itself which in the calm of reflection withdraws from error already committed, "having now recovered itself" by means of the awareness it has of itself. It is not a question of a method which is capable of improving itself. Sor Juana realizes, thanks to the "art" of thinking, that the intuitive act has "the defect of not being able to know the whole of creation." In the same manner, the understanding "checked in its very operation" has recourse to the discursive method, which Sor Juana describes in two phases: the first is the phase of ascent, "rising from one concept to another," which consists in moving upward, "step by step," from inanimate being in order to arrive by way of the vegetable and the animal realms to man, "the most portentous object" about which one can discourse. The other phase is one of reduction to the singular and the simple. Before the manifold and the diversity of objects the understanding "judges it suitable to bring itself down to the singular item, or to discourse upon things separately, one by one." [14]

Such is the end of the method, and in it consists the order demanded by the desire for knowledge. When everything tends to indicate that the poetess is in the midst of modern doctrines, there arises, very naturally, the well-known traditional explanation. It is a question, basically, of the abstractive power of the intellect which gradually forms more abstract concepts, which, because more abstract, are also of a higher order. Thus, one realizes that this order is not different from that of the Aristotelian tradition, and that things come "to be encircled in the twice-five artificial categories."

It remains clear then that the method is qualified by its own author as "metaphysical reduction which teaches us to form a science about the universals." [15]

All of which means that Sor Juana at this point establishes a theme which not only belongs to the tradition but is also a characteristic of the scholasticism taught by Veracruz, Rubio, and, above all, Mercado.[16]

C. THE FAILURE OF THE UNDERSTANDING

When Sor Juana asks herself whether this understanding, which proves inept before diversity and the absence of order, and which recovers itself when it considers matters one by one, really achieves the knowledge of the whole, she again shows her modern characteristics. She trusts its powers, but she is also aware of its limits; she launches upon the "intellectual flight," but in the act she restrains the audacity of wanting to discourse upon the whole. The desire for knowledge drives her on, but she feels the difficulties of the intellectual life. The soul, consequently, remains undecided: "sometimes it would like to traverse these levels; at other times it draws back, judging discourse upon the whole to be excessively daring."

The dazzling vision which the whole of reality produces gives occasion for oscillation, and in a special way the realization that the intellect "turns back" to "one object only" or that discourse avoids knowing "the impression" separated from the rest, as though it were independent and unique. How, then, justify the universal desire for knowledge?

To understand this very decisive point in the ideas of Sor Juana, it is necessary to point out the object to which reference is being made. To be sure, it is not a metaphysical object nor the universals. The poetess begins with the singular and precisely with the "natural effects": the subterranean stream of water, the shape, colors, and aroma of the flowers. The undertaking of the intellect is not to reflect upon the traditional matter of philosophy, but "to investigate nature." This is where the method is put to the test; and it fails because it does not understand "even the smallest, even the easiest, part . . . of the natural effects nearest at hand." The language she uses to this purpose clearly indicates that as she understands it: the object exceeds "the forces" of the intellect. The understanding becomes "diffident," discourse "cowardly," struck with horror.[17] But, become aware of its cowardliness, the intellect does not want to give up before "having entered the harsh contest." Taking courage, it recalls the story of Icarus, which fires its spirit, and it acquires "open paths to the boldness" to discourse upon the whole of creation. Nevertheless, it does not begin "the intellectual flight," for the audacity of the "Haughty charioteer" becomes a "warning," "a pernicious example" of the "arrogant soul" which seeks its own "destruction." And the desire for knowledge ends up by becoming a "crime," an "insolent excess." [18] These convictions seem to have their origin, rather than in the limits of the intellect, in the misgivings of the faith,[19] or perhaps in a moral conscience which rejects the temerity of undertaking impossible tasks. What is certain is that they avoid the reduction of realities to the categories, ending always with the uncertainties of knowledge. When the poem reaches this point, the dream which dreams of fulfilling the desire for knowledge and of finding the secure way ceases. "But," she says, "while I was foundering on the reefs, with confused choice, touching impossible moving sandbanks, in so far as I was trying to follow ways," [20] the world remained illuminated and "I watchful."

In this way the essay on the intellect, which the *Primero sueño* really is, means the bankruptcy [21] of knowledge in the only two ways possible for Sor Juana: the intuitive and the discursive. There is not philosophical skepticism properly speaking, even though the poem shows a relation to the contemporary theme on doubt, disillusion, and the dream, for, as José Gaos says, its purpose is not to seek a solution to the problem of "the effectiveness of knowledge" and even less "to philosophize in verse on the limits of knowledge." By referring to the experience of sleep and waking, which are "personally her own" and "not generically human," the *Dream* expresses this result alone: the "failure of her own desire for knowledge, toward which she had oriented her whole life." [22]

This means that the doubt does not destroy the truths or the "cosmovision" of the time. On the contrary, the poem produces, ultimately, the impression that Sor Juana is reconciled to the world illuminated by the Sun, abandoning to poetic fiction the illusion of discursive thought. Further, in the *Reply to Sor Filotea* there exists, alongside undeniably modern inquietudes, a complete justification of traditional knowledge. There two important things are stated: that the sciences depend on theology as its ancillaries and that she, the poetess, has always oriented her thought toward this discipline by the "stepping stones of the sciences and the arts." Rhetoric, logic, physics, arithmetic, and geology constitute orders of knowing, real, never problematic, which are necessary for the understanding of the "queen of the sciences." [23]

Nevertheless, it remains impossible to deny the influence of the *Primero Sueño* on the ideas of Sor Juana. As the introspection which the understanding directs upon itself ends in loss of confidence in the ways of knowing; as the awakened soul, restored to its proper character, fails in knowledge, she ultimately becomes reconciled to her faith and not with philosophy. With the intellectual flight impeded, the frenzied anxiety for knowledge finds salvation on the wings of theology. Because of her doubts about reason, she abandons, as is well known, books, maps, and instruments to devote herself wholly to the worship of God, an attitude which is not too far from certain well-known manifestations of modernity.

D. INDEX OF TRANSITION

For the reasons given above, the thought of Sor Juana, precisely because of its oscillations between the old and the new, is the first which in the history of Mexican philosophy indicates the transition to modernity. The controversy over her religious spirit has proved sterile. It is impossible to deny her traditionalism, just as it is to be blind to fail to recognize her modern attitudes. When the reader expects her to expound the doctrines of her philosophical environment, he is surprised by its coincidence with the matters and concerns of the century. Then suddenly, and in a most natural manner, without any effort she takes up the fundamental theses of the scholastic or theological culture. Expounding a nonscientific concept of the stars, for example, she states modern ideas. As in the authors of the transition, the doctrines rebound spontaneously from the system which is being abandoned to new positions. On the one hand, there is the concern for method and with the intellect turned in upon itself, seeking its inner nature; on the other hand, the ascent to God, the first cause, to which the human mind "always aspires," as well as reduction of reality to the Aristotelian categories. Perhaps the most important thing may be that Sor Juana, without having to admit influences or pointing out contacts with philosophers whose names do not appear, must be placed in the order of the "philosophy of the stove," formed by those who investigate the solitary "self" in contrast to the world. For this reason, the *Dream* must be placed "in the history of the philosophical poem from the Renaissance to the philosophical poem of the Enlightenment," as Gaos, following Vossler, says.[24]

If in the *Reply* the poetess creates the best prose of her period and already manifests the preoccupations which are to give historical meaning to the eighteenth century, in the *Dream* she contributes to thought in the Spanish language a philosophical poem so original that it can be compared with no other, either contemporary or later. "The literature of the Spanish language," says Gaos, "would be most poor in this genre . . . if it did not possess this, and this poem does not have in universal history the place and importance it should have because of the ignorance" of the historians.[25]

2. *Don Carlos de Sigüenza y Góngoro* (*1645–1700*)

In reality the thought of Sor Juana proves to be an anticipation of the modern ideas of Sigüenza. This student of the Jesuits, a scholar in the baroque manner, mathematician and astronomer, historian and man of letters, already cultivated the new learning. He does not write treatises in the scholastic manner, or is he a professor of philosophy; still, he writes on all subjects and in open competition wins the chair of mathematics in the university. His historical writings show a concern for national culture and for the fate of the indigenous culture; in them he employs modern methods of criticism, weighing the documents on every matter.

For our purposes the *Libra astronómica y filosófica,* which contains the "Philosophical Manifesto against Comets" and which replaces the lost mathematical *Belerfonte,* suffices.[26] It is a work written deliberately, as were so many of the eighteenth century, to combat errors, in this case the conception prevalent in his time of the movement, nature, and influence upon men of comets.[27] Thanks to this controversy, he left us a scientific treatise on astronomy which may also properly be considered philosophical because it contains an exposition of science, its methods, and achievements. Here we find, together with clear evidences of traditionalism and pure orthodoxy in religious questions, the decisive influence of the new times and, of confronting each other, two different conceptions, not only of knowledge but of life as well. There is also in the *Libra* an anticipatory model of the texts which our thinkers of the eighteenth century will later compose. It is one of the first books, perhaps the *first,* which, not disdaining the Spanish language for the exposition of scientific themes, strives for clarity, conciseness, the use of pedagogical forms, and the introduction of didactic figures. The fact, which Sigüenza himself recognizes, that both the science and the method which he follows are to be found in the mathematical writings of his time does not prevent his being the creator of scientific prose among us.

A. THE MEANING OF HISTORY

In the struggle against the old world Sigüenza develops his thought in two directions: the scientific, properly so called, and that other, which consists in dissipating the common errors diffused among the learned and the people alike. The dominant intention is to teach the truth, to endow man with a different attitude, to prepare him to be distrustful of the received meanings, opinions, knowledge, and, above all, prejudices. For this reason the *Libra* is combative and modernizing. Its pages appear innovational, with a polemical stance against everything which is old. And to this end he has such recourse to history that the scientific portion of his book occupies less than thirty pages. Why is history more important? Undoubtedly the reply is that the work represents the step from the astrological to the astronomical stage, from the mediaeval to the modern point of view; hence, to justify the rejection of the old, it was indispensable to show how error and superstition had originated. Only by discovering the causes of the science he was rejecting might Sigüenza disengage himself from a past which no longer had any right to exist and, at the same time, establish the new truths. History and criticism mutually support each other.

For the same reason history is indispensable for understanding the *rationale* of the new truths.

All the disillusions which the world owes to the scholars of this century are no less conclusive arguments against astrology. (370)

The contraposition of one age to another is expressed and repeated. Astronomy consists in a "meticulous science of movements" and of "natural philosophy"; and because the greater part (of them) had neither the one nor the other, and before this time no one had both, there is no cause to wonder that our predecessors brought this art into disgrace. (354)

In this way Sigüenza is the first to use history with the double purpose of undeceiving previous scientific opinion and spreading modern thought. It may in truth be said that there does not exist in Mexican literature of the eighteenth century another line of argument so instructive, so reasonable, and so clear against that fortress of the traditional soul, astrology in particular and backward science in general.

B. REASON AND AUTHORITY

In the same way as all of our moderns, but in anticipation of them, Sigüenza devotes special attention to another generalized vice of his time: the acceptance of an affirmation as true because it rested on authorities. He knows that he is endowed with an autarchic intellect, sufficient to itself, and that it ought to be used. "To take one's stand," he teaches, "only on what others say in philosophical matters open to discursive thought is to reveal oneself of sterile understanding." (131)

There is in the *Libra*, then, a new idea of reason. As in Sor Juana, it is a question of an active reason for which only its own knowledge is valid. It is a reason, further, which manifests itself in the field of science. The authority of respectable men, even that of Ptolomy or Aristotle, lacks sound bases in scientific matters because they did not know true natural science. But the question is not so simple as to be resolved simply by preference for novelties. The important point is that Sigüenza, in demanding the right to think and to use his intellect, is affirming that man, by reason of being man, must necessarily use his powers, an affirmation which signifies a radical alteration of attitude toward tradition. "It is certain," he writes, "that one who has understanding and discourse never governs himself by authorities . . . if the congruences do not support them." (76)

The prestige of the intellect itself demands the examination of the congruences, that is to say, the support which natural science gives to transmitted truths. What is modern is accepted, not because it is opposed to what is old, but because its conclusions are not opposed to "truth" and "reason." Sigüenza goes further. He thinks basically that earlier knowledge is the product of conjecture and not of "proofs" and "demonstrations." (225)

This was the beginning among us of the scientific movement, of antidogmatism and of the decay of metaphysics as well. The new model of knowledge is science, and true knowledge is that which can be established mathematically or that which is proved by experience. And it can be said that in the *Libra* there already exists that confidence in reason which is characteristic of our time. Reason finds truth by itself, in a struggle which destroys prejudices, lays bare falsities, dissolves doubts. It is impossible "not to realize that when there is doubt about the goodness of a thing, . . . there is no other way of freeing ourselves of that doubt than to place that matter in the balance of reason, as I have done here." (127)

Reason no longer has an ancillary character. In matters open to investigation and discussion, those which are not strictly theological or religious, reason is autocratic and autonomous.[28]

C. SCIENCE AND NATURE

The object to which the new idea of reason was applied was nature, which is not conceived by the Mexican scientist as a reality which is grasped by means of abstract concepts and even less as something unknowable which announces calamities and disasters. With regard to the errors of the vulgar about comets he aleady points out the regularity of nature. In this century, he points out, no greater number of comets has appeared than in past centuries, because since God created the world, "it is an established fact that there has been no change in the rise, meridian, and eccentricity of the Sun, the obliquity of the ecliptic and latitude of the Moon; whence it is inferred that it happened then in the same way that it happens now." (48)

Thus nature proves to be what it will be for our eighteenth century: a complex of realities and laws determinable by experimentation and mathematical calculation.

As a consequence, his concept of science is also new. The *Libra* abounds in expressions which create the conviction that Sigüenza y Góngora had reached a modern conception of science. For him science is synonymous with "method, rules, principles, and truth," just as modern authors understand it. The contrary is called suppositions, errors, ridiculous opinions; astrology itself, as a prediction of the future, is a "diabolical invention." (356) But this does not mean that he has detached himself from the fundamental concepts of the tradition. He continued to think that science is concerned with causes. Astrology is repugnant because one does not know and one cannot know the "innumerable number of causes" of all the stars. (338) One ought to make clear, however, that if indeed he taught, when the science of the age was still causal, that the knowledge of nature, of natural influences and powers, comes by way of causes, his meaning is by contrast modern because knowledge about the stars can only be secured by observations and mathematical calculations which the ancients knew nothing about.

José Gaos has made clear that the erudition of Don Carlos attests to his information about what was going on in the scientific world of his time. He taught the identity of heaven and earth and their composition from the four elements; the creation of an elemental chaotic matter; the age and the end of the world; the macrocosmos and the microcosmos.[29] He accepts the Copernican astronomy as an hypothesis, as was customary in Catholic circles so long as the Church did not consider it incompatible with the Bible. Sigüenza himself points out that his scientific information depends on the contemporary state of science. Frequently he refers to one or another point as not yet clarified, as when he writes about the lines of reasoning which might serve as a model for finding the parallaxes, "whose verification has, until today, been held to be practically impossible in the observations of these phenomena." (241)

In other instances he is aware of the limitations of the times. No one knows with certainty, he says, "of what and whence comets are engendered." (12) Of course, it remains questionable whether the author of *Libra* was aware of the very latest investigations or that he would have known how to discourse among the first-rank scientists and popularizers. Certainly, he knew nothing of Newton's investigations, published twenty years before the *Libra;* his observations seem ingenuous and his deductive arguments produce laughter among the well informed. What is of interest for our history of ideas, however, is the modern cosmovision which he upheld, for the first time, in the colonial world; his scientific desire to know and to explain; the modernization of point of view, which begins with what is precisely most characteristic of modernity, the new conception of nature;

the idea that science is useful and must renew, not only reason, but the whole of life.

D. THE EXPERIMENTAL AND MATHEMATICAL METHOD

Don Carlos, in many passages of the *Libra*, shows a determined preoccupation with method: he insists on the way in which a demonstration is to be conducted, that is, on the "method of arriving at the knowledge of the parallaxes" (241), or repeats the necessity of working out solutions "most geometrically and scientifically." (121) It is a question of finding the ways to prove or describe truths, and these ways are observations and mathematics.

In the same way that he appeals to reason scientifically, he also refers to experience, which comes to mean scientific knowledge and almost always is equivalent to the concept "observations." There are at least three types of observations. One type comprises those which are made with "sight and estimation"; to think that from these one can "conclude anything of importance" would be unworthy (252), since astronomy does not conduct "its operations so crudely that it might trust in the easily deceived sense of vision." Others are those which are made with defective instruments. The third, the only valid ones, secure knowledge with the aid of "very exact instruments." (246)

Basing himself perhaps on the importance which the *Libra* gives to experience, Gaos indicates that although the process of induction is never named, there are to be found "cases of the application of the rules of induction," for example, when he shows the lack of basis for generalizing from some latitudes to others, or when he insists on the lack of repetition of phenomena. In his desire to turn to making experiments, or in these words, "if they are to be maintained ... it was not enough that it should happen sometimes, and at other times not, but always," it is possible to find the principle of generalization. Unfortunately, that is all there is to the matter, cases of application, either of the inductive process which Sigüenza had assimilated in his wide reading, or of the Aristotelian logic, both recalled with reference to the facts which science was considering. On the other hand, the greatest number of his observations which are adducible are simple, and nearly always pragmatic in character. What is significant, it must not be forgotten, is the constant recourse to experience, as well as the methodic requirement of observation.

Something similar will have to be said about the consistent choice of the mathematical method to achieve knowledge. The *Libra* is characterized by use of geometrical demonstration which its author might have taken from Descartes or from other contemporary writers as well. There exists a certain pride in the "mathematical clarity which I followed in my works and which was the basis for what I asserted so absolutely." (381)

And it is not a matter of complicated elaborations, but rather of an explanation which is "so mathematically" made that any reader whatsoever is capable of understanding it. (245) Sigüenza's concern is not to compose a theory of method, but to show how true and secure knowledge can be acquired. Given this attitude, he places the greatest importance on the mathematical of all the ways which the science of his time offered him. Only one who is not ignorant of geometry, optics, and trigonometry, and uses them as the observations demand, is in a position "to discuss, apply, and resolve." (249) "Experience and observation" do not themselves constitute a solid foundation for knowledge. They demand "physical evidence and mathematical certitude." (334) The reading of the *Libra* dissipates any doubt on the matter: the ideal criterion of truth, the one which measures all orientations and allegations, is the evidence which provides validity to experience itself and which is turned into certitude when, in the proof or in the mathematical process, it engenders knowledge which is clear and secure, firm and totally determined, as well. Certitude is, for this reason, the concept to which Sigüenza has constant recourse; "evident" is the typical term by which modern knowledge is qualified.

The foregoing notwithstanding, it should be made clear that

Sigüenza claims certainty for the art of astronomy and that this has, so to say, the function of indicating not only the secure path to the knowledge of the stars but also the limits of the science of his time, which, he repeats, has not yet reached and could not reach this kind of knowledge about the nature, powers, and effects of the stars. Another pertinent observation consists in recognizing that the *Libra* is far from being a treatise in which the arguments or expositions follow a purely scientific course. On a good number of occasions there are to be noted in him the same faults which he imputes to the traditionalists, either because he proceeds in an unreflective manner, without observations, without concern for the data of science, or because he does not use the mathematical procedure, using instead ridicule, biting irony, humor, and even insult. In a word, a thinker of a time of transition, he fights with the same weapons as the enemy, so that he demands scholastically the correction of the plan to follow, expounds in syllogistic form, and destroys the sophism of false conclusions.

E. GOD AND PHYSICAL AGNOSTICISM

With these restrictions and with all the traditional formation necessary, the *Libra astronómica y filosófica* is the first document known which, by invalidating the old science, initiates the destruction of Aristotelian physics and of Aristotle himself. Rubio and Mercado, Alonso de la Veracruz himself, were only able to defend themselves from the Sumulae with weak reeds because they lacked any other idea of science, any other idea of method. One is not to think, obviously, that Sigüenza denies the data of Christianity. So long as the truths of religious origin do not collide with his reason, he accepts them in an integral manner; and when this is not possible, he interprets them according to modern science. The case of astrology is exemplary. To be sure, he accepts the infused knowledge about the world and, consequently, about astronomy which God gave to Adam. However, he says that such knowledge consisted in what man left to the exercise of his purely natural intelligence might have acquired in those times. Hence he concluded that Adam did not have knowledge of the stars, simply because he was incapable of having it. (334–339) On the other hand, since astrology refers only to sidereal things and is not "divinatory," "judiciary," or "prognostic," God could not have assigned it a task proper to reason. (329–331) And even further, the modern elements which Don Carlos uses make it possible for him to initiate a purification of Christianity, something which seems constant in Mexican modernity. As a matter of fact, he maintains repeatedly that it is "an enormous impiety in His creatures" to want to investigate the divine will as to the motives for which It creates comets. "I affirm, in a Christian manner, that they ought to be venerated as the works of such a supreme artificer, without going on to ask what they may mean." (12) Further, only to God belongs the knowledge of the stars, "since he counts them and gives them names." (332) The consequence of such ideas, of the purest traditional stock, falls within the tradition: if astrology does not belong to science, if the stars depend directly for their creation on God, astrology is of diabolical origin. The demon convinced men that they might become knowers of all the natures and of the future. (329–341)

Reflection on the texts of the *Libra* does not produce, it is just to say, a desire to understand the many traditional theses. Sigüenza, despite his continuous recourse to observations and mathematical rigor, despite constraining his adversary to proceed scientifically, begins his ideas with God and ends them with God. Even at the beginning of his book he must admit that perhaps the stars are not always subject "to the laws of nature, since they proceed directly from God by strict creation." (12) This position, if it were true, would render worthless the whole undertaking and content of the *Libra*. At any rate, Catholics, "possessors of the knowledge of the eternal truths and privileged of God," must accept the recondite mysteries which only God knows. It is satanic to try to penetrate the divine will or the divine ideas, "since what passes in the heavens will be known only to him

to whom the uncreated Wisdom should choose to reveal it." (38)
These convictions provide the basis for the limits which
Sigüenza assigns to scientific knowledge. The two secure ways
to knowledge, observation and mathematics, end up by not
procuring knowledge. The learned Mexican demands that all
certainty be secured by "physical or mathematical certainty."
However, he immediately discovers that neither in the field of
experience nor in that of mathematics is evidence achieved.
(12, 241, 338, 265, 372) It is not simply that the men of science
of the day had not achieved secure and evident explanations.
He has the theoretical conviction that "physical evidence" will
not yield knowledge, not only in the singular case of astronomy
but in science in general. He also believes that "mathematical
certainty" is impossible in hypotheses and calculations. What
follows on such an attitude? In the first place, the modern
meaning of knowledge escapes Sigüenza, not only since he
conceives of science as a knowledge of causes but also because
what he seeks by means of evidence is to seize natures, effects,
and powers, understood ad "quiddities," as essential ontological
contents. And it is obvious that such objectives cannot be reached
by means of experience of the mathematical method. In the
second place, there exists the determination, at once Christian
and modern, to make reality depend on the divine intellect and
will more than on reason. For these reasons the thought of the
author of the *Libra*, as José Gaos says, "is a physical agnosticism,
based on faith, instead of a metaphysical agnosticism which
establishes the fideism which is to be found in modern philosophy." [30]

F. WRITER OF TRANSITION

While the thought of Sor Juana is indicative of modernity, Carlos
de Sigüenza y Góngora already represents the transition from
scholasticism to modern times. Alongside the vacillations of the
pioneers his thought preserves the fundamental themes of tradition. Nevertheless, his ideas, his criterion, his preferences, an-

nounce what will happen in Mexico in the eighteenth century and, what is more important for the history of ideas, exhibit the tastes, the concerns, and the problems of later times. The very conciliation between Catholicism and modernity, which later will give rise to our peculiar eclectic thesis, is present in his work. Since he cultivates what is specifically modern, we must assign to the *Libra* the naturalization of the new science among us, even though his influence seems to have been lost until it emerges in the Jesuit Clavijero and in the learned Bartolache. Sigüenza, further, introduces the philosophy which will consolidate itself fifty years later.

From this point of view it is not very meaningful to ask whether he knew all the science of his period or whether he reached the height of contemporary culture. As a matter of fact, he quotes Descartes only once, from the *Principles,* Gassendi a dozen times on scientific matters, and we know that in the *Belerofonte* he explains the movements of the "Copernican hypothesis" or by "Cartesian vortices." It is certain that in more than one area he seeks original solutions; however, the truly significant thing is his determination to have done with the traditional intelligences, full of errors and superstitions. His undertaking consists in teaching modern, and abandoning the old, ideas about comets and stars. He is no reformer with a flaming sword, like Feijoo or Alzate. He is more a teacher who applies to the colonial consciousness the stimuli of European progress. He symbolizes a crucial moment, for then it was not a question simply of changing sciences; it was a question of changing the vision of the world, of the struggle to make man modern precisely in that in which he was most mediaeval, his vision of the world. Pierre Bayle was engaged in a similar undertaking: the comparison has been made by José Gaos. Both the one and the other explain prodigies as natural phenomena, recognize a universal legislation in science, and counsel the learned to cultivate a prudent attitude which will not admit unproved conclusions. Sigüenza does not have historical importance only because "he is an eighteenth-century Mexican and

Hispano-American . . . a man on the periphery of the prevailing culture, the French."

In any circumstance, one understands how the *Libra* can be "a fact of capital importance in the history of ideas in Mexico. However, if such it be, it is in part fundamental because it is the expression of a small part of the historical past, literally crucial, a moment of transition, at the same time between two ages and two worlds." [31]

It is equally the achievement of Don Carlos de Sigüenza y Góngora that he exhibits in the *Libra,* and in all his works, the transition to Mexican culture, which will become a permanent preoccupation of the thinkers of the eighteenth century. The themes of the nation appear even in the most unexpected questions. As he himself says, his intense intellectual work, his encyclopedic knowledge, are due to "the supreme love I have for our country." He struggles against the love of what is European simply because it is European, and the disdain for the Mexican simply because it is Mexican. Thus the *Libra* abounds in observations and mathematical calculations with a deliberate double purpose: that the learned men of Europe might compare Mexican science (381) and that they might recognize "that there are mathematicians outside Germany, even placed among the grass plains and the thorns of the Mexican lake." (244)

And even though the formation of the vernacular consciousness is imperfect, he is moved to write, as the later writers of the eighteen hundreds also will be moved, by concern for the discredit which would come to his country and the Spanish nation should silence be kept on earlier scientific undertakings.

II
THE EXPLOSION OF MODERNITY

In Sor Juana and in Sigüenza the new age appears with those notes of modernity which are most significant: concern with method, the self-sufficiency of reason, and the purpose of making of science the secure form of knowledge. How is it possible that they should treat these themes with such complete naturalness? In view of the fact that the historians have not, up to the present time, indicated any ideological antecedents, autodidacticism must be accepted as the answer; and these authors offer sufficient support for this reply. To this will have to be added their thirst for knowledge, a kind of second nature leading them to investigate natural phenomena and to break out of the molds of tradition. Even stranger is the fact that their influence, if they had any, was lost for half a century, during which time they had no followers. Modernity, as a matter of fact, appears only half a century later when the Franciscans, the Mercedarians, and above all the Jesuits, led by Campoy, cultivated not merely certain aspects but the whole culture of the modern world; sufficiently informed, these men also grasped the problems implied in the passage from the traditional point of view to the innovations of the age.

Various documents suffice to show the scholastic complacency of the first half of the eighteenth century: the journals of Castorena and of Sahagún, in which there appears not the slightest breath of anything new; the investigations of Bernabé Navarro into philosophical texts and manuscripts, which very faintly reveal certain inquietudes during the fifth decade; the researches of Miranda among the documents of the Inquisition, with negative results; finally, the fact that the presence of certain elements of modernity in prohibited books appears only with the beginning of the second half of the century, as Lina Pérez-Marchand has noted. Nevertheless, it is possible to suppose that even if there existed no influence of those who introduced the modern point of view, there must be, instead, some presence of modern ideas, whether in isolated thinkers or in small groups, which might lend continuity to the history of ideas. Certain established facts can be cited to prove that alongside the immense scholastic majority there are to be found nuclei informed of the new ideas. It will also be necessary to consider what is happening elsewhere, principally in literature, where the Jesuit Juan Antonio de Oviedo [32] thanks to his stylistic and esthetic innovations, created an environment propitious for the innovating movement of the second half of the century. Otherwise the influence of Sigüenza on Clavijero, and above all the vacillations between scholasticism and the modern point of view which are to be noted in the manuscript of the first fifty years, remain inexplicable.

Some spirit of modernity there must have been, since philosophers could not arise with tendencies already modern by a mere effort of the will. As a matter of fact, in 1706 the General Congregation of the Jesuits found it necessary to order that only the Aristotelian philosophy be taught and, at the same time, to attack thirty "erroneous propositions" of Cartesian origin as harmful in teaching. And in the last decades of the first half of the century there is to be observed a gradual change in the manner of exposition or in the attitude of certain authors. On occasions they took certain preventative measures, as though they had a presentiment of innovations and of the opponents of scholasticism; sometimes the reader receives the impression of a return to the ideas of Sor Juana and of Sigüenza. At the beginning the traditionalists reaffirm their doctrines against an opponent whom they do not identify; later they mention some modern writers who sustain opposing ideas, but only on certain points; still later they are already making brief criticisms and end up by expounding, in summary manner, the principal theses of modern philosophy without accepting any of them.[33] These concessions of the older point of view is followed by the explosion of the new.

The cultivation of modern ideas was carried on initially by individuals. Although Sigüenza was a professor of mathematics at the university, as a modern thinker he was a solitary instance. The new attitudes, consequently, arise outside the institutions and only later penetrate them. Once the conflict between the two spiritual currents had begun, the Jesuits Bartolache, Gamarra, and Hidalgo taught modern philosophy in colleges or in the university. The periodicals which at this time spread abroad the principal tendencies of the century were not allied to any institutions. And soon there were added the organizations, created by the government, to strengthen the cultivation of the sciences outside the traditional centers of teaching. It is necessary to emphasize this not only because, in general terms, this is the way modern philosophy was born in Europe but also because it affords an opportunity to reflect on the doctrinal sources of our authors. These are the texts of philosophy and, with constantly increasing frequency, the "acts" of the academies, the periodicals, the memorials, and the dictionaries, which were then the vehicles of the modern point of view. This circumstance, in conjunction with the reception of the most varied influences of the century, determines or accounts for the lack of profundity on more than one question. Paralleling the origin of philosophy among us, its forms of expression are those which we have encountered in Sigüenza. Gamarra continued the tradition of the Jesuit schools by publishing his treatise in the Latin tongue, but he wrote his *Errores del entendimiento* in Spanish. The periodical writers, naturally, wrote entirely in the vernacular.

It is not a question, therefore, of a period which presents any unity. It is full of struggles and controversies, of difficulties, and even of hostilities. The introduction of ideas takes place during changing historical situations which cannot be measured by determined dates; one attitude persists within the other, and the traditional proves to be an anticipation of the modern. It might be said that there are stages of transition, of the execution of plans which are both new and old. While the modern point of view in philosophy is to be found complete in 1769 with the publication of *Las lecciones mathemáticas* of Bartolache and, in the field of theology, in the year 1784 with the *Disertación* of the young theologian Hidalgo on the true method of studying theology, the *Elementos de filosofía moderna* of Gamarra, which constitutes at one time a greater acceptance of scholasticism and the exemplary systematic work of our eighteenth century, appeared in 1774. The Jesuits, though they introduced the fundamental themes in which the new tastes revealed themselves, do not occupy the advanced position which Sigüenza expounded with respect to the mathematical method or the identification of secure knowledge with scientific knowledge. On the other hand, the periodicals, inclined as they were to consider only science as philosophical, began to appear one after another, beginning in 1768, the year in which Alzate edited the *Diario Literario de México*. During the last six years of the century only the *Gacetas* of Valdés remained, and the modern impulse diminished considerably, in spite of the fact that the tasks of illumination continued. No teachers were outstanding, or did any works comparable to those of Clavijero, Bartolache, or Gamarra appear. To counterbalance this decline, there exists a greater activity on the part of enlightened despotism: beginning with the last quarter of the century, it establishes institutions like the "Amfiteatro" and the Chair of Anatomy, the Seminary of Minería, the School of Fine Arts, the Botanical Garden, and introduces educational reforms, all of which contributed powerfully to the creation of the scientific movement of which Humboldt speaks in his *Ensayo político*. All things considered, with the presence of the enraged scholastics and the lack of great philosophical, but not scientific, figures, the battle of modernity was peremptorily won at the end of the century. Little by little authority was yielding place to reason and experience, observation became an indispensable requisite for knowledge, and the cult of the new truth predominates in the colonial mind. In half a century of struggle the new philosophers changed the terms, the disputes, the ideas. Alzate and Bartolache, the two great scientists who prepared the dawn of Independence, tell us of the clubs which met in remote cities, in which philosophical themes were discussed and where there were persons able to take up the scientific questions proposed in the capital or to criticize botanical, medical, chemical, and geological discoveries.[34]

How were they able to overcome the attachment to tradition so characteristic of Spain and of the nations which had emerged from her? The fundamental principles of the new attitude were three: faith, experience, and reason. All reverenced religion and professed, at least, to respect its truths. Having come from the schools of the tradition and, in the majority of cases, enjoying intellectual and moral prestige within them, they were capable of changing the method of teaching and the content of the doctrines. The idea of philosophy changed insensibly. First, as in Clavijero and Abad, the useless questions of dialectic, metaphysics, or physics were excluded, and acquaintance with, and discussion of, the new theories increased. At the same time the modern physics of Galileo and Newton began to be considered as the true and only philosophy. Their distaste for the routine dialectic of the schools led them to cultivate experimental physics in a desire to know nature as it is in itself. Later, as in Gamarra, the fundamental points of the tradition were rejected, although on occasion they were taken up again. Bartolache, Alzate, and Mocino already rejected peripateticism as a whole. It can then be said that, beginning with the Jesuits, one finds a logic, a metaphysics, a science different from the corresponding disciplines of scholasticism. Bacon, the philosopher who restored wisdom with a new organon applied to experience, is the greatest teacher of our modern age.

For this reason it may be said that these changes are important. During the second half of the century, and always in more incisive form, accent is placed on what has already been observed in Sigüenza, namely, that modernity does not mean a mere theoretical manifestation of ideas, but above all an implacable war against tradition and at the same time the implanting of new doctrines and of a new vision of the world. A rent then appeared in the unity of colonial thought: on one hand were the innovators; on the other hand, the intransigent friends of the old, the "misoneístas," who at first were not aware of the danger of the new ideas, but later raised a cry on seeing their tranquil domain lost. In this atmosphere of conflicts it is important to point out the activity of the Inquisitors, who, before the continued attacks of the most recent books, especially from France, felt obliged to forbid their being read. Lina Pérez-Marchand has indicated, by means of the archives of the Inquisition, two ideological stages which are manifested in the failures and the ever-greater concessions to the penetration of the new ideas.[35] During the decade of the "fifties" the examiners evidenced a mind to destroy modern thought and are defenders, in opposition to the new works, of useless controversies and of a complete intellectual withdrawal from Europe; in the year 1770, however, they affirm instead that the illumination and good taste can be assimilated by Catholics. Principally in the closing years of the century the Inquisitors never left off persecuting the presence of new ideas when they contradicted the faith, Catholic customs, or the royal power. However, the persecution of the spirit of the enlightenment fell outside their reach, that spirit which was becoming ever-more dominant with the passing generations, to the degree that the Inquisitors themselves made use of modern writers to combat the modern point of view. There occurred, for example, a case in which they suspended the proceedings, in the year 1771, of an "act" in which the scholastic distinction between absolute accidents and modal accidents were rejected "because it is very probable that in the being of things there do not exist absolute accidents in the scholastic sense."

Along with the vigilant activity of the tribunal there existed, completing the "misoneísmo," the philosophy of traditional men, which may be considered to be represented by Coriche, Cigala, and Vallarta.[36] The first of these wrote a criticism of the famous discourse of Rousseau, which had been granted a prize by the Academy of Dijon; it bred naturalism, liberalism, and anarchy, which supported the theory that science and literature created obstacles to virtue. He defended man's reason and science against the "good savage," using history to explain the concepts of the philosopher of Geneva in relation to the evils of his time.

Cigala protected scholasticism from a greater danger than Malebranche or Diderot: Jerónimo Feijoo. Since he thought of theology as a perfect science, it was difficult for him to understand the message of the *Teatro círtico* or of the *Cartas,* and for this reason he considered those works as a kind of trap or snare which insensibly and heedlessly, as Eguiara says, would introduce "the abandonment of scholastic theology in order to establish the use of modern philosophy, which is mechanistic and entirely profane." Scholasticism for Cigala was practically national. Anything modern was foreign. The former was more useful to religion, in addition to the fact that it taught nature better than did mechanistic theories. The recent systems are weak; they rest upon probable opinions; their experiments are contradictory and never complete. The scholastics prove, in this way, to be superior to the moderns, since "to juggle nature" implies less genius than does the resolution of the difficulties about grace. In this defense he uses two concepts which he borrows from the century, truth and utility, but he encourages the conviction that the purpose of the innovators is to deprive the Church of her greatest weapons against heretics. The philosophy proposed by Feijoo, he says, "is useful perchance for society and the world of politics, but it does not lead to heaven and has no solid subtlety in scientific matters." These remarks clearly indicate the position of the peripatetic, who resists being modern and concerning himself with earthly happiness because he fears to lose the happiness of heaven. Vallarta will underline this direction of thought.

The genius of the Jesuit Vallarta, perhaps because he lived with the group which contributed most to the consolidation of the modern point of view, was suspicious, always careful of doctrines, engaged in ferreting out hidden errors against reason and against faith. He teaches in a funeral eulogy on the death of Eguiara that the wise man inspired by the divinity—he who unites religion and science, faith and knowledge, he who reconciles the successes of understanding with the data of revelation —he is the man who is the *wise* man, properly so-called. Philosophy, dominated by the senses, lacks divine light, falls into errors, and for this reason God rejects it. Expelled in 1767, the European scene confirmed him in his ideas. He wrote a book which can be considered the first philosophy of history, *Cartas*, on the hidden ways of philosophy, which is addressed to the Christian Filadelfo. He shows step by step how Catholics, even the alert ones, have been taken by surprise by the new ideas which had been introduced "in disguised form and by strategies." It is true that in his apology for traditional Christian thought he uses arguments, but the constant definitive criterion is faith. The modern philosophers are not wise men with the seal of God's approval, but malign and perverse, false and impious. Calling themselves lovers of truth, in mutual contradiction with each other, they are at one in denying Christ.

The works of these writers, which already contain a certain receptivity toward the new attitudes, as well as the records of the Inquisition, provide a pale image of the furious attacks of the traditionalists. They use all the means which a secular regimen provided them: pamphlets, accusations, even violence and insults. The dangers to the faith and to the Christian religion were always their handiest instruments.

In a certain sense the lovers of the old had grounds for opposing themselves to these innovations. In the conflict the moderns, too, used all occasions and all weapons—argument, irony, ridicule—in order to destroy the past. In reality there was no continuity between modern thought and traditional philosophy, although there was always conciliation between faith and the modern doctrines. The sense of opposition, which later will become a theme repeated *ad nauseam,* is already to be noted in Sigüenza. As time went on, modern philosophy became indispensable in order to satisfy the desire for knowledge but principally to solve the problem of decadence. The Jesuits, Bartolache, Alzate, and Hidalgo were convinced that the greatness of the nation could not tolerate, in a century of illumination, the peripatetic barbarity, the cause of cultural retardation which was apparent in comparison with the civilized peoples of Europe, especially England and France. For this reason the knowledge of modern philosophy and science not only created the desire to seek out the remedies for decadence but also provoked a nationalist reaction. They cultivated the wisdom which had given rise to progress in other countries, and they tried to establish scientific institutions like those of France and England with the hope that the Americans would cease being useless in the sciences and apt only for theological speculation. Philosophy became more and more the study of nature. They emphasized the capacity of the American in all types of knowledge, they scrutinized history for the scientific glories of the country, and they began to feel proud that they were Mexicans.

The modern philosophers are men tormented by their vocation, which they conceived as the task of saving neo-Hispanic culture from decadence. With the restlessness of innovators, they taught a new method, new truths, new orientations: and they wrung their hands in despair before the slow advance of ideas. Representatives, with whatever limitations one may wish to recognize, of the century of enlightenment, they made a philosophy for all men with the purpose of providing them with another education. For this reason they wrote in Spanish, an idiom considered up to that time completely unworthy for philosophy and science. Their words reached out to every region. The journalists especially, like Alzate and Bartolache, saw to it that the new ideas reached even the hairdresser and the shopkeeper, as may be documented from all the publications of the period.

The ever-more decisive predilection for reason and experience leads them to a distrust both of peripateticism and of system in philosophy. On the one hand, they are persuaded that syllogistic discourse is useless for the knowledge of nature; they know, on the other hand, that there are no ultimate explanations of facts, like those which the philosophers who create systems pretend to supply, for example, Descartes. Except for Bartolache they think that system is a limitation and an impediment to philosophizing. Hence it is that liberty of thought, together with the liberty of selecting doctrines from whatever source might seem prudent, is the basic principle of thought. There is nothing higher than the exercise of reason itself or the truths which experience proves. They are the ones who are to decide which are the true propositions and not prejudice, authority, or philosophical sect. Hence, they think that the eclectic is the exemplary philosopher. And surely with eclecticism, whose theoretician is Gamarra, they succeed in establishing an idea of philosophy which permits them to create the autonomy of this discipline among us without, for this reason, destroying their own faith, totally annihilating tradition, or subjecting themselves to the consequences of the modern doctrines which they accept. It is not a question of a philosophy of "accommodation" or of circumstances. They write their works with a sure hand, and far from those writers is that timid prudence of those who seek an adjustment or a conciliation. As a consequence, the solutions of the Jesuits Gamarra, Bartolache, Alzate, and Hidalgo are not those which their environment permits them, but those which, having accepted the historical limitations as their own, they will sustain after having made a selection in the light of their rational reflection. Even less does there exist in them a religious conflict which torments them for their modernity. Their religion is as true as science.

Thus, with all these attitudes modernity becomes a movement which rightly belongs to the Mexican intelligence. Naturally, the permanent influence of ideas coming from Europe is not denied, including in the first place the Spain of Tosca and Feijoo; even less can there be set aside the freedoms, the stimulus, the institutions provided by enlightened despotism. Nevertheless, any affirmation about the possible passive position of our reformers must be discounted. In truth, the texts leave no room for doubt; they do not imitate philosophers literally; they assimilate them, reformulate them in their own way, adapt them to Mexican culture, and show, as Samuel Ramos says in regard to Gamarra, that they are effective "in awakening the consciousness of our own character." [37]

They were not philosophers, original and coherent in the sense that the creators of systems are, but they left, taken together, a way of thinking with depth and sincerity about the philosophical problems of their times. This is also philosophy, and philosophy precisely as it was conceived in that century,[38] as may be learned from a typical document, the "preliminary discourse" of the *Encyclopedie*. It is only that this kind of philosophizing, just like the concrete case of the eclecticism of the eighteenth century, is not considered by the historians of philosophy as philosophy in the strict sense, as they should consider it.

To prove what has been said above it would be necessary

to compose an exposition, however summary, of the ideas of
the representative philosophers, the Jesuits, Gamarra, the scientists, Hidalgo.[39] In considering their thoughts we have not sought
to point out the dates of these authors but better to indicate,
from their own ideas, the degree to which they were modern or
traditional. We believe that in this way the modernity of the
eighteenth century becomes clear, and that the bases will also
have been laid for the historical understanding of the unity of
this century with the nineteenth century, which is characterized
by its love of science, its eclecticism, its antimetaphysicalism, no
less than by its love of liberty and progress.

III
THE JESUIT INNOVATORS

The group of Jesuits is principally formed of Francisco Clavijero,
Francisco Javier Alegre, Diego José Abad, Agustín Castro, Ray-
mundo Cerdán, Julián Parreño, and Andrés de Guevara y
Basoazábal. Their intellectual guide, the "Socrates of the new
Athenian age" in the happy phrase of Maneiro, is Campoy. The
most philosophical, director in part of the innovating movement,
and the one who most extensively presents modern methods and
science, is Clavijero.

All of them share the same basic attitudes; about 1748, when
they founded their clubs for discussion of new ideas with Tosca
and Feijoo as masters, they were about twenty-five years of age.
Their teachings extended throughout the colleges in which they
were professors: Tepotzotlán, Guadalajara, Morelia, Puebla,
Zacatecas, Mérida, and Querétaro. In addition to philosophy they
successfully cultivated literature, history, architecture, theology,
the sciences, all disciplines to which they also applied the taste of
the century. Before they left Spain they had published practically
nothing. In Italy, on the contrary, their many and varied publications had strongly attracted attention. However, their philosophical works, save one, remained in manuscript form, and some
have been irretrievably lost. Their adherence to modernity does

not leave them entirely immune. To the disdain and attacks from the ranks of the peripatetics, who tried to squelch the movement in its beginnings, there succeeded the loss of university chairs, censures from their superiors, and dismissal from the colleges.[40] They respond with integrity, without defecting from the new ideals, although they recommended to each other a certain hypocrisy and the use of old words to name new concepts. This Alegre tells Clavijero: "I am happy to see you determined to take so cautious a line, because with a little hypocrisy it will be possible to defend as many of the Aristotelian principles, which neither add to nor detract from sound physics, as one wishes."

Bernabé Navarro [41] has indicated that there exist three principal sources of their ideas: the biographies written by Maneiro and Fabri, two members of the group; the letters of Clavijero and Alegre to each other; and the philosophical courses of Abad and Cerdán, the special physics of Clavijero, and texts of secondary names. Thanks to these materials, which the author cites, expounds, and interprets very abundantly, we can here explain the methodical preoccupations, as well as the philosophical doctrines, of the Jesuits.

1. The Ideals of the Modern Point of View

The first thing which strikes one in reading the documents is the frankly modern tone. The orientation in teaching, the inclination toward what is new, and the attitude toward scholasticism are clear indications of the age. Not only did the Jesuits possess a wide acquaintance with contemporary philosophers and scientists but they also understood them with objectivity. What is even more revelatory, they realized that they too shared the theses sustained by those men, that is, the Jesuits prove that they wanted to be modern and that they were modern. Clavijero, for example, speaks in his *Historia* of "our philosophical century," and in his *Curso de filosofía* Abad says that he intends to expound "the new philosophy, indeed, even the most advanced philosophy of our day," that which "has so resounded in the ears of the people that it has even been circulated in the common tongue." [42] Of Clavijero his biographer Maneiro wrote that he had become so devoted to the so-called modern philosophy "so as to say, with a furtive love and cultivated it in his studies ..., reading ... as assiduously the works of Leroy, Duhamel, Saguens, Purchot, Descartes, Gassendi, Newton, Leibnitz." [43] But the foregoing does not mean that this group exhibited a radical attitude. Without stating as much, they distinguished the "learned and fashionable philosopher" who could, carried away by his reason, become lost in deviations, from the prudent philosopher who joins what is best and authentic in the tradition to what is to be recommended in recent philosophers. One understands thus that an historian Paw, because he wrote untrue things about New Spain, can be a negative model: "see here a truly frank manner of speaking, that of a philosopher of the eighteenth century." [44] The Jesuits are not as avant-garde as was Don Carlos de Sigüenza y Góngora. They belonged to a generation on which the truths of faith and fears of the new doctrines imposed limits.

This half-way modernity, which still continues to be one of our characteristics, appears under one form or another in all the work of the Jesuits. Thus, many texts refer expressly to, or at least imply, the abandonment of speculative prolixity and the abuse of logic; but in their works themselves they accept a considerable portion of the themes of the philosophical decadence. The rejection of the argument from authority is equally a measure of the new unrest. Although they do not indeed continue the school of the *Libra Astronómica,* they at least wrote express testimonies. Agustín Castro considered systems as philosophical parties and would follow none of them exclusively, "thinking unworthy of the wise man that custom of the Pythagoreans of assenting, not to reason, but to the authority of the teacher." [45] Clavijero wrote a dialogue between a lover of the truth and a friend of what is old for the purpose of inculcating the obligation of using in the study of physics "a method which leads us to the real investigation of the truth, and which in no way sustains any postulate arbitrarily established by the ancients." [46] He indicates that there is another criterion of truth, and that is, fundamentally, recourse to experience and the rights of reason.

In close connection with what has gone before are their repeated demands to have recourse to the sources, to the original writers and works, with the purpose of finding the genuine teachings of the peripatetics, since they are convinced that with repetition through different ages, those teachings were so deformed that they ended up by being irreconcilable. A similar desire, which partially includes the purpose of knowing modern writers at first hand, places the Jesuits in the line of those philosophers who use history in order to discover the errors of tradition. Common to our modernity is the case of Aristotle, of whom it is said that his doctrines had been shifted either by the interpretations of the Arabians or by the schemata of the schools. Of Campoy his biographer affirms that being very sharp in disputations, he venerated Aristotle, whom he considered his master, simply because in the schools he had learned "to vociferate on a wide number of theses, almost without any utility at all." From this admiration he conceived the desire to read the *Rhetoric* and the *Poetics*. On doing so, he was so completely astonished "he could hardly believe his eyes when he saw how different this Aristotle was, whom he was now reading and studying, from this Aristotle, disputer of futilities, whom he had come to imagine through the false legends of those who claimed that they were disciples of the prince of philosophers." Like the philosophers of our eighteenth century he learned by his own judgment, without the explanation of any teacher, the difference between the true wise man and the eternal disputer over trifles.[47]

Beginning with the Jesuits, the modern Mexican philosophers maintained the same attitude. They were all educated in the traditional themes and achieved high distinctions in them; when they became teachers or writers, they tried to eliminate useless themes and to substitute for them the "genuine philosophy of Aristotle." Some of them, like Agustín Castro, remained in the pure doctrine of the prince of the peripatetics, once he had been unearthed, without even expounding the insights which were contributed by Descartes, Leibnitz, Newton, and Gassendi. Abad, by contrast, and above all Alegre tried to uproot entirely Aristotle, as well as all intricate questions, from theology itself. To this end they dedicated themselves by drinking "from the true theological sources, that is, the Sacred Scriptures, the Holy Fathers, and the Councils," as well as from history and chronology.[48] This fact is important for the evolution of ideas, since it means that the Jesuits were already announcing the purification of theological method and that positive theology which Hidalgo advanced to its highest development.

The study of the sources means, on the other hand, a change in the manner of teaching and learning philosophy. The common method of teaching at that time consisted in passive repetition, in memorization, in copying and dictation; and the examinations were a literal repetition of the school texts. Campoy, who had meditated assiduously over the theological works of Saint Thomas, Suárez, Petavius, and Melchor Cano, was vetoed because he could not take seriously "the dictations of his teachers" after "the established discipline and customs."[49] One of the far-reaching efforts of the Jesuits, which will not end with the teaching of Gamarra, Bartolache, and Alzate, is to provide their students with the opportunity of exercising their intellects, of reflecting upon the old and the new in the light of reason.

The inclination toward novelties, the desire to investigate, the concern to avoid errors, the vigilant attitude to distinguish the certain from the uncertain, are so many other indications of modernity which exist in the Jesuits. They do not have, to be sure, Sigüenza's consciousness of method, and they also lack the intellectual criticism of Gamarra or of Alzate; however, they show in their works—on some occasions explicitly, on others implicitly —that they had made their own the fundamental attitude of the century. Alegre is the typical man when he is forever seeking new truths or when instead of concealing his wisdom he gives an account of his readings in his commentaries. Even more illustrative is Campoy, whose intellectual life is described in the following manner by his biographer Maneiro: "to consider as something sacred anything which he reads or takes up to learn;

to seek the truth in everything, to investigate everything minutely, to decipher enigmas, to distinguish the certain from the dubious, to disdain the inveterate prejudices of men, to go from one learning to another new one, to eliminate inept words." [50]

2. The True Philosophy

Despite the indications given above, the work of the Jesuits, taken as a whole, gives the impression that they were less advanced than their intentions. In their courses they had to treat the complete exposition which the teaching program demanded and not only that part of it which was most to their own tastes. Perhaps for this reason the texts which they wrote were fundamentally scholastic so far as they referred to logic, metaphysics, and the commentaries of the *Physics* of Aristotle. They are traditional because they insist on continuing the old themes, or because they pretend to present the genuine scholasticism and the true Aristotle, or, above all, because they accept the basic principles of the peripatetic philosophy. The only difference is that they offer some new points of view, that there is in their works greater clarity and simplicity; the questions are less useless and confused; here and there indications of a critical spirit appear; some direct readings of the classics is involved; and their own doctrines are reduced to the most important themes. Does this mean that the modernity of the Jesuits comes down to certain proposals, to an inclination for new ideas? Their contribution will have to be sought in the renovation they made in scholasticism, but, above all, in their treatises on general and special physics, since they belong to the days in which philosophy inclined to be the knowledge of nature which the true physics, the modern physics, provided. In order not to make them either too modern or too traditional, one must consider that theirs was a period of transition and that they are the first to teach courses with all the disciplines. "You know," Clavijero says at the end of his *Física*, "that all of the philosophers who have lived in America up to this time have abstained from teaching the true physics." [51]

Certainly, the Jesuits write on many occasions that the knowledge of nature is achieved by means of physics, to the point that they repudiate false physics, that taught by the scholastics with the pretension of understanding the whole of reality by means of deductive or suppositional processes, or very elementary, when not imaginary and fantastic, observations. The texts permit no doubt of this. They are physicists in the modern sense, even though they abstain at times from carrying out their proposals for reasons of a practical order, like the fear of imprudently revolutionizing the teaching program and the concern not to excite traditional souls. They are philosophers at the end of a period of transition. Their modernity does not prevent them from presenting at the same time both the scholastic and the most recent theses without deciding in favor of one or the other. They are also able to accept the old doctrines because their rejection would involve endless discussions, useless for educational plans. These reservations, however, find their compensation in the innumerable texts in which they openly praise and exalt the true physics.

As for the rest, they make their own the method proper to science, since they explain with complete clarity that "experience," "instruments," "the most exact observations," and "experiments" are the modes of knowledge which ought to be used in physics. A letter of Brisar to Clavijero reminds us of the statements of Feijoo in favor of the experimental method; in it, after having congratulated him for having obtained permission to give a number of lessons in modern physics, Brisar complains that he does not have "instruments and opportunities for experimental study and to record the hidden work of nature." [52] Clavijero himself states that almost no one ventures to defend the Ptolemaic system "after the very exact observations of the modern astronomers and the experiments of the physicists." [53] Abad affirms with conviction in relation to logical themes that "certainly a demonstration is much better when it is founded on the experiment itself." [54] Scientific experience is, then, the new criterion of truth which the Hispano-Americans propose to themselves in place of the metaphysics of the scholastics, a new manner of philosophizing that solves all difficulties and all problems. The conviction of modernity itself encourages in these Jesuits the belief that the true form of knowledge is the scientific and also that science offers difficult questions in which doubts are not always conquered.[55] Thus, to the desire to learn something new they add recourse to experience, or at least the desire to verify by experience what before they had studied in books. They even expressly accept mathematics as necessary for the understanding of physics or for the natural sciences. All these circumstances make them followers of Sigüenza and, at the same time, guides for Gamarra and the other moderns. The modernity of the Jesuits is not exhausted, however, by saying that they oppose experiments and the conceptions of their century to the qualities and virtualities of tradition. The very texts cited by Navarro [56] convince us that the philosophy defended by all of them is the modern science of experimentation and observation. One may even admit that there is "a certain sensistic or materialistic tendency, if things are looked at in isolation," in the ideas they expound.[57] Indeed, so overwhelming are both the number of passages and the meaning of their affirmations that there can be no doubt about the propensity of the Jesuits to consider the study of useful physics as the true philosophy. So great is their predilection and love for the sciences that it can be understood only by concluding that the true physics, for which they so eagerly sought, is the modern philosophy which they propound. The very authors whom they cite, especially Feijoo, whose point of view is experimental, lead us to the same conclusion. "Good physics," according to Maneiro, the apologete-biographer of the group, is their common aspiration. For example, the education which Alegre wants for the new age answers to the modern postulates: "we must go forward," he says, "permitting the seeds of all the sciences to fall, as Verulam says, insensibly upon the tender young minds." The "science of nature," of Clavijero, is, without doubt, "the sound philosophy." The taste for the true philosophy is satisfied in modern physics, which, as one of the Jesuits said, "must necessarily be approved by every rational man." [58] There is, it cannot be denied, too much scholasticism in them, but also too much modernity. Their merit, from the point of view of the history of ideas, consists precisely in the fact that they make the transition to the new philosophy without achieving it completely. That this interpretation is the correct one will be proven by the study of their science and their skepticism, which we shall treat in the following paragraphs.

3. *The True Science*

As a result of all this, it does not seem strange that they should defend and expound practically all the fundamental theses of modern thought, setting them in express contrast to the peripatetic tradition. In conformity with the order which scholasticism employed in the exposition of the parts of philosophy and even of the different questions, they proceeded to point out the old and the new ways of seeing things. [59] In this way there are present the most significant modern philosophers and scientists: Bacon, Leibnitz, Newton, Malebranche, Maupertius, Maignan, Losada, Feijoo, Copernicus, Galileo, Kepler, Tycho, Torricelli, Boyle, Cassini, and many others of secondary rank. The systems most extensively taught are those of Descartes and Gassendi, whose ideas on the first principles, or ultimate elements, of bodies, qualities, motion, the vacuum, substantial forms, the origin of ideas, and the nature of the world and of the soul are fully treated and always with marked opposition to the traditional positions. And while the Jesuits cannot be reproached with ignorance of modern thought, so far as the extent of their information is concerned, they can be reproached for the lack of a criterion for distinguishing authorities of the first rank from those of the second rank.

Their greatest failing, however, is that they do not know these authors directly in their works, a fact made evident by the total absence of direct quotations and citations. Even Descartes, so extensively treated and highly praised in their texts, is known only through the notices of him given by Gabriel Daniel and above all, transitional thinkers like Maignan, Losada, and Tosca.

This will eventually prove to be the distinguishing limitation of our modernity, from which not even Gamarra frees himself completely. Even after the ideas of the century have already penetrated our culture, only Alzate and, to a greater degree, Bartolache will be able to consult some of these works directly. Meanwhile, with no other training than that of their own restless curiosity, the Jesuits, autodidacts themselves, fulfilled their historic mission which was to open the old consciousness to the new; to present doctrines in an agreeable manner so as to make their acceptance possible, to place in crisis a body of knowledge widely accepted, and to implant in an almost imperceptible manner the attitudes, ideas, and theses of the new age. On the other hand, it is good to consider that, setting aside strictly scientific matters, these Jesuits were well informed not only about the preoccupations but also about the most recent tendencies in European science, which, it must not be forgotten, was at that time freeing itself from Cartesian physics and also suffering the vacillations of a period of transition.

As a matter of fact, they accepted a large number of contemporary findings: the ultimate elements of bodies, motion, the vacuum, the nature of water, the physiology of sensations, the composition of the moon, shadows and bright spots on the sun, corruptibility of the heavenly bodies, identity of earthly and heavenly matter, distance of the fixed stars, superiority of the orbits of the comets to that of the moon, the theory of gravity, weight and elastic force of air, the properties of the magnet, and the problems of optics, respiration, the heart and blood.[60] Each one of these truths is, in itself, an index of the modern point of view and of the sharpest opposition to peripateticism, which will continue obstinately to maintain its errors to the end of the century.

Nevertheless, modernity does not consist only in what has been accepted, for the traditional content far surpasses it at that time; it also appears in the way in which the new ideas are taught or in the devices used to introduce them. The main ideologists of the Jesuit movement—Clavijero, Alegre, and Abad—proceed in such a way that they do not expound any modern doctrine which does not modify something in the traditional mind, although immediately afterward they return to the beaten path. Certain determined arguments—those, for example, opposing corpuscles to substantial forms—at times seem to be enunciated simply in all their force; at others, are criticized; and on still others, accepted, but subject to certain conditions. On all sides one can see the hypocrisy which Alegre recommended to Clavijero, to the effect that he should defend the concepts of the true physics by using the words of false science. "I am of the opinion," he affirms in another place, "that when we think like everyone else, we speak like everyone else. That is to say that heavy burdens are imposed according to the capacity to bear them; nothing more is said than in a hidden quality. And this term may dispel all horror of what is new, and will bring it about that to treat these matters is not a horror and a spirit of partisanship against peripateticism." [61] In accordance with this determination, they created a screen, or web of words, in which the master thread could only be the modernizing intention and never the restoration of a radically decadent scholasticism. Thus one understands why it is that they constantly vest new ideas in old garments. Abad is modern when he establishes with scholastic arguments the equality of sublunary and superlunary matter, and is equally modern when in his treatise on philosophy he treats first "those matters in which the moderns agree with the peripatetic physicists and then those on which they differ most completely." [62] And the modern sense of his statement that his philosophy consists in providing the purest sources of ancient wisdom acquires an integral significance.

Another common device is to provide information about both the modern and the scholastic thesis, without adding anything in favor of one or the other. At times they adopt two very indicative attitudes: either they expound the recent doctrines in a favorable manner and, by the very fact of the exposition, leave them to be considered valid, or they oppose them, not with philosophical, but with religious arguments, as Abad does when he rejects the systems of Descartes and Gassendi due to the fact that the mystery of the Eucharist is explained by substantial forms, absolute qualities, and accidents which are different from the form. It also happens, by contrast, that they defend the modern doctrines by saying that they are more conformable to the meaning of Scripture and the Fathers or that they concur with the scholastic positions, either because they do not refute these latter or because they can be equally sustained. Very characteristic of modernity is the continuous rejection of Aristotelian and scholastic definitions, of prime matter and of substantial form, especially because they are too obscure and because they lend themselves to interpretation in the corpuscular theory of Descartes and Gassendi.

4. Atomism and the Copernican System

A special case, by reason of its importance in the debate between tradition and the new tendencies, is provided by substantial forms and atomism. Abad, who recognizes the necessity of admitting matter and form, writes that since it is not to his taste to dispute with the moderns, "let us suppose that there are substantial forms in the peripatetic sense." [63] However, in expounding the corresponding scholastic thesis, when everything makes us expect that he will remain in the traditional line of argument, he concludes in this fashion: form "must be maintained necessarily, not only by the Aristotelians but also by the partisans of Descartes and Gassendi," even though the respective parties differ in their definition of form.[64] The same thing happens in the case of the atoms. In order to explain them in a manner at once Aristoltelian and modern, he teaches that every body consists of "very small corpuscles, divisible *ad infinitum*," in each one of which "the essence of matter is saved." Matter is at the same time "a simple substance," in the traditional manner, and is "integrally composed of particles continuously extended" as the moderns demand.[65]

Denying the theory of the four elements, Clavijero, for his part, still calls "fire, water, earth, and air" elements, "even though we find them composed of elements." He knows well that "there are no other elements outside the atoms, since these are simple bodies, of which all things are composed and into which all things are resolved." However, to save matter and form, he distinguishes two kinds of bodies: one is the atom, "simple," a "complete substance, by its nature quantified and impenetrable"; the other is the "common and whole body," constituted of "integral parts" which are matter and form.[66] There does not exist in the texts above, or in those of Abad, anything but the greatest possible acceptance of the modern point of view, but with the intention of squaring the appearances with tradition.

Clearly, the indecisions, the return to the old, the veiled way of expressing oneself, the quantitatively overwhelming acceptance of scholastic theses, all prove that the full position of the new age has not been attained. This will happen only with the *Lecciones matemáticas,* which Ignacio Bartolache published in 1769, hardly three years after Clavijero taught his *Físca particular.* But where the Jesuits show a completely old-fashioned point of view is in the fact, repeated again and again, that they not only take into consideration the theological difficulties occasioned by certain doctrines but also return to agreement with the meaning of Scripture and tradition, and, even worse, adduce as valid proofs the motives of faith, instead of experiments and rational arguments. The singular attitude of Clavijero with regard to the system of the world may serve as an example, a question which, during the eighteenth century, was the critical point between moderns and peripatetics.

One of the first things which must be recognized in the Jesuit directors of this movement is a certain sympathy for the Copernican hypothesis, though later, for theological and scientific reasons, they seem to incline toward the acceptance of that of Tycho Brahe.[67] The sympathy appears above all when they reject the Ptolemaic system, a rejection which certainly cannot be taken as definitive, despite the inexorable statement of Clavijero, the Jesuit who gives especial treatment to this theme, that, "after the very exact observations of the modern astronomers and the experiments of the physicists, almost none cares to defend it, save a few peripatetics equally ignorant of astronomy and of physics." Before expounding the Copernican system, which he qualifies as "a very old disposition of the world," Clavijero himself clearly states that it can be defended *as an hypothesis only,* adding immediately that it is not possible to affirm it as a thesis because it contains opinions contrary to the Scripture and the Fathers. And further on, in strange contradiction, he assures us that it cannot be defended even as an hypothesis "because it is not conformable with phenomena." Nevertheless, at the end of the exposition he evidences a speculative perplexity between the three systems, which is not wholly congruent with his other expressions; "nor is it less difficult for me," he says, "to understand the movements of Copernicus than those of Ptolemy or Tycho."

In conformity with this last statement, after saying that Tycho Brahe "excogitated" his system because "the Copernican system did not accord with the Holy Scriptures or the Ptolemaic with the phenomena," Clavijero recognizes that in the form in which it is expressed by the moderns it is in conformity with astronomy but not with physics, for which reason it is not defensible. He seems to be concerned, not with considerations of faith, but with those of science. On the other hand, the force of tradition or disciplinary measures brings him not only to accept decisive questions of the Ptolemaic explanation but also to fall consciously into irrational theses. He writes, in fact, that the universe may be considered as a sphere whose center is the earth, as Ptolemy taught, "because even if this is not certain, it can easily be taken as an hypothesis." [68]

How can we reconcile the vacillations of Clavijero? How is it possible for him to affirm that the Copernican system has been demonstrated and later to say that it cannot be demonstrated completely? It becomes clear that we are not yet treating of a scientific position, but of a practical one. Clavijero knew that it was forbidden the members of the Society to teach the Copernican system. Even more, his own experience counseled him to take into consideration the scandals which might be provoked among the theologians. The solution, consequently, was to conceal his modern ideas.

5. The Eclectic Attitude

When things are seen in this light, the historian of ideas understands how eclecticism was the best solution, so that the philosopher might be modern and a modernizer in a country which firmly adhered to the traditional and opposed novelty. The Jesuits were eclectics, both in their expositions of the new doctrines and in regard to the teachings of their predecessors, though, indeed, they never used the term. They also recommended eclecticism for their students, since many times they left them free to select or choose among the modern, or between the recent and the old, opinions. To exemplify such a way of philosophizing, in addition to what has been said up to the present, a passage may be read in which Alegre expouds to Clavijero his treatise on physics: "From this point I went on to animated bodies: first, plants, in which matter I followed the thought of the moderns; then the animals, following Descartes; then man, which treatment I divided into the four faculties—vital, natural, animal, and rational—in which I inserted respectively the treatises on generation, corruption, and a compendium of anatomy. I treated the senses extensively and, with regard to that of hearing, the fundamental principles of music; with respect to vision, those of optics, dioptics, and cataoptics according to the three directions of light, in the explanation of which I followed Descartes. In generation, Maupertius seemed better to me; in anatomy, Heinster; in music, Erranso; in optics, Abad Nollet. In what concerns *the rational faculty, which is what we call the soul, I followed, most generally, Malebranche and Descartes.*" [69]

His modernity resolved itself into an eclecticism which responded to the drama which had arisen between his religious conscience and his consciousness of being modern. What is least important is scholasticism. B. Navarro and Eguiara y Eguren himself [70] interpret this movement as a restoration of, or as a reconciliation with, authentic traditional philosophy in such a way that the numerous modern ideas become incorporated into the peripatetic position. No. "They composed and harmonized new things in an ingenious fashion," but never according to the traditional point of view, rather according to that of the true physics. They follow this or that philosopher, making their own the ideas which seemed to them most probable; they choose the recent truths and also the old ones which accord with the new or the new which may be accommodated to the traditional; in the same way they select the theories which do not contradict faith, even though they may not be modern or do not enjoy the support of reason. Still there guides him, in all these processes, an attitude which is modern: boldness in knowing, a love of truth. Clavijero states it clearly at the end of the *Física:* "in it, without any intention of partisanship, but led by the sincere love of truth, we have chosen in each one of the questions the opinion which seemed to us to possess the greatest verisimilitude." [71] In a climate of philosophical struggles they sought the truth wherever it was to be found, independently of any school. Another time Clavijero says that innumerable facts must be known which are "the result of the centuries-long investigation of the wisest men and which are admitted by the philosophers without distinctions of school or system." [72] In order not to get lost in such a labor of intellectual innovation, they had a criterion ready at hand: the repudiation of peripateticism, the quest of the new as a philosophical attitude, and the method of experience and reason. In this way they could construct "a synthesis with an admirable order," in which "would be found concentrated and made clear with the greatest perspicacity the Greek philosophers, as well as all the useful knowledge discovered by the modern sages, from Bacon of Verulam and Descartes to the American Franklin." [73] It would be useless to ask more of this "original synthesis" of which the biographer Maneiro speaks. It is simply an eclectic philosophy, which deserves to be considered in history as a contribution to thought, even though at times its followers, even the greatest of them, in choosing their doctrines do not grasp the profound sense of the philosophemes, interested as they are only in gathering the data useful for filling out a mental scheme.

6. *National Culture and Humanism*

The thought of the Jesuits, of great importance in the history of ideas, receives a greater meaning when one considers that their works are the origin of our national consciousness. They loved their country almost excessively, so much so that, exiled in Italy, they preferred the city of Tacuba to cultured Rome. Practically all of them wrote on Mexican themes, now with the purpose of showing detractors the truth of our history, again with the plan of explaining, in an unobjectable manner, the American capacity for universal culture. Here is the cause which explains their anxiety to save the country from decadence by means of the reformation of method and the teaching of the new doctrines. Their concern is to bring Mexican studies up to the level of European culture. At every step they repeat that the greatness of the nation demands the cultivation of the modern sciences and the abandonment of those traditional attitudes which hinder her.

The Jesuits possess another merit equally great. In addition to being those who introduced modern philosophy, in addition to being Mexicans, they were humanists, because, as Gabriel Méndez Plancarte says,[74] they both affirm the rights and enduring values of man and descend to the study and remedy of his concrete necessities. With them anthropological thought, which would seem to have lost vigor after the sixteenth century, returns to the foreground, with the difference that now, thanks to the influence of the modern point of view, man begins to be considered as an end in himself. Out of an interest in man they seek in the historical past the greatness of the indigenes and the Creoles. They again speak of the covetousness of the Spaniards, write against unjust slavery, establish freedom as an inviolable right, and think that the people is the original subject of authority. About the social problem of New Spain they counsel the necessary establishment of crossbreeding. The very reform of studies and the new idea of philosophy have as their object the creation in the American man of an intelligence which, no longer deserving the name of barbarian, enables him to achieve earthly happiness.

Luis Villoro

V. THE IDEOLOGICAL CURRENTS OF THE EPOCH OF INDEPENDENCE*

Introduction

It would be improper to speak of "philosophy" in the epoch of the Revolution if we understood that term in a strict sense. The smooth rhythm of colonial development was suddenly broken, the revolutionary upheaval forced clear-cut decisions, there was no human life which was not affected by its contact. For the first time the Mexican mind felt its work closely bound up with the effective transformation of the community. A radical reversal of thought took place: it could no longer limit itself to the contemplation of reality, for now its expression was action, as well. Words demanded to be carried out, not repeated. The vehicle

* In my book *La Revolución de Independencia*, published by the Autonomous National University of Mexico in 1953, I treated the theme of this essay in great detail. My ideas regarding it have not changed substantially since that time; the reader will have to excuse me, therefore, for making extensive use of that work, summarizing here much of what I expressed there. On the whole, I have taken advantage of the opportunity to add some shadings of interpretation which I now see with greater clarity than I did at that time; I have also taken into consideration the investigations of other authors published after my own work.

185

of thought is no longer the treatise, but the manifesto, the periodical article, the political and historical essay. In this context the traditional philosophical themes lost meaning; no one would know what use to make of them. Philosophy as abstract speculation disappeared; its place was taken by concrete themes which illuminated and explained human action: political theory, religious criticism, or historical understanding. But in all this there still exists philosophy in a certain sense. In fact, if by philosophy we understand *radical reflection,* the concrete thought of this period will be philosophical according to the degree of its radicalism. In asking for the ultimate principles of social reality, which it seeks to make clear, it will acquire the dimensions of philosophy. Only in this restricted sense shall we be able to speak of "philosophy" during the Mexican Revolution of Independence.

The period which we are studying may be seen as the first effort of the Mexican mind to bring out into the open the origins of its community life. On the one hand, there is the liberation from inherited conceptions, from false systems which encumber the national truth; on the other, there is the conscious return to the bases upon which rests social life in its historical movement. To dig down to the depths of our own historical world in order to explain our action in it is a form, in the last analysis, of philosophical radicalism. It is "philosophical," no doubt, in a particular sense, since the purity and universality proper to abstract reason are abandoned in order voluntarily to circumscribe thought within a small segment of human life.

No matter how radical reflection succeeds in becoming, it never abandons the area of the concrete; for this reason it cannot be understood detached from the circumstance to which it responds. It translates rationally a movement which wide social groups carry out, and it is involved with their interests and projects. Its function is not separable from *praxis;* in seeking the principles of social life reflection undertakes to fulfill the function of clarifying and setting the norms for action. Thought clarifies action and action fulfills thought without our being able to know which of the two factors truly precedes the other. If theory frequently indicates courses of action, at other times action precedes thought and obliges it to express a discovery already made by action. In this alliance between thought and action the meaning of ideas varies with the function they fulfill. The concrete employment which is assigned them in a situation reveals their meaning. For this reason the mere historical origin of a doctrine ordinarily indicates little about its meaning. An imported doctrine of progressivist origin may, for example, fulfill in the new circumstances a moderating function; or, again, some traditional conception may, on being revived, acquire a renovating and even a revolutionary use. It proves more useful, consequently, to try to explain the acceptance of ideas by the historical attitudes of the men who employ them in a determined situation.

Ideological thought does not remain static during the period of Independence. We can notice a constantly more profound movement in the reflective quest of origins which corresponds to the growing revolutionary radicalism. The different stages of this process cannot be explained by the simple change in philosophical influences; on the contrary, the evolution of doctrines is clarified by the increasing persistence or steadfastness in one attitude toward reality. Let us examine the principal steps in this movement.

I
THE ANTECEDENTS OF REVOLUTIONARY THOUGHT

At the opening of the nineteenth century there already existed in New Spain what we might call an "enlightened middle class," made up principally of members of the liberal professions and of the middle and lower clergy, which felt that many of their aspirations bore an affinity with those of the rural Creole landholders. While the Europeans pre-empted practically all of the higher ecclesiastical, civil, and military posts, the Creole "literati" were obliged to compete for minor posts in the public administration and for canonries and curacies of second rank.

The principal political lever of this group was the municipal councils, which they dominated completely; its most powerful weapon, the Illumination, which rested almost exclusively in its hands. This Creole intelligentsia found itself culturally prepared for a change. Disgruntled with the colonial order, it will try to deny it and to oppose to it another order designed for its projects. In political theory it will pick out the doctrine which will serve to justify change at the required moment. There seemed to be, at the time, three principal currents which fed its thought. The most important was rationalistic natural law (Grotius, Puffendorf, Heinisius), which related itself without too great difficulties to the doctrine of the enlightened Jesuits; the latter, following Suárez, and, perhaps, Juan de Mariana, taught that sovereignty had its roots immediately in the people and that the people transferred its rights to the monarch by means of a pact. The union of these two currents clearly showed itself in Francisco Xavier Alegre. In his *Institutionum Teologicarum* of 1789 he argued that the proximate origin of authority resides in the " 'consensus' of the community," and its ultimate basis is in the "jus gentium." The sovereignty of the king, he asserted, is only mediated and rests on common assent. Quoting Puffendorf, he developed a doctrine which also coincides with the Suárezian line of thought: "all dominion, of whatever kind it may be, has its origin in a convention or contract between men." [1] The language which the first theoreticians of the Independence employed so clearly recalled this current that we cannot do other than see here its most important source.

Upon this basis of thought other influences accumulated. The enlightened Spanish authors, above all Jovellanos and Martínez Marina, with their purpose of assimilating certain modern political ideas to the legal political tradition of Spain, attracted the attention of the "literati" of New Spain. The continuous attempts to establish in Mexico "Societies of Friends of the Country" and the success enjoyed by the society of that character founded and directed by Jacobo de Villaurrutia in Guatemala suffice to attest the common preoccupations between the Spanish and the Mexican enlightenments. Finally, there was the influence of French ideas: Rousseau, Montesquieu, Voltaire, the *Encyclopédie*. We know that the new books circulated widely and were much discussed in select circles.[2] Some of their political ideas coincided formally with those mentioned above and were able to be assimilated to them, nourishing the impulses toward reform and renovation. Nor were there lacking cases of Creoles infected with Francophilism, like the Curé Olovarrieta, condemned by the Inquisition in 1802 for sustaining Rousseauan ideas. Another interesting case is that of the prosecuting attorney Posada, who held ideas "belonging to the Spanish tradition but, perhaps, too close to those of Rousseau."[3] On the whole, one should not exaggerate the influence of the French authors, as is sometimes done. From the simple reading of books a real ideological influence cannot be inferred. The records of the Inquisition show that most of those it tried were foreigners, not Creoles. On the other hand, the Spanish authorities and the Inquisitors themselves prove to be among the most avid readers of such materials. The diffusion of such works would only have a true meaning if the doctrines of the principal theoreticians of the Independence showed a clear similarity of thought, something that happens, as we shall see, only at a later stage of the Revolution. The initial attitude of the Creole seems much more to be to try to assimilate to his own line of thought those expressions of the French ideologists which coincided formally with it. In this way the Creoles prolonged and extended that selective eclecticism before modern ideas which distinguished so many of the "illuminati" of the eighteenth century.

In 1808 a singular event provided the occasion for the manifestation of the first ideas favorable to Independence. The continuity of the monarchy was broken, the disputing sovereigns Carlos and Fernando alienated their own kingdom because they were incapable of defending it. The metropolis was occupied by the troops of Napoleon, and it fell to the Spanish people to take the resistance into their own hands. *As a matter of fact,* the sovereignty had reverted to the people. Doctrinal discussions were useless; the different peoples of the peninsula had to organize on their own account and had to secure the constitution of the nation by their own efforts.

In New Spain two antagonistic parties were formed. On one side was the "Real Acuerdo" (the Royal Adherence), supported by the functionaries and business people of European origin; on the other, the "Ayuntamiento de la Ciudad de Mexico" (the Council of the City of Mexico) and the only Creole judge, Jacobo de Villaurrutia, through whose voice the American middle class made itself heard for the first time. Among the Creoles the effective disappearance of the monarchy made it necessary to open the problem of the origin of sovereignty. Fernando VII preserved the right to the crown; there was now introduced, however, an idea which changed the meaning of his dominion: the king cannot dispose of the realms by his choice; he does not have the power to alienate them. The abdication of Carlos and Fernando counted for nothing because they are "contrary to the rights of the nation, to which no one can give a king save itself by the universal consent of its peoples, and this in the single case in which, because of the death of the king, there remains no legitimate successor to the crown." [4] The rights of the nation are above the rights of the king.

Authority, the lawyer Verdad argued, comes to the king from God, not immediately, but by way of the people. [5] For his part, Azcárete recalled that a compact existed between the king and the people which could not be broken unilaterally. [6] This last idea was understood in the accepted sense of the social contract, which could be read in Vitoria or in Suárez as well as in Puffendorf. In a word, the original contract solemnized between the people and the king is irrevocable; if the monarch cannot renounce it, neither can the people snatch back from the king the donation of the kingdom which it has made to him. When the king finds himself incapacitated for government, the nation resumes the sovereignty; when, however, the king returns to his functions, the direct exercise of power by the people ceases automatically. Although the "Real Acuerdo" accused the Ayuntamiento of Mexico City of holding that the social contract is abolished during the interregnum and that the citizens are free to establish a new contract, the Ayuntamiento seems inclined rather to the doctrine of Heinsius, following his translator and commentator, Joaquín Marín y Mendoza. According to the latter "the pact solemnized by the people remains in force, and the Republic has not altered its primitive constitution by the fact that during the interregnum it has elected certain extraordinary magistrates. . . ." [7] The pact with the king remains in force, but the nation does not conceive itself alienated from the king. The original contract supposes that the nation is free to give itself the forms of government which are necessary and suitable for it. As a matter of fact, the basis of the society has been shifted from the king to the nation. While the lawyer Verdad on one occasion still speaks of "royal estates" which the nation must respect, Azcárete, with greater logic, inverts the terms and speaks of "goods confided by the nation to the king for administration by him." [8] For his part, Fray Melchor de Talamantes is more daring than his colleagues. When the king abdicates, he writes, "the nation immediately recovers its legislative power, along with all the other rights and privileges of the Crown." Then it is necessary to appeal to the voice of the nation, "that voice which all political thinkers, both ancient and modern, regard as the basis and origin of societies." [9]

In seeking the origin of society the Creole stops at the nation. What does he understand by that term? He is not speaking of the "general will" of the citizens, that sovereignty reverts to a society already established, organized into estates and represented in established bodies of government. It is a question of the idea of the authority of the "community" considered as an organic whole already constituted. Thus Azcárete calls into doubt the legitimacy of the junta of Seville because it was formed by the "plebs," "which is not the people, in the accepted meaning of law la, title 10, part 2, which expressly declares that there is no worthless class." [10] In a speech he develops this point with care. "On the occasion of the absence or the impediment (of the king) the sovereignty is lodged, represented, in the entire kingdom and the classes which form it and most particularly in the superior tribunals which govern it, administer justice, and in the bodies which express the public voice. . . ." These are ideas which the Ayuntamiento accepts in full, adding that the nomination of the viceroy belongs to the kingdom "represented by its tribunals and bodies, with this Metropolitan as its head. . . ." [11] Even Melchor de Talamantes, the man with the most advanced ideas among the Creoles, expressly opposed Rousseau, whose error was "to have assigned the exercise of authority to the people without proper distinctions, for it is certain that even when the people have a right to it, it ought always to be considered the lesser right." The same author takes care to call attention to the fact that he is not following "modern" ideas, but those derived from St. Thomas—by way, probably, of Suárez and Mariana, we would observe.[12] We ought not to forget that the thought of Rousseau, at this time, was considered bound up with Jacobinism; on the other hand, all Francophilism was associated with Bonapartean tendencies. Why, then, support this foreign current when in the Spanish tradition, both philosophical and juridical, sufficient elements were to be found to justify the projected changes? [13] Is this to say that French ideas are entirely absent? Perhaps not. José Miranda has observed that in certain phrases of Jacobo Villaurrutia and of de Talamantes there can be glimpsed a trace of the language of the French enlightenment.[14] If such is the case, they are no more than indications of a desire, either conscious or unconscious, to assimilate that language to their own line of thought.

The Creoles revived an ancient institution: national representation in a congress organized on the basis of classes and estates, to which were added the representatives of the cities. The junta which the judge Villaurrutia proposed would be "representative of all classes"; as a matter of fact, there would be a majority of the clergy, the military, and the nobility in it.[15] The Ayuntamiento for its part expressed another tendency: the junta should be made up of all the secular and ecclesiastical "cadres," and even the higher authorities of the government ought to be represented in it.[16] There is at work here an idea dear to traditional Spanish democratic thought: that of seeing in the autonomy of the "cadres" (cabildos) the bulwark of democracy and the force which might oppose despotism. In New Spain there was still preserved, without doubt, the recollection of the important role played by the "cabildos" in the first periods of colonial life and of the congresses, patterned on the Cortes, in which they used to meet.[17] The Ayuntamiento of Mexico City began a movement of return; beneath centuries of despotism it believed it saw the principles of a freer way of life.

In order to establish its pretensions on a juridical and legal basis, the Creole party did not rely on the laws in force. Forgetting the immediate situation, it retraced the course of history back to the first laws in quest of those opinions or decisions from which all the rest derived. In this way it came to the "Magna Carta" of Castille, granted by Alfonso the Wise in the Middle Ages. The "Leyes de Partida" offered one of the central arguments supporting the necessity of convoking a junta; from mediaeval jurisprudence they wrested democratic procedures which later were to be lost in the periods of despotism.

The same leap across time was achieved by the Creole in the history of America. The social contract was placed in the period of the conquest. The rights of the kings derived from the pact which they made with the conquistadores, who were the antecedents of the Creoles. Thanks to that compact, New Spain was united to the Crown of Castille on an equal footing with any of the Spanish kingdoms, endowed with the same internal liberty theoretically enjoyed by the latter. Let us listen to the arguments adduced by the lawyer Azcárete in the name of the Ayuntamienta of Mexico City, in order to deny recognition to the junta of Seville. "Seville by itself is not the Crown of Castille ... it is a conquest of Castille and León, in the same manner as New Spain." San Fernando wrested it from the Moors "in the way in which the most excellent Lord Hernán Cortés conquered Mexico by defeating the Emperor Moctezuma and his successor, Cuauh-

témoc. In exactly the same way Seville is a colony of Castille
and León; between the one colony and the other there is no
difference save that Seville lies within the same peninsula and
New Spain is separated from it." [18] America is dependent not
on Spain, but only on the king of Castille and León; when he
is seized and his territories occupied by foreigners, New Spain
should convoke the nobles of the kingdom in a junta as provided
for in the Code of the Indies. That Code, as a matter of fact,
gave New Spain the same power to convene the Cortes as
possessed by the other Spanish kingdoms.

The return to originative principles, both in Spanish law and
in American history, revealed the rights of the ayuntamientos.
The true popular representation lies in the "cabildo." "Two are
the legitimate authorities which we recognize," the lawyer Verdad
says, "the first that of our sovereign, the second that of the
ayuntamientos approved and confirmed by the sovereign. The
first may fail with the fall of the kings . . . the second is indefect-
ible because the people is immortal." On the other hand, the
ayuntamientos are to be found at the basis of the constitution of
New Spain. Those of Veracruz and of Mexico City were the first
authorities and dictated the first laws to the nation, "an example
which ought to guide us in the present period." [19] By contrast,
the "Real Audiencia" and the viceregency were established upon
a nation already fully constituted. The ayuntamiento is, therefore, more originative; to it we must now turn. The Creole attitude
implicitly carried the rejection of monarchical absolutism and
centralism, and the aspiration of linking themselves to the preceding period.

Disgruntled with an order in which he felt himself an alien,
the Creole wanted to recover a society in which he held a place.
It was necessary to reject the immediate past in order to make
contact with the beginning. The double meaning of "principio,"
"principle," became confused; it is at once the foundation of
society and the beginning of historical life. As a consequence,
it seems that in getting to the basis of society we also retrogress
in time; inversely, going deeply into the past is one way of reach-

ing the foundation on which society rests. The paradox of the revolutionary movement begins: the most progressive tendency of the time supposes, at the same time, a return to the past.

The return to origins, however, is not carried to its end. The quest for the real foundations of society stops at the already constituted nation. The "people" of which they speak is the people conceived as represented in the ayuntamientos, which in fact are formed in each city by the "hombres honrados," the "honorable men," of a certain education and social position, to the exclusion, naturally, of Indians and half-castes. In reality, it is the Creole middle class which dominates those bodies and which would gain control of the proposed Congress. On the other side, the return to the past reaches only the moment of the conquest. It is the Spanish "conquistadores" who made the pact with the Crown and not the aborigines. Those who direct the present struggle are descended from them, and they are at this moment as distant from the "peninsulars" as they are from the true people. In order for the movement to origins to proceed it will be necessary that other social classes, silent until now, become present.

This was the possibility which suddenly projected itself before the convocations called by the viceroy. After the lawyer Verdad had concluded at a meeting his speech maintaining that the sovereignty had returned to the people, the judge Aguirra, chief of the European party, asked him to make clear of what "people" he was speaking. We sense a moment of hesitation in the official, who ended up by replying, "the constituted authorities." Then Aguirre, "replying, in turn, that those authorities were not the people, called the attention of the viceroy and of the junta to the original people to whom, upon the principles advanced by the official, the sovereignty ought to revert; but he went no further in clarifying this concept ... because the governors of the Indian settlements were present, among them a descendant of the emperor Moctezuma." [20] The confusion was general. Archbishop Lizana, who had been sympathetic to the thesis of the ayuntamiento, changed sides and thenceforth supported the "Real

Acuerdo." It was not the attitude of the Creole which made the more conservative draw back, but the possibility it presaged. Through it there was felt the possibility of popular liberty, for the movement back to origins, once begun, could not be halted. Soon it would reach its term: the effective sovereignty of the people.

II
THE POPULAR REVOLUTION

With the popular uprising, begun September 15, 1810, by Don Miguel Hidalgo, the social context of Independence changes. Efforts at reform give way to revolutionary action. The Indians of the countryside, the workers in the mines, and the crowds in the cities rebelled in answer to the voice of an educated Creole. The explosion communicated itself like a ray of light; it spread to practically the entire nation. We stand before a unanimous movement of the popular classes without antecedents in the previous history of the whole of America and without parallel in the movement for emancipation in other countries of the continent, which gives a distinctive mark to that movement in New Spain. The revolution which exploded in 1810 is entirely different from the efforts at emancipation begun two years before by the metropolitan "cabildo." In its social composition it is fundamentally a peasant revolt with which the miners and the city masses associated themselves and which "caudillos" from the middle class tried to master and direct.

The political theories and historical ideas of the revolutionary movement reflect its social composition. The ideologists who express them belong to the group of "literati"; they are lawyers, ecclesiastics, members of the provincial ayuntamientos, and journalists; nevertheless, their contact with the people tended to transform the ideas peculiar to their class, and often they expressed tendencies which were clearly popular. Thus, as the revolution advances, the conception of the Creoles becomes more radical; then, surpassing the particular interests of their class, they express general interests of the community. This ideological transformation, due to the social context in which these ideas operated, will make the leaders of the movement constantly more open to "modern" ideological influences. The progressive radical-ization of the revolutionary action makes possible the acceptance of new doctrines, and not the inverse.

In a schematic way we can define two stages of revolutionary thought. They may be considered as two levels of increasing radicalism, which express the same attitude of negation of the past and return to the origins of the historical community. During the first years the ideas of traditional common roots persist: the theses of the ayuntamiento of Mexico are repeated and developed. However, others also arise, awakened by contact with the new situation. The first agrarian ideas, a certain social egalitarianism, and indigenist tendencies appear. At a second stage the educated Creoles become more and more receptive to democratic ideas, peculiar to European liberalism, in their French, or "Cadiz," form. Let us indicate the principal characteristics of each stage.

The first ideas of the insurgents are interlaced with the propositions of the Creole party of 1808. Allende sought, before September 15, 1810, a way of establishing the convocation of the "cabildos" stipulated by the old Castilian laws. He convinced Aldama to join him in order to establish a junta composed of representatives named by the ayuntamientos of the realm, which would govern the country until the restoration of Fernando VII. This is also probably the "Congress" to which Hidalgo alludes in his Manifesto, "... which is composed of representatives from all the cities, villages, and localities of this realm." [21]

After the capture of Hidalgo, Rayon and Liceaga sent a letter to Calleja; in it we have the first official declaration of the pur-poses which the revolution is pursuing. The document justifies the revolution on the grounds that Fernando was incapable of governing and that a congress was necessary which would protect the sovereignty of the king and would restore to the country the order which the *coup d'état* of Yermo and his followers had destroyed.[22] Dr. Cos developed his own arguments along the same lines. The basis of the movement is the absence of the sovereign, who could not be replaced by "a handful of men gathered in Cadiz," but only by the nation. The rights of the Creoles to a government of their own are based on a well-known interpretation: America is dependent on the Crown, but not on the Spanish nation. The "Plan of Peace" in its turn proposed: "1. Sovereignty resides in the body of the nation. 2. Spain and America are integral parts of the monarchy, subjects of the king, but equal between themselves and without dependence or subordination, one toward the other."[23] Quintana Roo makes clear for us the "nation" to which authority would revert. When the head falls, he says, the constituted bodies must take the government into their hands. And Carlos María Bustamante declares emphatically that he had sworn on the cadaver of the lawyer Verdad to vindicate his name and to take up again the thesis of the Creole: Spain is in an interregnum; sovereignty resides in the nation and in its most immediate representatives, the ayuntamientos.[24]

It is, however, Fray Servando Teresa de Mier who develops these ideas with greatest vigor. It is he who reveals to the Creoles the "Magna Carta" from which all their prerogatives derive.[25] America has its own social contract which establishes it as an integral part of the Spanish monarchy and which Charles V concluded with the conquistadores; after the junta of Valladolid in 1550 the juridical bases of the new realm were established by following the ideas of Bartolomé de las Casas. The king signed this original pact not only with the conquistadores but also with the Indians, whom he considered vassals, in exchange for the concession of exemptions and privileges. Included was a pact of the Crown with the liberated Negroes, concluded when in 1557 they laid down their arms before the viceroy. Since that time, despite subsequent despotism, "the kings maintained our fundamental laws, according to which the Americas are realms independent of Spain, with no other links with her than the king ... two realms united and confederated through the king, but which do not include each other." In a word, the sovereigns, so Mier holds, conceded to New Spain all the rights of an independent realm and endowed it with its own Cortes; with its Council of the Indies, separate from the Council of Castille and equal in rights with those of Aragon, Italy, and Flanders; with its own ecclesiastical jurisdiction; etc. The only link between America and Spain is the sovereign, and each country should govern itself as though this were not a common sovereignty, but one proper to each realm. Such is the original American code which Mier, using the terminology then in vogue, called "The American Constitution." In vindicating their position the Creoles had nothing more to do than to follow its dictates; it is the Europeans who are trying to abolish the social contract and substitute a tyrannical government. Through the tangled web of the code of the Indies, Mier, following the movement begun in 1808, believed he could discern the genuine principles, though it is difficult to reach them, since from the beginning an effort had been made to conceal them. The fundamental laws of America had been buried under later decrees. Shortly after 1550 the Royal absolutism had begun to dictate arrangements which abolished or weakened the Magna Carta. Trampling down the fundamental laws of the monarchy, Charles V dissolved the Cortes and started the movement toward despotism. Soon the Council of the Indies forgot that it was an American parliament and became dependent on the European assemblies. The viceroys imitated their sovereigns and consigned to oblivion the social contract to which they were subject until the American Constitution was reduced to a series of stipulations, in part unfulfilled, in part abrogated by later measures. Thus, the original constitution never had time, so to speak, to become effective; the first years of its existence were also those which witnessed its ruin. After some "lustra," these luminous principles, buried under a legion of insignificant decrees, could hardly be recognized.[26]

The same nostalgia for lost beginnings presided over religious thought. Shaken by the condemnations of the ecclesiastical hierarchy, the Creole intellectuals and the insurgent lower clergy equally resented the scorn of the theocracy toward their authentic religious faith and turned toward a purer conception of the Church. Hidalgo is the first to protest against the excommunications which were launched for purely political reasons and indicated that their cause resided in the worldly interests of the clergy and the distortion of religion into political ideology: "They are not Catholic, but for political reasons. . . ." [27] Mier, Dr. Cos, and, above all, Morelos underlined the damage which the attitude of the higher clergy causes to the Church itself and the necessity of separating religion from all earthly concern. Ideas of Church reform easily accumulate; even Ignacio Allende declared that it was suitable that "the ecclesiastic state should regulate and reform itself, especially the religious orders, which should return to the primitive rigor of their patriarchs and founders." [28] In Dr. Cos this idea acquires greater scope. The attitude of the higher clergy has had as its consequence, he says, the placing of the Christians of New Spain in a position in every detail similar to that of the primitive Church, in which the clergy communicated directly with the people and the ecclesiastic dignitaries were elected democratically by the assemblies of the faithful. When an opponent protested that the Church in America would fall into heterodoxy if it reached the point of separating itself from the Spanish Church, the insurgent writer answered that, on the contrary, "religion would emigrate from Spain to take up its residence among the Americans in all its purity and splendor; the happy days and years of the primitive Church would be reborn; the priesthood would be venerated as it is not venerated at present." [29] We believe that we have heard the same tone of voice in other quarters; there comes to memory the old dream of a Motolinia, of a Las Casas: that of founding a new Church in America, purified of earthly corruption, reviving the first days of Christianity.

Teresa de Mier directs his criticism to the evils which afflicted the Church in America. The same question which led him to the discovery of the "American Constitution" took him back to the moment of the birth of the Church in New Spain. He saw the beginnings of its corruption in the equivocal methods of evangelization, the lack of spirituality, and the league between the clergy and the secular interests of the colony. His criticism acquires greater universality when it is placed within the framework of the general study of the historical evolution of the Roman Church. He examines the origins of caesaropapism and the temptation to realize the kingdom of God in a mundane or worldly society, which he traces to the eighth century. In the tendencies of the French "constitutional" clergy and the teachings of the Bishop of Blois, Henri de Grégoire, he believes that he sees an encouraging sign of return to the original spirit of the Church. He fights for a religion of the people, a Church poor, without privileges, ruled by tolerance and respect for the ideas of others, free of retrogressive ideologies. In the natural ideal of equality and liberty for all men, he sees a correspondence with gospel teaching. The work of Mier is without a doubt the most original effort to unite in a doctrinaire manner the need for the spiritual purification of Christianity and the new ideas of liberty and equality.

Alongside these ideas direct contact with a people in arms imposed others. Social—and not merely juridical—egalitarianism, the agrarian measures of Hidalgo and Morelos, do not appear to issue from earlier political doctrines, but express the real experience of the revolution and obey its impulse. The case of Hidalgo is significant. The wise Creole appeals to the liberty of the people. In the same instant he sets himself up as their representative. And the people surround him, they absorb him into their movement to the point of converting him into the spokesman of its desires. Hidalgo takes all measures in its name "in order to satisfy it," his own expression. In appealing to the "common voice of the nation" he is probably using this term in the sense which it had for the enlightened Creoles from Azcárete to Quintana Roo.[30] Nevertheless, the "nation" which had *in reality* acclaimed him was not the "constituted bodies" or that represented in the ayuntamientos, but the Indian peasants who proclaimed him "generalísimo" in the plains of Celaya, the great masses which from that time onward supported him. In fact, "voice of the nation" acquires in this context the meaning of "wish of the popular classes." By legislating in their name Hidalgo establishes, in practice, the lowly people as sovereign, without distinction of estates or classes. Thus, his employment of them in revolutionary *praxis* gives a new meaning to the political formulas of the enlightened Creole. *Before* any theoretical evolution the people has established itself as the origin of society. The decrees of Hidalgo do nothing more than express this effective sovereignty. The abolition of the taxes which weighed on the people, the suppression of slavery and of all caste distinctions, are signs of the disappearance of social inequalities. Included is the first agrarian measure: the restitution to the indigenous communities of the lands which belonged to them. The rumors current are even more radical; many attribute to Hidalgo the intention of dividing all the lands among the Indians and of appropriating the products of the ranches in order to distribute them equally among the people.

It is, however, in José María Morelos that the influence of the popular ideas is most evident. His agrarianism is even more clear. He abolishes the community depositories so that the farmers "might collect the revenues from their lands as their own," and he threatened the Europeans that he would prosecute the war so long as "you do not leave to our farmers the fruit of the sweat of their brows and of their personal labor." [31] In his *Sentimientos a la nación* the people's leader sketches a new system colored with an egalitarian and Christian humanitarianism. He demands that employment be for Americans, that "the laws should moderate opulence and indigence," that "they apply to everyone without exceptions of privileged groups," and "that slavery be proscribed forever and caste distinctions as well, so that all might be equal, so that only vice and virtue might distinguish one American from another." [32] The revolution tended to an order of equality and social justice, based on the abolition of privileges and on the farmer's ownership of his land. Among the papers abandoned by the insurgents in Cuautla there is to be found a "plan," probably written by one of Morelos' partisans, which clearly reflects the popularist ideas. In it is the demand that "all rich people, nobles, and employers of the first order, Creoles or natives of Spain," be considered enemies of the people, that all properties be attached and the mines be destroyed. These measures, anarchistic in appearance, have, nevertheless, as their object "to establish a new liberal system in opposition to the royalist party" and serve a precise, even highly ingenious, project, namely, that the goods expropriated from the rich should be equally distributed among the neighboring poor in such a way that "no one should be enriched in particular, but all relieved in general." The measure to which the greatest importance is attached is the following: "All of the great haciendas, whose workable lands measure two leagues or more, should be destroyed because the greatest benefit in agriculture is realized when many dedicate themselves to the cultivation of separate small tracts." [33] No matter how rudimentary the ideas may be they are directed to a change in the economic structure of the colony: an agrarian order of small landholders and of social equality would replace great mining and rural exploitation, the source of economic inequalities.

All of these ideas are presented under an unmistakable seal: the hope of a total change in the social order and the desire for a more humane era in which man would be brother to man. Let us hear his announcement in the so-called *Decreto de Tecpam*.[34] In the face of hatred and violence, Morelos urges that "there be no distinction of quality, but that we all, in general, call each other Americans so that, united as brothers, we may live in holy peace such as Our Lord Jesus Christ left us when He made His triumphant ascension into heaven, from which it follows that all should know Him, that there is no reason why what are called castes should seek to destroy each other, whites against Negroes, and the Negroes against the natives." The future advent of equality would signal the return to pristine Christian peace, in which we were all made brothers by the bond of charity.

The experience of the revolution, in which the people set itself up as sovereign and rejected the imposed order, also increased the radicalism of the historical conception of the educated Creoles. Alongside the conception which appealed to the fundamental laws of the kingdom, there appeared the tendency to deny the colonial juridical order en bloc. The negation of the past no longer stopped at the Conquest; it embraces the colonial period as a whole. Their own world began to appear to the insurgents in sombre colors: they see only despotism, ignorance, and poverty across three colonial centuries. The Inquisition, which impeded all intellectual progress; the lack of schools and culture; the fatuity and laziness of a dissipated nobility; the misery of the Indian and of the castes—all showed through the illusory opulence. The movement of negation refers to a period marked out with precision, its extreme limit is the conquest, and its chronological duration embraces a little less than three centuries. "Dependence on the peninsula for three hundred years has been the most humiliating and shameful situation in which the resources of the Mexicans have been abused with the greatest injustice . . . ," says Hidalgo.[35] These three obsessing centuries will haunt all the insurgents. Dr. Cos will remember the cruelties of the "conquistadores," and the injuries which both the Indians and the castes, like the Creoles, have suffered.[36] Morelos, after noting the "supreme ignorance" and the "absolute oppression" of the colonial world, tells us "America knows that what you think and what you do is closely related to our servile education, criminal conduct, and ancient barbarism." [37]

When a spatial metaphor is used, it seems as though the rejected epoch formed a circumscribed interval between an earlier and a later space, which did not fall under that negation. "Arouse yourself to the sound of the chains which you have been dragging along for three centuries," Maldonado exclaimed.[38] The colonial period is likened at times to a period of imprisonment and servitude; at others, to a period of dreaming. New Spain is an obscure stage, with a precise beginning and end, only an episode which has come to interrupt the course of a different life. If the colonial period was a dream and a captivity, had there not been, perhaps, another period free of this yoke and this deception? The Creoles remembered little of that remote existence; nevertheless, nostalgia for those lost years began to invade them. The eighteenth century had begun the re-evaluation of the pre-Cortés civilizations; the hope of the "intelligentia" did not rest only on vague presentiments but also upon this new evaluation of what their enlightened predecessors had created. Everywhere there is to be noted the influence of pre-Columbian themes. Teresa de Mier takes up again the arguments of Clavijero in defense of the indigenous civilization and questioned the legitimacy of the Conquest. When the justice of its beginnings is denied, the whole colonial period proves to be a fraud, an adventitious and bastard dominion, a usurpation of rights. With this, the vindications of the Indians are recognized as justified: "The Indians believe that the land and everything else in America is theirs and has been usurped by the Spaniards, against whom they may wreak a just reprisal." [39] The bold rejection by the Creole of all that constituted his own past led him to extend his hand to the indigenous people and to vindicate their rights; he battles then for the Indians, "ancient and legitimate lords of the country, whom an iniquitous conquest has not been able to deprive of their rights." [40] But what happens then to the ancient "American Constitution"? Must not this also be abandoned before the much more original rights of the Indians?

The "indigenism" of the insurgents had about it nothing of a romantic movement for the restoration of the remote past. It does not seek in the indigenous civilizations values which might replace those of the colony or does it try to revive conceptions of the world which have been lost forever. The Creoles sense that their period resembled the pre-Columbian exclusively because both wanted to be cleansed from a colonial past. Their coincidence is merely negative; the Indian and the Creole insurgent meet because both are situated within the confines of the same historical order which both reject. Out of this situation there developed a curious and significant symbolism. The conquest was the negation of the indigenous society; Independence, the negation of this first negation. The new awakening of the indigenous people is a movement against its subjugation in the Conquest. The War of Independence appears—vaguely, in some writers; clearly, in others—as a reversal of the Conquest. The term "reconquest" falls from their lips without their seeking it, and comparisons with those times occur spontaneously to many minds. Morelos called himself "One commissioned for the reconquest and the new government of America." [41] Mier sees in the revolution the end of Spanish power over the Indians and God's revenge for the injustices which the "conquistadores" and colonials had perpetrated against them. And Bustamante made fashionable the idea of a war which would reproduce, in negative form, the adventures of Cortés and his companions, down to the smallest events. In the Congress of Chilpancingo Morelos was to deliver a speech, probably written by Bustamante; before the constituents of the Congress he was to invoke the ancient emperors: "Genius of Moctezuma, Cacahma, Cuauhtémoc, Xicoténcatl, and Calzontzin, celebrate your ritual about this august assembly as you celebrated the war dance in which you were attacked by the perfidious sword of Alverado, the solemn moment in which your illustrious sons have congregated to revenge the insults and outrages which you have suffered. . . ." Independence opens anew the dilemma of the Conquest. "To August 12, 1521, there succeeded September 8, 1813. On that day our chains were fastened on us in Mexico Tenochtitlan; on this day they are broken forever in the happy city of Chilpancingo." [42] One atom of time is placed upon another, inverting their meaning; the moment of the Conquest seems to repeat itself, but in the inverse direction, three centuries later.

These ideas hardly agree with the older, traditional conception which, doubtless, subsisted for a time along with them. The fact is that both can be considered as different levels of profundity in one continuous movement. The purification of the past carried to its extreme the historical attitude initiated by the Ayuntamiento of Mexico City in 1808; it is presided over by the same nostalgia for that first yesterday, anterior to the slag-heaps which time had accumulated. Then as now, the beginning was sought in the double meaning of the term: the foundation on which the social order rested and the beginning of the historical community. In 1808, however, the movement was not followed out to the end. Society was accepted as established in its essential bases; the origin was pursued only to the point at which might be encountered the basis of the constituted bodies and their temporal beginning in the conquest first: and later in the "American Constitution." With the revolution begun by Hidalgo there stood revealed, in practice, the ultimate origin which justified those social bodies: the liberty of the people. Once it had emerged, the Creole could not ignore it. At the same time he would be driven to pursue the investigation of historical origins beyond the Conquest. The quest for the historic principle in the pre-Cortés period corresponds to the revelation of the people, Indians and half-castes, as the social foundation, just as the appeal to the "American Constitution" corresponds to the purpose of establishing society upon the ayuntamientos. For this reason both conceptions could subsist jointly at the same time; they are two stages of the same historical attitude, the return to origins. On reaching its term this attitude will tend to set aside the principle on which the colonial order was founded and all conceptions inherited from it. It will be necessary to constitute the nation anew on the freedom of the people, on the model proposed by liberated reason. The insurgent ideologists thus opened themselves to new political doctrines, whose acceptance will be prepared by their negation of the past.

The political conception of the middle class quickly passed over to a liberal modern conception. One of the most important vehicles for the diffusion of the new ideas is the liberal writing of the peninsula and the work of the Cortes of Cádiz. From 1809, for example, Julián de Castillejos invoked the "numberless publications which came to us from the peninsula" in order to maintain the thesis of popular sovereignty. The American deputies to the Cortes will also be an important point of contact with the new ideas. In Cádiz they were surrounded by an ideological climate to which they were not fully accustomed; the Cortes often imitated the French National Assembly: its terminology, its arguments, and its themes repeated those of the great revolution. The Americans took up this language and the new meaning which it gave to political conceptions. This assimilation was all the easier because the Spanish Cortes also presented itself, in its beginnings, as a return to old democratic institutions buried under despotism, in this way it followed the tendency of Jovellanos and Martínez Marina to unite modern, enlightened principles with the Spanish juridical tradition. The convocation address to the Cortes, for example, in 1809 spoke of the "three centuries of disasters" suffered by the Spaniards and of the need for rebuilding the august edifice of our ancient laws."

Guridi y Alcocer, a Mexican deputy, in Rousseauan terminology, maintained in Cádiz that authority rested on the "general will" of the people. Even more, by defending the rights of citizenship of the Indians and the castes, by demanding the abolition of slavery and advocating freedom of production and trade in all the Hispanic countries, the American deputies showed themselves much more in accord with liberal principles than the Spaniards; while the latter did not venture to apply those principles integrally, fearing the independence of the colonies, the Americans could apply them universally.

The Cádiz influence is responsible for two propositions which, although they may appear irrelevant, point to an important transformation in the meaning of the ideas which were being manipulated: first, the equation of the struggle for Independence with the general struggle which the peoples were waging against despotism in the name of individual liberties; second, the attribution of sovereignty, in the absence of the monarch, to the general will of the people. Neither of these ideas was in accord with the political ideas previously maintained by the Creole party. Apparently, it is a matter only of a trivial change in terminology; this change, however, is a sign of a much more important alteration. Above all, the American revolution has remained bound to a European movement from which it could not easily detach itself. Also, the new terms were not inoffensive. The "despotism" was bound up with the political institutions of the realm, with the entire traditional juridical structure; "despot" is a mask which hides the true name, absolute monarch. Before it we no longer encounter Spaniards jealous of their fundamental laws, but a congress of citizens defending their individual rights. Again, the appeal to the "general will" involves the rejection of the traditional institutions and the pretense of establishing the nation anew. Soon the "Representative Constituent Congress" replaces the "Congress of the Cities," the "Liberal Constitution," the old "American Constitution," and this successively, until we find ourselves with a different political conception.

The Constitution of Cádiz proved for some of the Creoles to be an unexpected ideological weapon. The able and clever writings of Fernández de Lizardi, editor of *El Pensador Mexicano,* are outstanding; this journal may be considered the first liberal periodical published in Mexico. In it the Constitution is hailed as the light which reveals their rights to an oppressed people: "Did we know perhaps that there existed civil liberty in the world, property, independence, or all the other rights of the citizen? We knew only of imposts, excise duties, and a humiliation like that of slaves" until the new Constitution came to turn the slaves into vassals.[43] The sovereignty of the nation is acclaimed because "it beats down the ancient despotism." The absolutism of the Spanish kings is attacked as being responsible for poor government and the arbitrariness of viceroys and functionaries. Liberty and enlightenment begin to be associated, and in the ignorance which up to that time had reigned in America there is seen the most solid bastion of despotism. For this reason *El Pensador* defends the liberty of the press, through which means, it was sure, the Illumination would come. However, the most important thing about its position is that it places the popular American revolution in the framework of the general struggle for liberty against despotism and the ignorance of the old Spanish system.

In the Congress of Chilpancingo we clearly perceive the triumph of a new political concept. Lacking antecedents in New Spain, and unable to appeal to any earlier meetings of the Cortes which might have served it as a guide, it could do no less than to take its inspiration from the French Assembly and the Cortes of Cádiz. From the beginning it disowned the monarchy and, instead of basing independence upon the ancient laws of the kingdom, based it upon the idea of popular sovereignty. Consistently carrying to its logical term the negation of the past and the return to origins, the Congress of Chilpancingo denied all legal title to the Conquest and undertook to re-establish the sovereignty usurped from the ancient inhabitants of Anáhuac. It was no longer possible to speak of a nation already constituted, but rather of the authority of the people which abolished the social constitution derived from the colonial system in order freely to reorganize itself anew. From its first sessions the Congress did not restrict itself to dealing with urgent measures of government, as Morelos probably desired, but set itself to establish the nation. This meaning of the deliberating body did not coincide with the ideas of the first stage of the movement. We are no longer in the presence of a junta of ayuntamientos or other corporations, destined to protect the sovereignty and to govern the country according to its fundamental laws; the idea of establishing the notion on the basis of the deliberations of the representatives of the people appears now for the first time in our America; it corresponds to the total negation of the past and to the purpose of establishing another, new historical life on a new act of free election.

The Constitution of Apatzingán, fruit of the Congress, found its principal inspiration—as José Miranda has shown—in the French constitutions of 1793 and 1795.[44] For the first time it sets up a national system of representation, the separation of the three powers, the rights of the citizen, and freedom of expression. Article five affirms that "sovereignty resides originally in the people and its exercise in the national representation composed of deputies elected by the citizens." On other points, too, its language was that which would correspond to the new ideas. Article two, for example, indicated that the end of government is to guarantee man the enjoyment of his natural and unprescribable rights. Article eighteen defines law as "the expression of the general will directed to the common happiness"; the twenty-fourth article explained in what that common happiness consisted: "the happiness of the people and of each one of the citizens consists in the enjoyment of equality, security, property, and liberty . . . ," fundamental rights of man in society. The expression is typical of bourgeois European liberalism. By contrast, the Constitution does not underwrite any of the agrarian measures decreed by Hidalgo and Morelos, or does it indicate the bases of any further economic reform.

Under the system of representation agreed upon at Apatzingán, all political direction would remain in the hands of a collegial body, dominated by the middle class. As a matter of fact, the only candidates for the Congress were moderately enlightened curés, lawyers, and writers, the only ones who possessed the literacy and the intellectual prestige which the rhetorical disputes of the assembly required. Thus, at the time that the middle class was carrying the return to origins to its logical term, imposed by the presence of the lower classes of the people, it immediately transposed this origin into its own representation. The shift of supreme power from a popular leader in direct contact with the people, accepted and followed unanimously by them, to a deliberative assembly betrays the purpose—unconscious, perhaps—of the middle class to replace its ally, the peasantry, in the direction of the revolution: the idea of representation is the instrument of this substitution.

In the following years the influence of French ideas and of the liberal bourgeois conception grew. Their attraction is such that even a writer like Mier, who in his *Historia* of 1813 had harshly criticized Rousseau, manifested the influence of Rousseau by 1820. He then agrees that individuals must give up a part of their rights in order to secure in society the guarantee of the rest; to this end they must submit themselves to an authority elected by themselves, the Congress. The Congress is the "organ born of the general will." [45] The fact is that by 1820 the panorama of the revolution is very different than it was in its beginnings. With the defeat of Morelos before Valladolid in 1813, the people had lost their most vigorous leader; this event also marks the pre-eminence of the middle class in the direction of the movement. At the beginning of the year 1817, with the Congress dissolved and the chiefs given over to an internecine struggle, the peasant revolution seems to be at an end. The fleeting expedition of Francisco Javier Mina did not succeed effectively in reanimating the popular spirit. Of the powerful force unleashed by Hidalgo there remained in the year 1818 only a few nuclei of troops organized under the hand of Guerrero, and the popular revolution had, in fact, come to an end. Neither, however, is the political conception of the Creoles the same. With the idea of the constituent congress, the middle class believed that it had come to the end of its quest; the project of establishing the national representative assembly obsessed its spirit. "Congress, congress, congress, then after that, after that. . . . Thus is the talisman which is going to cure our ills," wrote Mier in 1820.[46] After Iturbide came to power the middle class, drowned before in the great popular movement, will find its most effective weapons in the Congress and in the liberal conception. The first act of the new assembly will be to declare that sovereignty is embodied in itself. Thus the Revolution of Independence will terminate under the sign of a political conception different from that which set it afoot.

III
THE EMPIRE AND THE REPUBLIC

The close alliance of the elements which composed the conservative party did not cancel out, in any way, the differences between them. The insurrection set afoot by Hidalgo succeeded in lulling them to sleep, but not in extinguishing them. They reached their critical point in the year 1820 with the re-establishment of the liberal constitution in Spain and the decrees of the Cortes which touched the interests of the clergy. Then there revealed itself openly an historical and political conception proper to the higher Creole classes—higher clergy, higher officers of the army, landholders, and mine owners—which had been in process of gestation since 1808. This conception proved at the same time contrary to the popular revolution and influenced the Independence. It finds its greatest expression in the movement of Iturbide.

The movement of Iturbide proposed no radical transformation of the older regimen; on the contrary, it vindicates themes grateful to those who were opposed to the innovations of liberalism. Above all else it was a matter of defending the clergy from the reforms which threatened them and Catholic ideas from "contamination" with the liberal philosophemes. To the defense of religion there was united fidelity to the Spanish monarchy. Only the rejection by Fernando VII of the Treaty of Córdoba made it necessary to look for another candidate for the Crown. The proclamation of Iturbide himself as emperor cut the last political link to Spain, leaving the monarchical structure standing.

The Iturbidist movement had its source in the same current of thought which the Creole party had employed in 1808. On the whole it found its justification in a peculiar conception of historical evolution which imparts a characteristic meaning to political ideas. We may sum it up in two words: "maturity" and "transition."

In the circle of a private club one of the principal counter-revolutionary writers, the canon Beristáin, let it be known that "the justice of the insurgents' cause was undeniable, but we were not yet worthy of independence and liberty." [47] The paradox of Beristáin gives us, without actually stating it, the key to the historical idea which will preside over the Iturbidist movement. Independence is just and desirable; however, we are in no position to assume it. Thus, it seems that we must hope for some change in ourselves in order to be able to be free. Something must grow and develop in society before the human will imposes a new order of things. In the meantime, haste helps not at all, things must be left to come to a head, the situation must mature. It may be said that society slowly follows its own course, responding to its own impulses. Left to itself, society's development is gradual and smooth and without leaps; it links together the stages of development just as the growth of a man prolongs adolescence into youth, and youth into adulthood. On reaching, in its slow progress, the full development of its powers, society undergoes a powerful change: maturity. Only then is it able to determine itself, only then can it become "worthy" of independence. "The nations which were called great by reason of their extension over the globe," Iturbide said, "were dominated by others; and so long as their own lights did not permit them to determine their own fate, they did not become emancipated. The European nations which reached the highest illumination and policy were slaves of the Roman empire; and this empire, the greatest which history has ever known, is like a "pater familias" who in his advanced age sees how his sons and grandsons leave his house because they are now at an age to establish other households of their own, reserving to himself all their respect, veneration, and honor, as being their first origin.[48] An idyllic picture, indeed, of societies which grow without violence and gradually awaken to the age of reason. When the "lights" of a community reach a certain development, we can diagnose its virile age. But it does not seem to reach this stage as a result of voluntary effort, but as the result of spontaneous and incalculable forces which preside over its growth. The act of determination by which a nation declares itself independent would not be the cause but the consequence of its maturity. New Spain has not reached its age of majority because it has declared itself independent, but it ought to be independent because it has reached its age of majority. The nation must, therefore, be left to grow until it reaches its adequate moment. Thus, the past was gradually approaching independence until the new historical age detached itself or emerged in its time, like the fruit from the tree which sustained it. "Now the branch is equal to the trunk," exclaims Iturbide;[49] it is time to cut it so that it may give its own shade.

Maturity, far from supposing the negation of the stages which preceded it, is determined by them. Each stage is linked to the previous stage, and is nothing save in relation to it. This is not to say that transformations do not take place. The colonial age is preserved in the new age without preventing independence from inaugurating a different form of society. Such is the mystery of maturity; the appearance of a metamorphosis due to the continuation of preceding life. In a like manner, independence means a change in American society such that it is, at the same time, the fulfillment and the persistence of the colonial order. It is reached not by foreswearing New Spain, but by prolonging its growth. Hence it is that the social and spiritual structure of the past is preserved under the new political form; there subsist its hierarchy of classes, the privileges of determined groups, the monarchical government, the values of the Catholic religion and of the Spanish tradition, while at the same time its political and legislative forms and its international status change. Paraphrasing the accepted formula of the Treaty of Córdoba, we may say "loosening but not breaking" the link with the past.

The mutation is achieved without sudden breaks. It is not realized all at once because it is brought to completion not by lucid stroke of liberty, but by the irrational impulse which guides the life of nations. "Nature produces nothing by leaps, but everything by gradual steps. The moral world follows the rules of the physical world." [50] It is human liberty which introduces decisive novelty into evolution: catastrophe or revolution. But can there be catastrophes in the ordered growth of a society in which all is preserved and nothing perishes? Change does not show itself at a decisive point in history but must traverse various stages. Before achieving a more just social order, Iturbide believes, we will have to pass through a period of transition. The constitutional monarchical regime, proclaimed in Iguala, is conceived as an intermediate condition or institution of indeterminate duration between the colonial age and a more liberal state. Republican government may perhaps be good, the Iturbidists think, "but it is necessary, of course, to inquire whether the Mexican state has reached that stage of illumination which places the passions within bounds." [51] Before reaching the last stage, we must exhaust the intermediate ones.

The colonial system is the "primitive origin" of the independent society, Iturbide holds. In whatever moment we consider it, society is found to be constituted on the immediate past, which, in its turn, rests upon an earlier condition, and so on, in succession in a chain of historical foundations. Society is given in each anterior moment and not simply proposed for our action; rather it is a given figure which varies at each moment. For the middle class in the Congress of Chilpancingo everything must be proposed to the sovereign will of the deputies, whose task will be to form a new contract as the constitutive origin of the future society. For the Iturbidists every transformation whatsoever must take its origin in society such as it is found already established in the immediate past. The Plan of Iguala and the Treaty of Córdoba are, in this case, the fountain and source of all subsequent right; they indicate the norms on which the new society must rely and indicate precise routes to the free planning of the Congress. But these treatises are based, in their turn, on stipulations of society as constituted in an earlier moment (the rights of the crown, of the clergy, the viceregal authorities, etc.) and so on successively. The origin of society is to be seen, not in present human action, but in the social structure constituted by its immediately preceding action.

For this reason, behavior as well as planning must adapt itself to the situation given at each moment, instead of being lifted to the stature of planning. The liberal constitution, Iturbide maintains, was abstract and put together piece by piece, without taking into account the weight of the reality which it pretended to modify. It must prove, eventually, inadaptable for New Spain. Its enemies would commit the same mistake: they legislate for a possible world and disdain the real world. The Republicans, he says, "have been my enemies because they were convinced that they could never bring me to take part in the establishment of a government which, despite its attractive features, is not suitable to the Mexicans." [52]

It is curious to observe that despite his opposition to this conception of liberalism the influence of the new ideas is so great that Iturbide himself used at times the language of Rousseau. He considers himself the representative of the "general will," accepts "the sovereignty of the people," the "social contract," etc. [53]

Rousseau is also used as an ideological weapon against the pretensions of the Congress. Iturbide believes that he can justify its dissolution by the doctrine of the philosopher of Geneva that the general will cannot be represented and, therefore, that no assembly can assume to itself the plenary exercise of sovereignty. "The reef on which we have foundered is that of the supreme power, which, by the most impolitic of errors, they have tried to transfer from the mass of the nation, to which it belongs exclusively, to a constitutent congress." [54] A clear example of the way in which one self-same doctrine can acquire distinct meanings according to the use made of it: while the thesis of the sovereignty of the people is serving as the basis of the struggle of the democrats against the monarchy, its nontransferable character is being used by the latter to buttress its power.

The proclamation of political independence does not end, naturally, with the revolutionary process. The empire prolongs, to a certain degree, the colonial regimen. The old insurgents united again to continue the struggle. Once more it is the middle class that takes the lead. Now, however, the popular revolution is at an end, and the "literati" have lost true political contact with the people. Its instrument in the struggle is the Congress. The deliberations of the assembly replace revolutionary action; the effective sovereignty is transferred from the masses in action to the assembly of Creole deputies. The Congress, thanks to the decisive intervention of the ayuntamientos in the elections, was dominated by a middle class determined to combat the groups which provided the principal support of Iturbide: the army and the higher clergy. From the first session the Congress voted that the sovereignty resided in itself. As a matter of fact, it acted as sovereign, taking itself to be the real foundation of society. We are in the presence of a case of "dual sovereignty." On the one hand, Iturbide claimed to base his authority on the treaties which had brought him to power and which he considered the direct expression of the national will; on the other hand, the Congress declared itself sovereign and was in a position to cancel any earlier agreement. The contest was inevitable; in the end the Congress party won out. The abdication of Iturbide and the re-installation of Congress, in March 1823, may be considered the end of the Revolution of Independence because they mark the accession to power of the Creole middle class which had initiated the movement.

In the struggle against the empire the liberal ideology strengthened itself, following the general lines which were fixed in Chilpancingo. The diffusion of French ideas continued. For example, the first translation of the *Social Contract* appeared, published by Severo Maldonado. It is significant that it is presented as the appendix to a work of Martínez Marina; even then the doctrines of the citizen of Geneva were more readily accepted if they appeared in relation to the purpose of reconciling its novelties with tradition, an effort represented by Martínez Marina.

In the struggle between Iturbide and the Congress two historical attitudes of very different character clearly met face to face. The followers of Iturbide see the origin of sovereignty in the society constituted at an earlier moment, in such wise that all further evolution must be measured with reference to it; the liberals thought that they could establish society anew on the basis of rational planning. The rejection of the colonial system and the return to origins indicates for them the beginning of a new historical epoch which ought to realize human values that the colonial system was not able to realize. The Congress proposed as its goal a democratic representative republic in which the citizens would be equal before a law which respects the fundamental rights of the individual, promotes prosperity and enlightenment, and assures economic liberty of expression, and in the bosom of which such values as illumination, equality, property, personal security, and self determination could be realized. But the image of this society is, in many aspects, contrary to the existing society. It must, therefore, be planned and established deliberately according to our own projects. The liberal sets in contrast an irrational and enslaved past and a rational and liberating future. The achievement of the latter is found to be dependent on its own reason and will. No impulse toward social development can be hoped for from the past; all progress whatsoever must have its origin in rational anticipation of the future. There is nothing strange in the fact that the first instrument of this transformation is located in an institution planned according to ideal norms of government: the assembly of representatives. The faith in the capacity of the deliberations of a democratic congress to change the reality is bound up with confidence in the free reason as the real motive principle of development. To the doctrine of the slow transitional evolution of society is opposed that of progress regulated by reason. The transformation of political and juridical institutions and, above all, education, will be the moving forces of this progress.

The "lights" are not simple rewards or gifts of the spirit, but the impulse charged with impressing a progressive movement on society. We are in the presence, consequently, of a predominantly intellectualistic conception which leads one to think that the dead weight and ballast of the past can be dissolved by discussion, knowledge, and organization.

The Iturbidist and the liberal movements correspond to attitudes toward history charged with entirely inverse movements. The educated Creoles are concerned to elevate reality to a projected possibility. For the Iturbidists the movement must be exactly the contrary: to adjust political institutions to the situation, to restrict rational projects to the level of the circumstances in which we find ourselves. The two movements, as has been noted, have inverse directions. While the one takes its point of departure in freely chosen possibility in order to transform reality, the other establishes itself on this reality and limits possibility by reference to it. For the first, man—after the image of the rowers who, leaping to the shore, tow the boat forward—ought to go ahead of the spontaneous movement of society in order to impel it toward the future; for the second, on the contrary, man ought to move in accord with social growth, taking care not to get ahead of its pace, as the helmsman ought to adapt his movements to the combined forces of the elements which drive the ship forward. Antagonistic conceptions of the task or mission of liberty in history, which are going to confront each other in Mexico all during the nineteenth century.

Leopoldo Zea

VI. POSITIVISM

I
PROGRESS AND RETROGRESSION

On September 16, 1867, in the city of Guanajuato, an address was delivered that was to prove the beginning of a new and astonishing stage of Mexican thought and philosophy. The author of this address, this "civic oration," was Dr. Gabino Barredo, and the theme was an interpretation of the history of Mexico, its philosophy of history, a philosophy which followed the guidelines of the "Father of Positivism," Auguste Comte. Dr. Barreda had come to know the French philosopher while following the course which the latter had given at Paris in 1845 on the general history of mankind. Other Hispano-Americans followed the same course, and these, too, would become notable as propagandists of the positivist doctrine.

Even more, this year 1867 was a special year in the history of Mexico, for that history interpreted by Barreda from the positivist point of view. It was the year in which the invading army of France withdrew; the year in which the abandoned and disillusioned Austrian emperor fell prisoner and was shot on the hill named "Campanas de Querétaro." It was the year of the final triumph of the "Reform" movement, of liberal ideas. It was the year in which a new phase of Mexican history began.

A new order was finally going to take the place of the old colonial order, defended to the very last moment by Mexican conservatism. It was this old order which had symbolically fallen on the hill of the Campanas in 1867.

Gabino Barreda spoke of this history and of the forces which had triumphed, the forces which were going to give rise to a new order, the positivist order. It was the triumph of the liberal forces at war with the conservative. The metaphysics of liberty was triumphing over the theological spirit implanted by the colonial order to give place to a new order. It was the triumph of the positivist spirit advancing the march of Mexico along the road to progress. The struggle of which Mexico was the scene is but a phase, a part, of the struggle developing in the entire history of mankind, between the negative spirit and the positivist spirit. The triumph of Mexican liberalism is but the triumph of this spirit in the history of mankind. The forces in Mexico opposed to progress, showing their relation with that great negative force which impeded the progress of mankind, had held it necessary to resort to outsiders in order to prevail and to impede that progress. The Mexican conservative forces, defeated by the forces of progress in Mexico, had found it necessary to seek the aid of one of the greatest representatives of regression in the history of humanity, Napoleon III. The French intervention in Mexico is nothing else but the intervention of the negative spirit which triumphs in the world in order to crush the last redoubt of the positive spirit. Mexico became, in Barreda's interpretation, the last redoubt of progress. It would be here, in this last outpost, that there would be decided the destiny not only of Mexico, but of humanity menaced by the conservative forces, which refused to yield place to progress.

For this reason, in Barreda's opinion, the battle of May 5, 1862 and the Mexican triumph were but the expression of the titanic struggle between the powerful forces which disputed the destiny of mankind.

The soldiers of the Republic in Puebla [says Barreda] saved, like the Greeks at Salamis, the future of the world by saving the republican principle which is the modern ensign of Humanity.

Europe, and with Europe the entire world, had fallen before the powers opposed to progress, and only Mexico stood firm and confronted the champion of negativism, Napoleon III.

In the conflict between European retrogression and American civilization [said the Mexican positivist] in the struggle of the monarchical principle against the republican, in this ultimate effort of fanaticism against emancipation, the republicans of Mexico stood alone against the entire world.

Gabino Barreda explains, in this famous speech, the form assumed by those forces which in disputing the future of Mexico were disputing the future of humanity. On one side are the clergy and the military, the two great bodies of the interests inherited from the Reform, the representatives of the negative forces, the forces corresponding to what Comte called the "theological stage." On the other were the social groups which, embracing the liberal ideology, confronted the conservatives in order to establish a new economic, political, and social order, different from that established by colonialism. The stage corresponding to these struggles is that which Comte called the metaphysical stage, a stage of combat, necessary to destroy and to displace or dislodge the forces which opposed progress, the establishment of a new order, the positive order.

The triumph had been achieved; now the need would be to create the ideological bond which would make the new order possible. The metaphysical forces of liberalism, as Barreda said, were acutely conscious of this necessity and were preparing themselves to meet it. The combative phase was finished; now there was beginning the phase which would make possible the order that would lead the Mexican nation along the road of progress. It was a question of a new order which, while respecting the ideals for which the Mexican liberals had fought, would make it possible to attain the envisioned progress; an order in the service of the most authentic freedom, which had nothing in common with the anarchy in which the Mexican people had wallowed for half a century. Expressing this liberal ideal, which is not considered foreign to the new positive order, Barreda says:

That in the future a complete liberty of conscience, an absolute liberty of expression and discussion, giving room to all ideas and field to all inspirations, would permit light to spread in every quarter and make unnecessary and impossible all commotion which was not purely spiritual, every revolution which was not purely intellectual. That the material order conserved at any price by the government and respected by the governed should be the certain guarantee and the secure way of walking always in the flowery path of progress and civilization.

The stage of revolutions had ended. The goal of the liberal revolution had been achieved. Now would come the order which would make possible the progress aimed at by those revolutions. Liberty would be guaranteed within the material order, which was the goal of progress. Thus was anticipated an idea which would prove the axis of the positive interpretation of Mexican history.

The material order, supreme object of every government as the instrument of society, would be foreign to the idea of liberty of the individual himself, something which belonged to his internal forum, the tribunal of his conscience. It was clear that this liberty would be finally subordinated to the supposed ends of society on its march toward progress. However, before reaching this stage, positivism would openly support the postulate of Mexican liberalism with respect to liberty of conscience. Gabino Barreda in his "civic oration" places the accent on this postulate. Its realization depended on what he called the "emancipation of conscience." It was necessary to free the conscience of Mexicans from its mental servitude to colonialism, to theologism, as Comte would say. Mental emancipation by means of an adequate education would be the immediate goal to achieve, an education which would liberate Mexicans from old servitudes, from old habits inherited from the colonial state. The new order would depend on this change.

II
Positivist Liberty

On December 2, 1867, three months after this positivist discourse, the triumphant Republic, under the presidency of Benito Juárez, promulgated the law which oriented and regulated public instruction in Mexico, from the elementary to the professional level, including what was called "preparatory education." The man who was called upon to collaborate in this reform was Gabino Barreda. The reform would proceed along Comtian lines.

What moved the leader of the liberal Mexican reform to pay attention to the Mexican positivist by asking his collaboration? Many chance circumstances are spoken of in this connection, among them the friendship of Barreda with one Dr. Pedro González Elizalde, who had also been the person who had encouraged Barreda to attend Comte's course in Paris. It has likewise been said that it was the discourse of Guanajuato that attracted the interest of President Juárez. Whatever the reason may have been, what is certain is that the leader of Mexican liberalism had seen in the ideas of the Mexican positivist the ideology capable of forming the Mexican of the future, putting an end to the long period of anarchy in which he had lived from the moment of his emancipation from colonial status. In the future, the near future, there would become apparent the differences, the profound differences, which would separate triumphant Mexican liberalism from the positivist ideology taken as its instrument to create an order to replace anarchy. Gabino Barreda himself had taken good care to make these differences apparent in the discourse already cited.

Liberalism, we insist, represented the necessary metaphysical stage of which Comte had spoken, capable of destroying the old theological order and of making possible the new order which was to be constructed, the positivist order. Positivism was thus only a new expression of triumphant liberalism, its constructive image, once its combative mission had been concluded.

Already in the "Civic Oration" Barreda changes the Comtean motto *"Love,* order, and progress" to *"Liberty,* order, and progress."* Liberalism was triumphant, but now it had to carry through the task of establishing an order which would lead to progress. Such was the dream of every liberal, and the positivist philosophy led the way to the realization of this dream by forming through education the men who would make it possible and who would create the society for which their ancestors had fought. However, the goal of liberty would change its meaning within the ideology of those who fulfilled it, the positivists. Liberty, taken in the sense of laissez faire as in the initial phase of liberalism, was becoming impossible. This idea proved contrary or opposed to the idea of a liberal *order.* Order and liberty had to be reconciled. Hence, liberty could not be a simple matter of laissez faire. Barreda expounded the liberal ideal of positivism in the following fashion by saying:

Liberty is commonly represented as a faculty of doing or seeking anything whatsoever without subjection to law or to any force which might direct it; if such a freedom could be achieved, it would be both immoral and absurd because it would make all discipline and, consequently, all order, impossible.

Liberty is compatible with order, the authentic liberal order, if given a positive meaning. The Mexican teacher says in this regard:

Far from being incompatible with order, liberty consists, in all phenomena, both inorganic and organic, in submitting fully to the laws which determine those phenomena.

In accordance with this idea something is *free* when it follows its natural course, that is to say, without obstacles, without hindrances. And this course, the path followed, is to be found in the law or laws which determine that thing. Law, order, is proper to the nature which moves within it. Its liberty expresses itself in freely following what its laws indicate. Barreda cites a physical example, saying that when one speaks of a body which falls freely, one is speaking of a body which follows the laws of gravity:

down directly toward the center of the earth, with a velocity proportionate to the time, which is to say, subject to the laws of gravity.

When this happens, it is *then* that we speak of its *falling freely*. The same is true in the moral field. In this field man will act freely if he follows his moral impulses which, by being such, will mark out for him the distinction between what *is* and what *ought to be*, between good and evil. It is man's task to take freely the path which does not impede the realization of moral goals. And it is here that society enters in its highest expression, the state. It is the state which by means of education fortifies the impulses which follow the moral law and limits those which oppose obstacles to it. In this way there is achieved the free development of the altruistic impulses.

Freedom, as one may see, is only the expression of the unimpeded march of the higher moral sentiments toward ends in which they achieve their greatest development. It is not a laissez faire or a laissez passer, but rather a conjunction of guided impulses which society, of which the individual is a part, needs for its development and progress. The individual is not free to do what he wishes; this doing what he wishes might become an obstacle to the free development of altruistic sentiments which bind the individual to the society of which he is a part. If one were to understand liberty in the sense given to it by liberalism, all that would follow would be disorder and with it the destruction of the highest social goals which make a true liberal order possible. Disorder, the product of liberty in the anarchistic sense, would be an obstacle to the development of liberty in the positive sense. Liberty in the liberal sense would mean the stimulation of the egotistic sentiments and by the same token a rein on altruistic sentiments. For that reason, the freedom which does not attain to ends which fortify society and with it the individual who makes society possible, is an egotistic liberty which must be made subject to the laws of the development of society, to the order of freedom in the sense of the free development or progress of society. The egotistic liberty of individuals must subordinate itself to social order.

Hence the reason why the state must intervene, like the instrument of society she is, in the moral education of Mexicans. She must prepare Mexicans to be good servants of society, stimulating their altruistic sentiments. Mexicans, as individuals, may be liberals or conservatives, Catholics or Jacobins; this means nothing. What is important is that, independently of this individual attitude, they must be good citizens. That is, they must submit their individual goals to the goal of the society of which they form a part. In doing so, they will also realize their individual goals. In other words, the individual may think he wishes, but he must work in accordance with the interests of society. One may hold freely whatever ideas he may wish; what he cannot do is to hinder, by these ideas, the free movement of society and of the individuals who constitute it.

III
THE THEORY OF ORDER

However, how far *does* the state, or *may* the state, go in its intervention in the service of society? No further than the social order necessary for the development of society, a development which stands in direct relationship to the material development of each individual member. The important thing for the ideologists of positivism will be this social order, the order which will put an end to the anarchy in which the country had wallowed from the beginning of its political emancipations from Spain, a political order which will permit the material development of the most apt individuals among the Mexicans; a political order at the service of the material development of Mexican society that rests in the material strengthening of the individuals who compose it.

The socialism here advocated goes no further than the social order which makes possible the material development of the class which had been emerging since the initiation of liberalism itself, "the Mexican bourgeoisie," as Justo Sierra calls it.

This order, purely political in character, would be inoperative in the economic field. Barreda himself maintained that the state should not intervene in the organization of private property. Only through education, with the development of altruistic sentiments, would it be brought about that its possessors should direct private property toward a greater development of society. However, nothing more. The state should not attempt any other intervention. It would, of course, be able to regulate the political order which would put an end to anarchy, but not the economic order which would remain at the free disposition of individuals. The only thing it could do would be to make the possessors of wealth see that

the rich, although they are morally authorized to hold the same capital which the social order has made it possible for them to increase and conserve, all that is necessary for their real needs and also for the maintenance of their rank and dignity, should seek to cultivate and use the excess, under pain of moral responsibility, as a public power which society has placed in their hands for the good of common progress.

Moral responsibility, the conviction that wealth ought to result in social benefit at the same time that it benefits its possessors. Moral responsibility, which does not imply any intervention of the state except as a simple counsel for the greater use of such wealth. Barreda says it will not be necessary to regulate wealth; what ought to be done is to "humanize the rich." The rich man can do what he wants with his wealth except to divide it up, for to do so would dislocate and disjoint the possibility which resides in wealth. Wealth and the rich are instruments of the material development of society; for the sake of society and its development the state, far from placing obstacles in their way, should open roads to their greater achievements. Even the fact that the rich man is considered a depository of the wealth of society is no reason why the state should be able to intervene, save morally, in the regulation of that deposit.

Such intervention would prove an impediment to the free development of that wealth which would redound to the social benefit. Society, which intervenes in education, cannot intervene in the regulation of wealth. The society which ought to lay the foundation of a political order that would put an end to all possible anarchy will be bound to abstain from impeding the material development which must be the outcome of the free play of the interests of wealth. Wealth is an instrument of social progress, and it is found in the hands of those who understand the laws of its development; it must be left where it is. The only thing which should be of interest to society is that this wealth should also serve social progress. Wealth, because it is the instrument of progress, must, for the same reason, be protected by the state.

So far as the abuses which the possessors of wealth may commit are concerned, the most that can be done is to appeal to the moral responsibility implied in the possession of wealth. Nothing more can be done, for to attack wealth and those who know how to increase it would be to diminish and to extinguish their stimulus and with it the progress which the development of wealth implies. The important thing for positivism, as may be seen, is the political order. To the establishment of that order all of its powers should be directed, the order which would permit the free development of the best of its individual members and, in this way, of society itself. The state has no mission of transcendental character, such as it claimed in the theological and metaphysical periods; even less has it the economic mission that socialism claimed for it, such as the division or organization of wealth. Its mission concerns only the conservation of the social order; for this end it intervenes in the educational field in order to create the kind of men who might make this order possible. The state as the instrument for the service of society should not concern itself with the existence of men who are more or less rich, more or less poor, but rather only with the existence of men of order who make possible, without impeding the freedom of thought of each of them, the free development of wealth.

Let Mexicans think whatever they want to think; let them exploit others or permit themselves to be exploited. The important thing is the order which makes social progress possible along the path indicated by the free play of interests in which, according to the Darwinian doctrine later maintained, the fit prevail. Behind the neutrality of the state in the area of personal ideologies and of private property, defended by Barreda, there already emerges the outline of the interests of what seemed to be going to become the nucleus of the Mexican bourgeoisie. This class leaned upon a doctrine which justified its economic and social situation and at the same time created the political instrument which would prevent the alteration of the order that served its development.

IV
THE POSITIVIST GENERATION

The fruits of positivist education directed to the political order made themselves felt immediately. Porfirio Díaz had risen to power after a revolution which unseated the heir of the exalted Benito Juárez, President Sebastián Lerdo de Tejada. By 1878 there arose in the capital of Mexico a new political group which made its voice and its ideas heard in a periodical entitled *La Libertad* and which carried the Comtean banner "Order and Progress." A number of its editors had been students under Gabino Barreda or had been formed in the system of education which he had established under the reforms introduced by President Benito Juárez in 1867.

This new group began to stir up public opinion about one idea, that of *order*. However, theirs was a new type of order which resembled in no feature the colonial order which had been broken by the liberal triumph, a new kind of order which was not the order upheld by the conservativism which had been annihilated on the hill of the Campanas. The new group called itself conservative; however, a liberal conservativism. Our purpose, it declared, is liberty; however, our methods of achieving liberty are conservative. We are before all else conservators of order as an instrument for the achievement of authentic liberty, which is not, cannot be, the anarchy which weighed upon the country for half a century. They called themselves conservatives because their methods were contrary to all other methods for attaining liberty. Liberty, they held, is achieved by way of the free natural development of which Barreda spoke and which his disciples called evolution. Not revolution, but evolution. This is change in accordance with laws within a determined order.

What is urgent for the achievement of an authentic liberty is the establishment of an order which makes that liberty possible. This is what Mexican liberals had not been able to understand and still did not understand. They had tried to give the people liberties for which they were not ready; the result had been anarchy. The first thing was to educate, to create in the mind a knowledge of liberty and of the obligations which liberty implies. So long as Mexicans did not have this knowledge, all utopian laws and constitutions would be useless, alien to the reality of the situation. The liberal constitutions and laws these must be, were not capable of creating the liberty of which they spoke; theirs was a simple-minded utopianism, proper to minds without a sense of reality, without a practical direction of spirit.

Finally, however, thanks to the educational reforms of positivism, there had arisen a generation capable of directing the nation along the best roads, a practical generation, positive, realistic. The generation about to come to power would establish the social order from which would arise the liberties which the liberals had ineffectively pretended to establish. This was a generation capable of creating the bases of a democratic government resting upon authentic social freedom. Meanwhile, as this generation was creating those bases, the important thing was *order,* the political and social order which would make possible, in the near future, the dreamed-of liberal government. It was necessary to put an end to widespread anarchy, which continued despite the triumph of liberalism over colonial conservatism. There stood as the principal obstacle to the abolishment of anarchy the liberal Constitution of 1857. The ideal liberty advocated by that Constitution could be reached only after the creation of the habits and customs which would give it life within each Mexican. Before that it was impossible of fulfillment.

What most makes one indignant, wrote Francisco G. Cosmes, one of the editors of *La Libertad,* is that there still exist men of such retarded mentality that they still believe in the ideas maintained by the legislators of 1857:

after half a century of constant struggle for an ideal which, once attained, had produced only lamentable results for the country, it is a cause of great sadness, in truth, to see that while the atrocious wounds which the revolutions and the civil war have inflicted upon the Republic are still bleeding, the revolutionary ideal still finds among us those who defend it.

And Justo Sierra, director of the same journal, wrote in criticism of the constitution-makers of 1857:

Our fundamental law, made by men of the Latin race who believe that a thing is certain and realizable since it is logical; who try to make human, brusquely and by violence, any ideal whatsoever; who pass in one day from the domain of the absolute to that of the relative, without transitions and without shadings of color, and seek to force people to practice what is true only in the domain of pure reason—these men (perhaps we are of their number) who confuse heaven and earth, made for us a noble and elevated code of alliance, but one in which everything tends to diffusion, to the autonomy of the individual raised to the highest degree, that is to say, to the stage at which it would seem that the force of social duties ceases and everything is converted into rights of individuals.

Utopia must come to an end. A new period of history was approaching, a realistic period directed toward an order whose final term would be the realization of that which had only been a mere utopia. Toward this end would march the forces of the new generation, a generation conscious of its historical mission. No longer following Comte, but rather Darwin and Spencer, this generation would maintain the necessity of strengthening Mexicans for the struggle for life and for passing from the military era, the era of order, to the industrial era, the era of work and of the triumph of the individual.

To utopian and anarchistic liberalism there had to be opposed a realistic liberalism, a liberalism of order, a conservative liberalism. We desire, said Justo Sierra,

the formation of a great conservative party, composed of all the elements of order that in our country possess the capacity of rising to public life. We do not carry as our banner a person, but an idea. We plan to gather about it all those who think that in our country the period of seeking to realize its aspirations by revolutionary violence is over, all those who think that the definitive moment has now arrived for organizing a party more devoted to *practical* than to *declamatory* liberty, and are profoundly convinced that progress resides in the normal development of a society, that is to say, in order. . . .

"We do not carry as our banner a person, but an idea"; in these words was enclosed the ideal of the new order, an order whose force did not depend upon the will of a "caudillo," but an impersonal order derived from the very minds of Mexicans. However, this order remained, for the moment at least, one more utopia. Above all it was necessary to educate the people for such an order. In the meantime any kind of order would be good. The problem seemed insoluble: one sought to abandon an order which depended on the will of a "caudillo"; nevertheless, someone of sufficient personal prestige was needed to lay the bases of the new order. This "someone," of course, would be nothing else but a simple instrument, something transitory until Mexicans could acquire the mental habits necessary for an autonomous order, that is an order free from any force external to it.

For the moment is was necessary to limit liberties which were manifestly utopian. It was necessary to create confidence in the country, the only path along which it might initiate a process of regeneration:

Rights! [exclaimed Francisco G. Cosmes] Society already has rejected them; what is necessary is bread. In place of these constitutions filled

with sublime ideas, not one of which have we seen realized in practice
. . . I would prefer peace, in whose shade or shelter it would be
possible to work tranquilly, with some security for its interests and to
know that, instead of launching themselves into the hunt, the flight,
of the ideal, the authorities would hang the exploiters, the thieves, and
the revolutionaries. Fewer rights and fewer liberties, in exchange for
greater order and peace. No more utopias. I want order and peace,
even at the price of all the rights which have cost me so dearly. And
more, [he went on] the day is not distant when the country will say,
I want order and peace even at the price of my independence.

How to achieve this order and peace for which they called out
in such urgent need? Not by means of arbitrariness, they said; not
by way of the governments of persons which have been so harmful to the country.

There is nothing more odious [said an editorial in *La Libertad*] or more
contrary to progress among us than the dominion of one, or several,
men without "regla fija." That is what we think about dictatorship.

Nevertheless, the Mexican reality, the state of affairs, had given
rise to dictatorships, to tyrannies. To have done with them, it
is necesasry to transform that reality. Meanwhile, however, one
has to put up with it. In order "to have done with dictatorship
in fact . . . we must establish a practicable constitution"; however,
since that is impractical in the prevailing circumstances, "we are
content to seek extraordinary authorizations for these extraordinary circumstances." And Francisco G. Cosmes said in another
of his articles:

We have already realized an infinity of rights which produce only
misery and distress in society. Now we are going to try a bit of honorable tyranny to see what effect it might produce.

This "honorable" tyranny would prove to be that of General
Porfirio Díaz.

V
FROM COMTE TO SPENCER

The generation educated by Gabino Barreda, that of men who
were going to lead the destinies of the nation along the road of

progress, would find itself too confined within the limits of Comtian positivism. This doctrine, no matter how hard Barreda had tried, could not justify the kind of liberty which might have the greatest interest for the future Mexican bourgeoisie, the liberty to enrich itself, with no limits save those of the capacity of each individual. Comtianism, in the strict sense, subordinated the individual to society in all the fields of material good. This was the meaning of the "sociocracy" of Comte; such is what his positive politics would establish. Comte's politics, like the religion of humanity, had not been accepted by the Mexican positivists because they considered them contrary to the interests for which positivism itself had been accepted. The important thing was to form the directing class of the Mexican bourgeoisie, which was more and more powerful as time passed. The model to which this class should conform was offered by the Anglo-Saxon countries.

The theoreticians of the Mexican bourgeoisie very soon found a theory which might justify their interests. This was offered by the English positivists John Stuart Mill and Herbert Spencer, especially the latter, and, with them, by the evolutionism of Charles Darwin. This doctrine seemed most completely to coincide with the interests which needed to be justified. These men were, moreover, the highest expression of that practical spirit which the Mexicans so much admired. According to these doctrines it was necessary to educate the Mexican people. English positivism, far from opposing the idea of individual freedom in the greatest number of its expressions, justified it. The great examples of this fact were the liberal regimes in England and in the United States: Spencer opposed the coercive state, and Mill defended individual liberty. In the theory of both the state proved to be nothing else than what Mora desired: an instrument of protection for all and each of the individuals who made up the society. Even more, the Spencerian idea of progress would make it possible to offer, at least for the future, an ideal of liberty, that for which the people had struggled on different occasions. To establish this promise, it was necessary only to make a determined degree of progress.

And here we return to make connection with the group of young positivists who, from the pages of the periodical *La Libertad,* demanded a new order and aspired to establish an honorable dictatorship. This group no longer followed Comte, but rather Mill and Spencer. How then could they justify ideas which seemed to be contradictory? They would find this justification in Spencer's idea of evolution. The fact would seem to him beyond doubt, Sierra would say, that society is an organism which, though different from others (the reason why Spencer called it a superorganism), has undeniable analogies with living organisms. Equally with animal organisms, society is subject to laws of evolution. In accordance with these laws, all organisms realize a movement toward integration and differentiation in a process which goes from the homogeneous to the heterogeneous, from the indefinite to the definite. In the social organisms the movement is from social homogeneity to individual differentiation, from complete order to complete liberty.

In this form the idea which the older liberals had held about liberty was not denied; what was denied on the basis of the *Principles of Sociology* of Spencer was that Mexican society had reached the high level of progress which was necessary to obtain that freedom. These men did not think, as had the Comtians, that this freedom belonged to a stage of metaphysical transition; rather, they were convinced that it was a goal to be achieved. It is not something *past,* but something in the *future.* In order, however, that such a condition might come about, it is necessary first that society should *evolve* in that direction. For this reason the new conservatives opposed the Constitution of 1857, considering it utopian, that is, outside its proper place in time. Such constitutions can be good only for countries like the United States, given the high degree of progress they had achieved, not in countries like Mexico, which found themselves at an inferior stage of development. "Is it not against good sense," they asked, "to raise a mighty edifice upon muddy ground without first casting solid foundations?"

The first thing to be done was to look to the material future of the country. Liberties are useless in a materially depressed country. When that future is reached, liberty in its many forms will come about by addition, by natural evolution.

The day when we are able to say that the basic charter has procured us a million freeholders, we will have found the constitution which is suitable for us; then it will no longer be a word on our lips, but a plough in our hands: the locomotive on the track and money in everyone's pocket. Freedom of ideas will come. We prefer normal and slow progress to precipitating matters by violence.

These men stood for progress by way of evolution, not revolution.

The urgent, the immediate thing to be done is to strengthen society, to integrate and to homogenize it. To the degree that society becomes integrated, becomes homogeneous, the more will it become differentiated and defined. To the degree that social order becomes more permanent, the more will individual liberty take form. Up to this time, the positivists thought, Mexico had been a land without order and, therefore, a land which had not complied with the laws of progress as revealed by Spencer. For this reason it is necessary, before all else, to establish order. It is not possible to go from anarchy to true freedom.

Now the demand for a strong state becomes natural and justified, a state which would assume the task of setting up the order so necessary for the progress of Mexico. Now it becomes natural, as Justo Sierra says, "for a people . . . who exist in the most miserable conditions of life, to seek the invigorating force of a center which would serve to increase the power of cohesion." Otherwise, "to the contrary, incoherence will become every day more pronounced, the organism will not integrate, and the nation will be aborted." It is disorder, Sierra goes on, which makes of the Mexican nation one of the most feeble and most defenseless social organisms within the orbit of civilization. While Mexico goes on destroying itself, "there lives alongside us a marvelous collective animal, for whose enormous intestine there does not exist alimentation enough and which is armed and ready to devour us." Before this colossus we are exposed "to being a proof of Darwin's theory, and in the struggle for existence we will find all possibilities against us."

VI
POSITIVISM AND THE REGIME OF PORFIRIO DÍAZ

"Political evolution," the evolution of liberty in the field of politics, was to be sacrificed on the altar of what Sierra used to call "social evolution." That is, on the altar of the social evolution of the Mexicans, indispensable in order to arrive at that supposed political liberty, all this liberty was to be limited. To uproot the habits of disorder from the mind of the Mexican was a very difficult task.

Unfortunately, [Sierra said] these congenital habits of the Mexican have come to be a thousand times more difficult to uproot than the domination and the privileged classes it established. Only the progress in the conditions of work and of thought in Mexico would be able to bring about so great a transformation.

Only a strong state would be able to bring about such a change. On the day a group or party succeeded in maintaining itself as an organized body political evolution would continue on its march.

And the man, more necessary in democracies than in aristocracies, would emerge; the function would create the organ.

All political power, and with it the freedom of Mexicans, would be turned over to a strong man, to General Porfirio Díaz.

In order that the President [Sierra continues] might be able to bring to completion the great task which he has taken on his shoulders, he needs the very greatest concentration of power in his hands, not only legal authority but *political authority* as well, which would permit him to assume the effective direction of the political bodies, legislative bodies, and governments of the states; of *social* authority, constituting himself supreme judge of peace in Mexican society by general assent . . . and of *moral authority.*

However, all of these delegations and abdications of power to one man had to be compensated by the action of the state in the field so important to the leaders of mental emancipation:

education. The honored tyranny was an educative form by means of which the Mexicans were going to learn the meaning of freedom.

On November 26, 1876, General Porfirio Díaz, who had risen in arms against the government of Sebastián Lerdo de Tejada under the cry of "no re-election," made himself interim president after the triumph of his troops. On December 5 of the same year he ceded power to General Méndez, but reassumed it, provisionally, on February 16, 1877. On September 25, 1880, with his consent, General Manuel González was elected; however, in 1884 Díaz returned definitively to the Presidency in which office he was to remain until May 25, 1911, on the triumph of the Mexican Revolution. About General Díaz were grouped all of the political forces of the country. His figure came to symbolize that peace and order for which the men brought up in positivism had clamored so loudly. Materialism and dehumanization were converted into models of life by the generation which was formed during his regime: industry, money, railroads—and always more money. Progress seemed to triumph definitively. Social evolution seemed to march forward with giant steps; however, in this euphoria there was forgotten that for the achievement of which, so it was claimed, order had been established: freedom. They conformed to a very special kind of freedom: the freedom of enrichment. It was a freedom in which not all classes could participate.

The absence of authentic liberty, Sierra was to protest, had necessarily brought about the abortion of everything that had been gained in the field of evolution.

A new type of Mexican arose with "porfirism," who, by comparison with the liberal generation which had preceded, described themselves in the following manner:

We are charged [they said] with our lack of beliefs, with our positivism, our poorly hidden disdain for the institutions of the past. All that is true; however, it is due to the different education which we have received. You [they went on with reference to the liberals] nourished yourselves in philosophical matters on Voltaire and

Rousseau, on the Encyclopedists, on the "Choix de Rapports" of the French Revolution, and the most advanced among you, in the lofty metaphysics of the German school, while we study logic in Mill and Bain, philosophy in Comte and Spencer, science with Huxley and Tyndall, Virchow and Helmholtz.

A different education would produce men equally different.

You [they continued] came out of the lecture rooms drunk with enthusiasm for the great ideas of 1789 and, citing Danton and the Girondonists, hurled yourselves at the mountains in order to combat the clergy, consolidate reforms, demolish the reactionaries, and outline our laws upon the beautiful utopias which were then current in philosophical transactions. We, by contrast, less enthusiastic, more skeptical, maybe more egotistical, seek a new explication of the binomial theorem, dedicate ourselves to natural selection, study sociology with enthusiasm, concern ourselves little with the celestial spaces, but a great deal about our earthly destiny. We concern ourselves with questions which cannot be submitted to the slide rule of observation and experience. The part of the world which interests us is that part which we must study by means of the telescope and other instruments of scientific investigation. We do not know the truth, needless to say, at first sight. In order to come to it we must make long voyages to the regions of *science;* we must give ourselves to arduous and constant labors, to laborious and patient investigation.

The new generation considered itself destined, by reason of its capacity, to guide and direct the country. Its methods were sure, perfect, and precise. They were the methods of science, those they had learned in the schools as Gabino Barreda had reformed them. Those methods, they said, would be applied to the solution of all the problems of Mexico, including its political problems. In 1881 they were already speaking in Mexico of the "scientific school of politics." In 1886 a number of its members entered the Chamber of Deputies. Some of them were to become outstanding figures in the regime of Porfirio Díaz: Justo Sierra, Pablo Macedo, Rosendo Pineda, Francisco Bulnes, and others. All of them, together, would impress their mark on the period which is known by the name of "porfirism." There began the era of the "scientists."

VII

POLITICAL ORDER AND ECONOMIC FREEDOM

In 1892 the political party called "Union Liberal" issued a manifesto in support of the fourth re-election of Porfirio Díaz. In it was formulated a program intended to satisfy the interests of the ever-more powerful Mexican bourgeoisie. It spoke of analyzing the Mexican social situation, its problems, and their solutions from a scientific point of view. For this reason the opposition and the mass of the people in general, whose political rights had been trodden underfoot for all practical purposes, began to call that party by the disrespectful and ironic title "Party of the Scientists."

The manifesto also spoke, among other things, about the necessity of conceding greater liberties to Mexican society, since Mexico seemed to have reached a higher level of progress. It seemed that at last the promised freedoms were to be granted. Earlier it had been necessary to grant a greater power to the executive; at this moment, however, it seemed that the hour had come to grant greater liberties to the people.

Our party [the manifesto reads] is already fully in a position to impose a rational discipline upon itself which permits it to be completely clear in the expression of its will within the constitutional formula and to participate more actively in the direction of public affairs, marking out the courses which lead to its supreme ideal of liberty in enduring conjunction with order.

Recalling the slogans of the old liberal party, this new union believed that liberty is not possible until a certain level of order has been attained. Now, however, this order seemed to be an achieved fact, thanks to the government of Porfirio Díaz. With order established it would be possible to take a further step in the achievement of liberty. What would this step be?

We believe the moment has arrived to begin a new era in the historical life of our party [says the Union]; we believe that the transformation of its directive organs into organs of government has already been achieved; we believe that just as peace and material progress have achieved this end, it's now the task of political action, in turn, to consolidate order, it behooves it to demonstrate that from this day forward revolt and civil war can only be an accident and that peace, based on the interests of the will of a people, is the normal state. For that reason it is necessary to establish peace as the cornerstone of liberty.

With this increase of liberties it would become possible to decide whether or not Mexican society had attained that level of order necessary to obtain still greater liberties. The new political party proposed a series of liberties for which it thought the Mexican people had now become ready; however, among them electoral liberty is not to be found because it was thought neither important nor opportune. The people could have other liberties more important than that.

The nation [the manifesto adds] would desire that its government might find itself in a position to demonstrate that it considers the present peace as a definitive state of affairs by the economic reorganization of certain branches of the Administration. . . . It would desire that national *freedom of commerce* might, through the suppression of internal tariffs, be established as fact and no longer be but an aspiration periodically renewed. . . . Only in this way will peace be assured to future generations of Mexicans, whose resources have been tapped to create our credit and our progress, the means of continuing that progress and even of *accumulating a reserve of capital* which might be transformed into greater well-being and vigor. In such conditions peace would never appear costly.

What does all this mean? It is asserted that greater liberties must be granted, but immediately it is said that electoral or political liberty is the least important among them. What is immediately sought is freedom of trade and, more inclusively, an economic liberty which would permit the accumulation and formation of capital. What is sought is the reduction of the interventions of the state in the economic field, not in the political area. Political liberty is betrayed or sacrificed in exchange for liberty of enrichment, a liberty, obviously, which could only benefit those who possessed resources capable of being incremented. It can be seen, consequently, that there was no question of granting the kind of liberty which had been of interest to the older Mexican liberals.

Political order and economic freedom: such is the ideal of the Mexican bourgeoisie. Political order, maintained by General Díaz, was to be placed at the service of the economic freedom of the bourgeoisie. As far as political rights were concerned, the bourgeoisie would reserve its power to demand them only for the occasion on which an attempt might be made against the freedom of enrichment. Political freedom, the right to the election of the governors, could be limited for the good of an order which satisfied the interests of the Mexican bourgeoisie, and since the government of General Díaz insured peace, its re-election was necessary.

In this way the bourgeois order identified itself with national order, and the bourgeois party with the people. With national order achieved, it would be necessary to ensure the liberty which served its interests. Díaz was the man called upon to concede this liberty and to see that it was not obstructed.

The Republic [the manifesto says] is aware that it is the efficient cause of its progress and tranquillity; however, it also knows that a certain man has collaborated in the first stage in giving practical form to general tendencies, and he is the citizen whom the convention has elected to occupy the Presidency again.

The authors of the manifesto affirm that if he is being re-elected for the fourth time, it is not because he is considered an indispensable man, but rather because in his previous three terms he had given proof of his capacity to govern in accordance with the interests of the nation. In this manner the bourgeoisie had succeeded in making of Porfirio Díaz the "honored tyrant" who would satisfy its interests. For this reason it had supported him and would continue to support him so long as he remained so. From the beginning the theoreticians of the bourgeoisie had distinguished between what they called "personal dictatorship" and "social dictatorship." The first was of the type of dictatorships of which Mora had spoken, that type which serves the interests of a determined group or social body, such as the clergy or the military. The second was, simply, the dictatorship established to protect what the bourgeoisie called the interests of society, that is, its own interests.

For his part, Porfirio Díaz, a power-orientated man with a mentality similar to the kind which the educators of the bourgeoisie had sought to extirpate, was not satisfied to be a mere instrument of the bourgeoisie. He rejected the limits which it sought to impose on him, so far as his political power was concerned. He was not disposed, consequently, to maintain the order which suited the Mexican bourgeoisie, but rather demanded the total transfer of that power to himself.

Justo Sierra, with the genial intuition which made him outstanding among the members of his generation, understood that this delegation of political liberties to the person of the dictator was dangerous, "terribly dangerous for the future because it *imposes* habits contrary to those of self-government, without which one may have great men, but not great peoples." And he vowed that at this crossroad of its historical life the Mexican people would not err.

Fernando Salmerón

246

VII. MEXICAN PHILOSOPHERS OF THE TWENTIETH CENTURY

THE ATENEO DE LA JUVENTUD

In the year 1909 Pedro Henríquez Ureña wrote these words:

In Mexico the philosophy of Comte, mingled with the theories of Spencer and the ideas of Mill, is the official philosophy, as it has been dominant in instruction since the reform directed by Gabino Barreda, and it is invoked as the ideological basis of the political tendencies in vogue. Although the positivists have not succeeded in implanting here, as they did in Brazil, the ecclesiastical rites of the religion which Comte annexed to his philosophical conceptions, Mexican Comtism has its press organ, the *Revista Positiva* (Positivist Review), in support of which there is displayed a tenacity similar to that displayed in favor of the same cause by the celebrated Juan Enrique Lagarrigue in Chile. *Sotto voce*, a part of the youth is already following other courses; nevertheless, criticism of positivist ideas (not the conservative Catholic criticism, but the advanced criticism which takes its inspiration from the contemporary intellectual movement) has barely begun with the memorable discourse of Don Justo Sierra in honor of Barreda (1908) and one or another of the works of the recently organized Sociedad de Conferencias.[1]

The criticism of the positivist conception initiated a new stage in the history of ideas in Mexico. As a matter of fact, since 1874 Don Justo Sierra had rejected the doctrinal content of positivism and had set himself against certain of its essential theses. In his speech in homage to Barreda, he expressed his skeptical attitude toward Mexican positivism, toward its rigidity and routine, rather than criticize the philosophy of Comte. He presented, as incitements to renovation, some ideas about the limits and relativity of scientific knowledge. Further, the old and venerable scholar publicly saluted the efforts of the young men to whom Henríquez Ureña makes reference and stated that Gabino Barreda himself

would have turned with profound attention and a no less profound, though unquiet, inclination toward this same movement which we are witnessing today, this precipitous and tumultous arrival of the new generation.[2]

Upon this new generation we must present some notes.

At the beginning of 1906 a group of young writers and artists established the review *Savia Moderna* which was the continuation of another famous review of the preceding century. The new review did not appear for very long, but long enough, however, to mark out a tendency to abandon two accepted norms: nineteenth-century France as a literary model and positivism in philosophy. About it there gathered a number of young men who were to remain united in various intellectual undertakings and, above all, were to live, during a time of life decisive for their training, through the most outstanding event of contemporary Mexico, the Mexican Revolution. Among them there stand out, from the point of view of their interest for the history of philosophical ideas in Mexico, José Vasconcelos (1882–1959) and Antonio Caso (1883–1946). The third great figure is Alfonso Reyes (1889–1959), a very prolific man of letters, who in his later years dedicated a number of outstanding studies to themes on the humanistic classics and literary criticism, in which he touches upon matters in the history of ideas and the philosophy of language and literature, besides writing some essays of outstand-

ing value on themes in social philosophy and Hispano-American
culture. The limits of the present work make it necessary for
us to omit Reyes and another figure who, to this date, has not
received from critics the attention he merits, Ezequiel A. Chávez
(1868–1946). Chávez belonged to an earlier generation than
that of the "Ateneo de la Juventud"; nevertheless, drawn along
by the antipositivist movement, he accomplished a work which
shares the characteristics of and, on many points, may be considered parallel to that of Vasconcelos and Caso.[3]

On the demise of the review, *Savia Moderna,* the same group
established the Sociedad de Conferencias (Lecture Society) at
the beginning of 1907. The principal purpose of this association
was to spread ideas and foment artistic activities in the middle-
class spheres of Mexico City. About 1908 a conservative journal
provoked by its attacks on Barreda the reaction of the young
men of the Society, who organized in memory of the founder
of the Preparatory School a "true philosophical meeting," as
Alfonso Reyes described it. The speakers at the "mitin" made
evident their solidarity with the liberal works of Barreda, but
at the same time they made very clear their independence of
positivism.[4] In the following year a series of seven lectures on
the history of positivism delivered by Antonio Caso in the very
lecture halls of the National Preparatory School clearly succeeded in defining the final attitude of the young intellectuals
toward the official doctrine. On October 28, 1909, a new association was formed, called "El Ateneo de la Juventud" (The
Athenaeum of Youth), which immediately began its activities
with fortnightly meetings, lectures, and public discussions on
philosophical themes in the lecture halls of the Preparatory
School.

A sense of renewal, a feeling of change, were accentuated
with the celebration of the first centenary of the Independence
of Mexico. The Ateneo de la Juventud actually possessed a
character of its own as a center of free discussion, and its members were aware of the fact that they were giving social form to
a new way of thought. With full official endorsement the group

took part in the festivities of the centenary with a series of conferences on American themes. José Vasconcelos delivered one of these conferences on the subject "Don Gabino Barreda y las ideas contemporáneas" (Don Gabino Barreda and Contemporary Ideas); this speech constituted a true intellectual "manifesto." [5] With profound respect for the memory of Barreda, Vasconcelos expounded "the contemporary ideas," and in so doing he laid bare the first lineaments of a personal work in philosophy and made clear the intellectual leanings of the group.

Compared to the intellectual generations immediately preceding, that of the Ateneo presents certain features proper to itself. Although none of its members renounced literary creation and many made of it a preferred activity, all of them are characterized by a deep interest in philosophical and social problems and also by a conviction, perhaps inherited from Justo Sierra, that the problem of Mexico was a problem of education. All held Greece and the Latin poets in the greatest esteem; at the same time, however, they valued an extensive acquaintance with modern culture and entertained a constant concern for everything Mexican and Hispano-American. Further, they all exhibited seriousness, not only in their activities but also in considering the intellectual occupation a true vocation and not an activity marginal to the real tasks of life. This last was the case despite the fact that they had received the greater part of their formation outside the university halls and in spite of all those personal traits which Henríquez Ureña had already pointed out in Antonio Caso as early as 1909 and which to a greater extent prove applicable to his compatriots. With reference to a declaration of "intellectualism" made by Caso, the Dominican writer described the difficulty of a person who was

spontaneously accessible to the distractions which constantly drew him away from intellectual rigor: conversation, affectionateness, artistic feeling, attraction of the mysterious, data of conscience, sense of reality. . . .[6]

Nevertheless, the most characteristic trait of the generation remains, without question, its nonconformity to positivism.

The most alert and generous minds of the positivist movement of the first years of the present century were those who incited them in the process of alienation from the positivist philosophy, such as Sierra, Chávez, and Macedo, who had been the teachers of the members of the Ateneo in the Preparatory School and in the Faculty of Jurisprudence. To this was added the influence of their readings, a good part of which were group readings and public discussions. The young "Ateneistas" studied, in group readings, the great classics, Plato and Kant principally, James, Croce, Nietzsche, and Schopenhauer, who, according to Vasconcelos, possessed in a number of his formulas "the seed of the whole modern age." Above all they studied contemporary French writers, Boutroux and Bergson in the first place, but without excluding, probably, the "modernism" of French Catholics, which exercised so much influence in those years.[7] With such weapons they launched the battle against the official doctrines of the Porfirian regime.

In the first of two articles which in 1909 Pedro Henríquez Ureña dedicated to commenting on the lectures of Antonio Caso on positivism, he elaborates some of the criticisms of the philosophy of Comte which were to emerge, among others, as starting points of the two great thinkers of the generation of the Ateneo, Vasconcelos and Caso. Resting his case on quotations from other critics of the philosopher, the Dominican writer argues that Comte's attacks on metaphysics are, in fact, directed against scholasticism, that is to say, against the intention to explain phenomena by means of entities, causes, or essences which are themselves not to be found in experience. And when Comte praises the investigation of laws instead of causes, he did not ask himself whether the principles he sought to establish were any less metaphysical than the scholastic entities. What Comte did not notice was that the mark of metaphysical truth is not so much that it makes use of those scholastic elements of explanation as it is the tendency toward the unification of experience, the tendency to consider things as a whole. It is this confusion which makes positivism so ambiguous a philosophy.[8] Conceived as an effort or attempt to achieve a totalizing vision of the universe with roots in scientific thought and free of Comtian criticism, metaphysical thought becomes the intellectual program of the new generation.

Another of the targets of the attack on the positivist doctrine is the famous law of the three stages. In his lecture on Barreda, Vasconcelos insisted that the so-called three stages of knowledge have nothing to do with progress, but concern only the utilization of different methods adapted to the different fields of reality. By showing the limitations of positivism the argument opens the possibility of advancing along other paths of knowledge, those of religion, art, and life.[9] On the other hand, the influence of pragmatism in pointing out the instrumental value of reason and its limits contributed to the justification of metaphysical doctrines with nonrational bases.

The return to metaphysical concerns, the enlargement of human experience, the affirmation, without vacillations, of liberty as the foundation of the spirit, in a word, the exaltation of man is what gives to the lectures and the writings of the "Ateneistas" the tone of Christian optimism and generosity, of liberty and sympathy for the people, which distinguishes them from the texts of the positivists.[10] This idea is imprinted not only in its writings but rather in all of its cultural undertakings and especially in its greater ones—the establishment of the Mexican Peoples' University, the introduction of free, philosophical investigation into the National University, headed by Antonio Caso, and, years later, the educational work of José Vasconcelos, which succeeded in reuniting various elements of the group. The Peoples' University, established in December 1912, was the first free institution of culture devoted to the spreading of ideas in factories and in popular centers and continued its work for ten years despite the unstable situation brought about by the revolution.

The most characteristic traits of the Ateneo group took form in opposition to the positivism of their teachers. According to Lombardo Toledano the new generation set up against

social Darwinism, the concept of free will, the power of the sentiment of human responsibility, which must control conduct both individual and social; against the fetishism of science, the investigation of "first principles"; against bourgeois conformity, of the survival of the fittest, the joyous Christian nonconformity of a full life, shared by rich and poor alike, by the learned and the unlearned, by the proud and the rebellious. It was rightly thought that it was necessary once more to draw the spirit close to the pure sources of philosophy and the humanities and that it was necessary to spread these ideas, not only among the enlightened classes but among the people as well.[11]

The opposition to positivism was not, however, a mere theoretical divergence; it has political consequences. What these consequences were and to what point they appeared clear to the young critics of positivism is a matter on which we must say a few words.

Positivism, as all the members of the Ateneo later came to recognize, functioned as a political instrument:

it was the doctrine of the dictator Porfirio Díaz and exercised notable influence on many of the acts of the ex-president of Mexico.[12]

As a doctrine, positivism was really exhausted, a fact which was proven by the rapid accession of the new generation to the commanding position in the culture of the capital of the Republic, the correlative of which was the de facto loss of the teaching profession by the elders with the sole exception of Justo Sierra who, by his inclusiveness and youthfulness of spirit, was able to keep the young subject to his influence and loyal to the regime of President Díaz.[13] The regime was historically liquidated, to the point that it constituted an actual obstacle to the development of the country: a privileged sector of the national bourgeois, a group of landholders and directors of the public finances, had seized economic and political power and worked behind the back of the interests of the rural population, of a proletariat much in the minority of a middle class which found itself in ever-more reduced circumstances.[14]

Madero took account of the situation of the middle class and was able to personify its ideas of renewal, liberalism, and practical democracy without, however, breaking with what he considered the values of "Porfirism" and much less with the idea of provoking a popular revolution and of changing the structure of the national economy. That society, however, could not advance a single step more without violent changes, and positivism, as a doctrine, would have shown itself unable to adopt itself to a new historical situation. The task of the new intellectual generation consisted in making this change possible in public opinion, as they impressed a new orientation in the area of thought, breaking with an ideological past which conceived the Mexican people as an entity which, although produced by a process of historical evolution, was definitively constituted and rendered incapable of any new transformations. This task, in its origins and in its intentions, is strictly parallel to the "Maderist" movement, insofar as it is a matter of critical attitudes arising from the middle class and directed against a group which, in the name of order, was paralyzing the progress of the country. This parallelism has caused a certain historian to affirm that the leaders of the Ateneo were the "intellectual precursors" of the Mexican Revolution, though not its political directors.[15]

The truth is that the Mexican Revolution had other precursors in the intellectual order: those who criticized "Porfirism" in the political and social fields, a criticism which not only took place on the margin of academic circles but also, in one manner or another, proposed concrete measures for the reformation of social usages, political institutions, or economic arrangements.[16] The members of the Ateneo were, in 1910, too young and too lacking in sufficient social influence for their doctrines to go beyond the cultured groups of the middle classes. Moreover, those doctrines did not exist except as projects of philosophical creation in the heads of young thinkers; what existed was simply a need for intellectual liberty, for the right to discuss metaphysical "first principles," and for a criticism of the fundamental ideas of positivism. The negative and critical attitude toward positivism and the need for intellectual freedom are the two facts of culture parallel to the "Maderist" movement which constituted a first step in the Mexican Revolution.[17]

Those projects of philosophical creation were to find completion some years later, after the periods of violence had passed, when their authors found in the new social conditions opportunity to derive attitudes and opinions on some of the real problems of the country, principally those concerning educational policy. Nevertheless, during that "Maderist" period of the Revolution, which corresponds to the years in which the Ateneo de la Juventud began to function and in which the group defined its character as an intellectual generation, its influence was "nil" in relationship to the real problems of the country, even though its desires for a humanist revival possessed such clear correspondence with the political ideas of the middle classes of that period. This correspondence permitted the intellectual youth to identify itself with the Revolution after the triumph of Madero.

The relations of the young men of the Ateneo with the regime of Porfirio Díaz, to which we have alluded above, did not impede their efforts at intellectual renewal to the degree that they did not pretend in any way that the renewal would reach other aspects of the national reality; in the same manner Madero, when he wrote *La Sucesión presidencial de 1910,* intended nothing else than a renewal of political procedures. This is not to say that the members of the Ateneo remained on the margin of all political action, but that they acted as individuals and not as a group.[18]

On the triumph of Madero they returned to unity, changed the name of their group, which came to be called "Ateneo de Mexico," and elected as president José Vasconcelos, who had from the beginning been associated with the partisans of the new government. With the complete triumph of the intellectual opposition to "Porfirian positivism" and the completion of the political transformation as well, they rejoined forces, in order, in Vasconcelos' words, "to swear a new oath to the ideal of our generation" and to announce its disposition "to cooperate in order to establish a higher enlightenment on bases independent of politics." Nor did they fail to indicate to the new government that it ought to "be prudent in reforming" that same educative regime under which the "Ateneistas" had studied and against which they had fought so steadily.[19]

The generation of the Ateneo de la Juventud found in the

change brought about by Madero a favorable conjunction of circumstances, though one not entirely free of dangers, for their ideals of evolution and progress, for

the development of that which may come to be a national character, a well-defined profile, perhaps the principle for the creation of a mental state which promises to integrate itself by realizing the expression of our race which has been mute for so long a time. . . .[20]

Later, other times would come. The death of Madero opened another stage of the Mexican Revolution which extended the armed struggle to the whole country and brought to the fore the interests of the largest masses of the population: the peasa.its and the workers. Mexican society, divided into clearly defined groups, suffered the effects inseparable from all armed revolutions, and among the revolutionaries themselves profound differences appeared. When peace was re-established, there reappeared contractions and discrepancies of standards; periods of energy were succeeded by others of pause and recession. Still, this stage of the Revolution, that of constitutionalism and the struggle of factions, surprised many and certainly took the young men of the Ateneo by surprise, costing them a great effort to adjust themselves to the change. It was difficult for the young men of that time, according to the trustworthy testimony of Alfonso Reyes, to admit that the national heroes might be some humble neighbor or other or an ignorant rancher.[21]

The members of the Ateneo dispersed. Some abstained from political action altogether; others intervened sporadically either in a direct manner or by assuming technical or diplomatic duties. Still, during those years both groups were fulfilling an intellectual role which turned them into the greatest masters not only of the thought but of the whole Mexican culture of the present century.

Now, it is indispensable to consider the work of each one of them in order to see in what form they developed that common nucleus of youthful ideals and in what manner they succeeded in assimilating the fundamental fact for that generation, the

Revolution. This will also permit us to describe to what extent the thought of each one exercised influence over Mexican life, and especially over the ideological field of the revolutionary process. Still, since the undertaking is too large for the limitations of space which are imposed on this essay, we must leave aside the detailed and complete exposition of the thought of each author in order to confine ourselves to making clear two things: first, what we consider the essential nucleus of this thought and, second, the efforts undertaken to resolve the real problems of the country on the basis of that essential nucleus.

José Vasconcelos

Lawyer and philosopher, mystic and politician, writer and teacher, he is, without question, the most inspiring intellectual and human figure which Mexico has produced (Eduardo García Máynez).[22]

Vasconcelos was born in Oaxaca on February 27, 1882. Lawyer and philosopher, mystic and politician, writer and teacher, he is, without question, the most inspiring intellectual and human figure which Mexico has produced. In 1897 he established himself in Mexico City and began studies in the National Preparatory School and later in the National School of Jurisprudence, receiving the legal degree in 1905. In the last years of the Díaz government he opposed the dictator, not only by his pen but also by taking part in an assault on a barracks of Profirian troops. During the insurrection he collaborated with Vázquez Gómez by representing Madero in Washington. On the triumph of the movement he returned to Mexico without, however, assuming any position in the government; but on the death of Madero he abandoned his legal work and again acted as a representative of the Revolution, first in Washington and later in London. On the defeat of Huerta he returned to Mexico and took part in the National Convention, where he allied himself, as Minister of Instruction, with Eulalio Gutiérrez, who had been appointed provisional president by the Convention itself. On the triumph of the constitutional movement he left the country and remained in exile until the fall of Carranza, when Obregón named him Rector of the National University and later, Minister of Education. At the close of Obregón's regime Vasconcelos resigned in order to oppose Callas' candidacy for the presidency, taking part as a candidate in the elections for the state of Oaxaca. Unsuccessful in the elections, he again went into exile. On the death of Obregón he accepted the candidacy for the presidency of the Republic; after an agitated campaign, in which personal assaults were not absent, he lost the election and called on the people to revolt. His call remained unanswered, and he again went into exile.[23] He returned to Mexico at the end of the government of Cárdenas and from 1943 on devoted himself entirely to the public life of the nation as founder-member of the National College and as director of the Biblioteca México until his death in 1959.

The enthusiasm which the figure of Vasconcelos awakened at one period has not ceased to be an enigma to later generations.[24] If we agree that that period coincides with the political campaign of 1929, the first thing we are obliged to recall is that in that year there appeared the first edition of the *Tratado de metafísica*.[25] Not withstanding the fact that it hardly had opportunity to become defused in those months, it must be taken into account that with the appearance of that volume the system called "metaphysics of aesthetic monism" ceased to be a mere project. The treatise explains what the system undertakes to do and develops its first part:

being in its rational manifestation, differently from being as action, the examination of which will be developed in the *Ethics*, and in opposition also to *Esthetics*, in which being appears as actualized and fulfilled in an eternal undertaking or rather as surrendering itself to rhythms of supernatural movement and ascension.[26]

It begins with what the author calls "an examination of the immediate evidence" and then devotes some chapters to problems of method, becoming, existence, and other concepts in order thence to enter upon the central undertaking of the book: the theory of the transformation of energy. Convinced of the necessity of basing philosophy on science, Vasconcelos introduces into his system this first part, the metaphysics of nature. The treatise closes with a classification of the kinds of knowledge, which allows him to order all of the branches of learning into sciences of description (physics), sciences of invention (ethics), and sciences of synthesis (esthetics), which together embrace all that exists. Religion, or theodicy, falls outside the classification; it is the fourth term which goes beyond philosophy. Ethics is defined as "the science of those disciplines which are necessary for the consummation of the projects or ends of life," [27] and the disciplines grouped here range from biology and natural history to law, morality, and economics. Finally, certain pages try to relate the content of this book to practice, the doctrine of which is unfolded in *Ética* (Ethics), the second part of the system. However, these pages constitute no more than mere indications and barely permit one to glimpse the general line of thought which will unite later developments. Thus we learn, for example, that law must be based on ethics rather than on reason:

the discipline which defines its projects with honesty, directed by a criterion of the emotion of justice, of human sentiment, leads to the *Law as the esthetic fulfillment of a high transcendental mission,* that is to say, rather than the code, the Gospel. [28]

Before the *Tratado de metafísica,* Vasconcelos had issued other publications, [29] but his prestige does not seem to have been due to these as much as to his public activity as Rector of the National University and, above all, as Minister of Education. This activity and the repercussion of two of his books, *La raza cósmica* (The Cosmic Race) and *Indología* (Theory of the Indies), gave Vasconcelos prestige, principally outside Mexico, as the intellectual representative of the Mexican Revolution.

La raza cósmica is a great utopia of the Ibero-American race. A humiliating and strange book, it takes its point of departure in the idea that the mixture of similar races is fertile, while the results of the mixture of more distant races are dubious. This enables the author to explain the backwardness of the Hispano-American peoples in virtue of the fact that:

the mixture of very dissimilar factors is very slow in taking form. Among us, the mixture was suspended before the racial type had been completely formed, by reason of the exclusion of the Spaniards, decreed after Independence.[30]

Nevertheless, even the more contradictory mixtures may be carried out satisfactorily as long as the spiritual factor contributes to their elevation. And Vasconcelos declares that in Hispano-America the spiritual and material conditions are present to make it the cradle of a fifth race in which all peoples might be integrated in order to fill out the four which had, in isolation, been forming history.[31] Spain, Mexico, Greece, and India are the four particular civilizations which have most to contribute to the formation of Latin America.[32]

The myth of the new race is taken up again in *Indología,* which is in a certain way an enlargement of *La raza cósmica* in so far as it tries to offer a characterization of the collective Hispano-American existence on the basis of its differences in geography, history, and race from North America. These differences make it possible to conclude with all clarity that Latin America is not a vague geographical denomination, but a perfectly homogeneous ethnic group.[33] The idea of race and the tone of universality which is expressly opposed to the usual concepts of the fatherland,[34] in addition to the affirmation of the spiritual unity of the Hispanic race in Spain and in America, constitute the central motif of the book in which Vasconcelos accumulates historical data and scientific information of every kind: arbitrary generalizations resting upon a formidable ignorance of the social and cultural realities of Hispano-America, side by side with sure insights and very keen observations deriving from a direct knowledge of the life in the great cities of America.[35] However, alongside this tone of universality, which does not always seem to be sincere, the experience of the intelligent traveler and a sensitivity toward the works of the past compensate us with pages which proudly vindicate the autoctonous values.

In addition to these generalizations, the theory of the future race is supported by a philosophy of history no less meandering, which is summed up in the *law of the three social stages.* The stages represent a process which is gradually liberating man from the empire of necessity and submitting his whole life to the higher norms of sentiment and imagination: the material, or warrior, stage in which the sole unifying principle among peoples is physical force; the intellectual or political stage, in which reason tends to prevail, correcting the errors of force, organizing customs and submitting everything to laws, tyrannies, and political convenience; the third stage, whose advent is announced here, is the spiritual, or esthetic, one in which conduct will not be orientated about reason but about sentiment and imagination.[36]

This last point is connected with the prophetic announcement of the coming of the new race which is being born in Hispano-America. As every race must establish its own philosophy, Vasconcelos recommends the abandonment of philosophies learned from other races because the body cannot be redeemed before the spirit is liberated.[37] This explains the inclusion of the chapter on "Hispano-American Thought" in *Indología,* which in the first place discusses the possibility of such an Hispano-American philosophy. While by definition this philosophy must embrace the whole of the culture, it is nevertheless a truth which in part at least implies a manner of thought proceeding from collective life and rooted in it. His exploration of the Ibero-American culture is thus justified, as is also the announcement of the appearance of a new philosophy which, corresponding to an emotive race, senses the principles of an interpretation of the world founded on emotion, like that initiated by Vasconcelos himself.[38]

Still, beneath the myth of race and the arguments which accumulate about it what there is of truth in it is the decision to reject socialism and especially Marxism and to oppose to them the concept of "consciousness of race." In the book the opposition does not seem entirely clear because the author defends a vague humanitarian and Christianizing socialism, which sets up as the first and most urgent need the purification of the moral environment.[39]

The fifth chapter of *Indología* is devoted to public education.

Here the author ventures a brief history of education in Latin America with special emphasis upon Mexico and above all on his own work which, he held, had been developed in accordance with the ideas which had up to that point been expounded.

With the passing of the stage of armed combat, the revolutionary regimes began to apply the new laws and to test out their programs of government. President Obregón reorganized the public administration, gave strong impulse to agriculture and agrarian reform, but above all he seemed to be disposed to make the whole future of the country rest upon one base, education. In this way education took on the meaning of a social regeneration, which destroyed the status of privilege of the school in order to make instruction a benefit to all social classes. Vasconcelos, as minister of this branch of government, succeeded in impressing upon it the tone of a religious crusade, so that the problems of education were discussed publicly and enthusiasm broke out of teaching circles to give a stamp of animation to the intellectual life of those years.[40]

It is important to keep in mind the moment of revolutionary enthusiasm in order to understand that the educative work of the period, which in reality lacked any true plan, could not be undertaken by one man, as Vasconcelos himself came to believe during his years of exile.[41] With Vasconcelos there collaborated, in addition to the young intellectuals of the generation of the "contemporaries," other persons of great experience in matters of education who brought it about that ideas might find the channels necessary for their application to the actual condition of the country.[42] Nevertheless, the directive ideas which presided over that educative work were imposed by Vasconcelos.

The same ideas which had animated the meetings of the Ateneo de la Juventud appear in the discourses and documents of Vasconcelos, sometimes more precise, sometimes rendered turbid by political utopianism: humanism as the exaltation of man and freedom as the foundation of the spirit, the cosmopolitan meaning of culture and the love of the classics, which becomes deeper in the traditions of Christian inspiration as well as discovers rules of hygiene in wisdom; the interest for Hispano-America and for Spanish culture crystallized into open utopia, in the dream of a federation founded on the basis of common blood and language, Hindustani, but with ideals rather mystical than political; the interest in our own culture appearing as a rescuing of the values of popular art without, however, any trace of nationalistic sentiment; Christian generosity converted into the desire for social revindication of a vaguely socialistic flavor; and all this shot through with an evangelistic fervor in the undertaking of redeeming the Mexicans by means of education.[43]

No sooner had Vasconcelos left the Ministry of Education than the enthusiasm decreased, and the multitude of detailed changes in his educational plans clearly showed the lack of precision and the inability of those ideas to deal with the actual problems of the country. The change of orientation of the educational system marked the definitive end of his personal influence on the formation of institutions. Nevertheless, the prestige gained in his undertakings appeared at one time sufficient to begin his political campaign for the presidency of the Republic.

The crisis precipitated by the death of Obregón made possible the cooperation of nonconforming groups with the revolutionary government. Vasconcelos, who since his exile had maintained an attitude of opposition by means of his periodical articles returned to his country in order to place himself at the head of the discontented.[44] At no moment of the political campaign did Vasconcelosism appear to represent a danger for the government. The program of the candidate offered no real popular attraction; it was limited to the promise to maintain the legislative and practical advances of the revolutionary governments in the areas of agrarian reform and the protection of the working classes, and added, as its single original stroke, the creation of an atmosphere of moral dignity in all public life. What might have been of great interest in 1910 had no revolutionary meaning in 1929; nevertheless, the circumstances in which the campaign developed called forth, on the one hand, unnecessary violence and the abuse of force on the part of the groups in power and, on the other hand, an almost mystical enthusiasm on the part of the young which offers no point of comparison with any other similar situation in contemporary Mexico.[45]

The abandonment of active political life made it possible for Vasconcelos to bring to completion a very rich work as a writer, distinct from the group of his philosophical and historical works. Further, there ought to be mentioned a short treatise on questions of education and a group of writings which may strictly be classified as literary efforts. Among these literary pieces there are, in addition to the essay, stories and travel accounts, theatrical pieces and poetry; however, it is not possible to say that among them are to be found the most enduring pages of Vasconcelos. Rather the contrary is the case if exception is made for certain really remarkable travel pieces; they emphasize incredibly negligent stylistic defects and an absence of clarity and structural rigor in each work which can barely be compensated for by an extraordinary verbal facility that at its high point succeeds in rounding off a phrase into its perfect expression.[46] Curiously, the literary gems, the best examples of an effective style, are to be found in the group of writings that we have classified as historical, where stylistic negligence combines with polemical violence and the direct experience of political passion.

The historical works, in addition to constituting a considerable portion of the intellectual achievement of Vasconcelos, are also a part of his political undertaking. To this circumstance must be attributed the fact that their value rests precisely upon what they contain as political documents, besides the literary value alluded to, and in no sense upon the historical content. The famous *Breve historia de México* (Short History of Mexico), the author's greatest publishing success, is an "Hispanic" interpretation of the national history, which judges all its heroes by submitting them to a single criterion:

The criterion is this: those who, knowingly or unknowingly, have been instruments of the Poinsett Plan, which proposes to replace the Spanish with the Anglo-Saxon in the dominion of Latin America, and those who in full consciousness or occasionally have opposed the Poinsett Plan. . . .[47]

A personal vision of our history, written with the desire for retaliation, not only alters the value of contemporary figures but also subverts the entire liberal tradition of Mexico, even in those instances in which it does not do violence to the historical facts. The other historical works of Vasconcelos are biographies that amplify chapters of the history of Mexico, complements to the Hispano-American meditations of which we have already spoken or autobiographical expositions which in their structure approach closer to literature than to history. The studies in the history of philosophy deserve a chapter by themselves; these studies, like the allusions to other philosophers contained in his works, prove useful in discovering the imprint of these readings on Vasconcelos himself and in learning his reaction to another's thought. Yet these studies are useless in making us aware of the content of that other's thought because of the complete lack of objectivity of these studies and, in many cases, the absence of direct knowledge of the sources,[48] although, on the other hand, Vasconcelos is not a man to conceal the influences he has felt. Bergson is his master *par excellence,* although his thought had, in addition, benefited from the whole history of philosophy. Plotinus and Pythagoras, Schopenhauer and Schelling, the Christian tradition and, in his last years, contemporary American and English philosophy, have in his books left traces of differing importance, but always noticeable.

A book on education, *De Robinson a Odiseo, pedagogía estructurativa* (From Robinson to Odysseus, Structural Pedagogy), was published in 1935 and is a study, at ten years' distance, of the problems raised during his tenure as Minister of Education. The passage of time permits the author (as it would seem, for the first time) to clarify with precision his educational ideas and to bring his thought to confront, in polemical form, the reforms carried out after his period in office and especially the influence of Marxism and the pedagogical theory of Dewey and of Decroly.

Seeking roots in Hispanism and in Catholicism, Vasconcelos opposes to all forms of empiricism a pedagogy of metaphysical ideals based on a philosophy which pretends to treat matter as experience and spirit as wisdom. Man must educate himself as a means to life and needs a life which will be a path to salvation. A pedagogy which does not linger at one of the stages of life but which concerns itself with the whole of destiny must be structural, must organize the moral and mental structure of the "educandus," incorporate his consciousness into the plan of humanity, and develop the most essential gift of human nature, the unitive faculty, the faculty of organizing all knowledge into a system:

To hold always present the essential purpose of education, which is *to help construct our destiny*, will also be the most effective means of freeing ourselves from particularist methods which far from contributing to the integration of our personality, disperse it.[49]

The group of philosophical writings complete the system announced in the writings of his youth and of which mention has been made above. The first part of that system is the *Tratado de metafísica* (Treatise on Metaphysics); the second part is the *Ética,* published in 1931; the third, the *Estética,* the first edition of which appeared in 1935 and the complement of all of them, in the study of method, is the *Lógica orgánica* (Organic Logic), which appeared in 1945. With these four bulky volumes and some short works, Vasconcelos has tried to construct an entire "vision of the universe which begins in the magnetic wave and ends in the Trinity which St. Paul defined." Trying to summarize this vision in a few pages would seem to be an impossible undertaking unless we content ourselves only with indicating certain essential points which lay bare the nucleus of this thought, the method according to which it develops, and the firmest lines of its architecture, without losing sight of the fact that these notes cannot pretend to be a complete exposition.[50] On the other hand, Vasconcelos himself brought together his ideas, reaffirming and clarifying what is fundamental in his earlier books in a fifth volume: *Todología, filosofía de coordinación* (The Theory of the Whole: a Philosophy of Coordination) published in 1952, which may now serve us as a guide in the present treatment. Vasconcelos presents the *Todología* as

the conclusion of his personal experience in an effort to reach the
harmony of total understanding—of philosophy, of science, of
revelation—without losing sight of the fact that for him these
modes of wisdom and the stages of a complete life are inseparable. Bearing this in mind, he postulates for this achievement
an irrational method:

a living experimentalism in which concur, each one in its own function, the data of the senses, the rules of reason, the projects of the
will, all in a harmony which engenders love. The ambition to bring
into concert all the resources by which consciousness disposes to
relate itself to the world and to penetrate more profoundly its own
depths. And finally, to assist in the encounter with God; such is the
desire of a philosophy which I have called *Esthetics,* understanding
by "esthetics" an art of composing and coordinating cognitive
values. . . .[51]

It is a question of a philosophy of synthesis, a type of philosophy that does not want to eliminate a single one of the properties of things and that, by the same token, accepts alongside of
its own truth, truth as identity referred to the static and abstract
condition of being, whose modes are exemplified in physical
science. The truth of esthetic philosophy is conceived as a
"musical chord" rather than as a logical result. To think is an
effort toward unity, a discovery of the relations among beings
which can respond to systems of reason, but also unity agree-
ing with love. Compared to the passive knowledge of logic, the
active knowledge which unfolds itself by means of rhythm,
melody, and harmony delivers facts to us in their reality, the
truth of the living thing.[52]

To avoid the translation of my panorama into abstraction, I do what
the artist does: I observe in my small portion of reality its relations,
its proportions, its lights, and that which my emotion and memories
add to the panorama. It is a question of a conjunction made up of
images and states of soul, bound together by various systems of order:
the system of scientific experience which tells me how the things
which I hold before me came to be and how they are related to each
other in a physical sense. In like manner there acts an entire moral
system which establishes relations between objects and my conduct.

Moreover, I enjoy conforming to the laws of beauty which are the origin of the satisfaction caused in me by the intervention of my consciousness in the natural order which I contemplate. By living within the concrete order, by the projects of my will and the joys of my contemplation which distinguishes, assimilates, and orders, I participate in a mode of life which I have called paradisal. . . .[53]

Since the theme of this philosophy is reality itself, the seizure of reality will enter according to the order in which the senses, reason, and later the imagination and revelation, all in a clear hierarchy, give it to us. Alongside the forms of sensibility and the categories of the understanding we have within ourselves an "ethical a priori" constituted by judgments of value and an "esthetic a priori" whose modes of apprehension—rhythm, melody, harmony, counterpoint—permit us to arrange in an ordered fashion, and in unity, heterogeneous elements, while we respect their whole integrity because knowledge by coordination finds it obvious that all living unity is the result of the concurrence of differences.[54] No portion of being escapes from their form of knowledge, not even that which is irreducible to "rational reason." [55] The knowledge of the totality of reality, of the relations of its parts among themselves, and of the parts with the whole, is what makes possible the truth which saves, the orientation of personal destiny.[56]

As truth is a process of functional coordination, reality is the coordination of structural elements. The immediate "datum" of the most authentic experience, a point of departure achieved by the "experientialist" method, is "existence," which is not an empty being, but the conjunction of concrete beings, a multiplicity in movement submitted to hierarchical orders. Everything which exists is structured energy. Alongside of existence Vasconcelos speaks to us of being (ser) and its varieties. The notion of being belongs to the experimental order; it is reality itself, the synthesis whence all proceeds. On the basis of these two notions there are established tables, categories, branches, cycles, classifications, and hierarchies, which cross each other with some complexity.[57]

We shall linger only over the categories of being, since they coincide almost completely with the structure of existence and reveal an image of the world as energy in activity, in an ascending movement toward the absolute. The quantum wave and the atom are the first constructive efforts of the cosmos. A second step in this struggle against dispersion is achieved in the molecule which joins heterogeneous atoms. The third step in this progress toward coordinated heterogeneity is constituted by the living cell, which gives origin to the animal species. The human person represents a fourth step reached, like those before it, by a qualitative leap, and is characterized by consciousness, which has as its specific power the capacity to coordinate heterogeneous elements.

Within the world of souls, Providence brings about the Incarnation in order to give encouragement to the higher forces of history. Before the panorama of existence two things clamor to be clarified: the relations of the parts among themselves, the task of science, and the relations of the parts with God, the task of theology.[58] This "esquisse" of the universe corresponds better than others, Vasconcelos thinks, to the cosmovision of the Gospel, assuming that a philosophy not in accord with Revelation is false or incomplete.[59] It is important to emphasize that each of these leaps implies a change in the quality of energy in the direction of a superior degree of integration and receives the designation "revulsion of energy" after the work of 1924 which bears this title.

So far we have recounted the essential points of this so-called system, which is *monistic* because beneath the division of orders and methods it discovers a single energy which moves in different rhythms in inanimate things, in living beings, and in souls, and is esthetic in its manner of dealing with the cognitive processes.

Still Vasconcelos believes that he engendered this system by his life, as poets create poems by singing.[60] Upon this assumption, a reading of his works does not seem to confirm his thought; his autobiographical writings may be moving, but at no point do they reveal a direct relation with the content of his philosophical system. In the same way his system does not seem to bring the reader often in contact with the times in which Vasconcelos, the statesman, moved. There exists, no doubt, a fundamental bond bringing together all members of his generation: the rejection of positivism, whose meaning has already been indicated. But in the restoration of humanism and liberty, in the quest for a national character and the roots of a lost tradition, Vasconcelos, who sees in positivism a philosophy expressive of the Anglo-Saxon character, undertakes to elaborate a philosophy of his own which would be at the same time universally valid and salvation for the Hispano-American situation.

The incorporation of these themes into Mexican thought was a complete revelation, and the undertaking could not be clearer or more keenly felt. However, the times were not propitious for meditation, or was Vasconcelos' temperament apt for living on the margin of the times. Further, the absence of discipline and of a solid intellectual formation were the gravest obstacles to the elaboration of a doctrine of universal validity; the incidents, speculation without restraint, the passion of the moment, a spirit arbitrary and hurried, impeded all attitude of reflection and analysis, alike in the philosophical works and in the political writings. The serene elaboration of the problems of Mexican life and of the international situation was replaced by the facile sketch, utopia, myth, and enthusiasm.

There was a moment, under the presidency of Obregón, in which it was possible that with those general sketches Vasconcelos personally collaborated in the transformation of the country. But when it was necessary to adjust these ideas to national realities, the philosopher was unable to distinguish the meaning of social transformations from the struggle between political groups and wasted his intellectual energy in superficial pamphlets and in the elaboration of a speculative metaphysics wholly devoid of contact with the human sciences. Not even his most serene and realistic books have a direct dependence on his system; moreover, their diffusion in the country came about late, when they could no longer have any influence on intellectual life, and even less on political life. During the last years of his life Vasconcelos delivered courses on political philosophy in the National College which made clear once more his lack of knowledge of the democratic advances in the country. He defended a division of society after the mediaeval manner and an exercise of power after the manner of a Roman consul: an inspired governor, called to govern by popular plebiscite, but master of all powers and with no more restraint than his own conscience.[61]

Nevertheless, his philosophical undertaking was important and noble, and the passion expended on it did not fall short of the goal it sought. This circumstance and the fact that his pages were written in the valiant and free tone of an emancipated man, with the appearance of offering the reader at each step the ultimate depth of the personality of the author, made of him one of the most-read writers of recent years.

Antonio Caso

Antonio Caso represents an entire Mexican era. The champion of indispensable reforms and guardian of essential traditions, he is to be found situated at the critical point of the catastrophe. When there supervened the intense social upheaval which, among many evils, also destroyed many good things, there providentially fell upon him the role of "sóter," of savior, of continuator. To men like him, from one generation to another, there falls the task of preventing the unravelling of the fabric, always being woven, of our national consciousness. This is the way history must consider him (Alfonso Reyes).[62]

Antonio Caso was born in Mexico City at the end of the year 1883. Like Vasconcelos, he studied at the National Preparatory School and then graduated as a lawyer from the National School of Jurisprudence. Differently from Vasconcelos however, Caso dedicated himself to the academic life and only occasionally fulfilled some important public assignment. In the years of his youth he engaged in some wholly irrelevant political activity, to which reference has been made;[63] nevertheless, his competencies and his prestige as a brilliant orator kept him much of the time in contact with public life, and it was his task to carry out certain important missions.[64] In 1921 President Obregón named him Extraordinary Ambassador of Mexico to Peru, Chile, Uruguay, Argentina, and Brazil; Caso toured those countries from June to November, seeking political solidarity for the revolutionary government. On Caso's return President Obregón personally testified to the success of his tour.[65] However, teaching from his university chair proved Caso's most personal mode of expression above everything else; the brilliance of his exposition attracted large groups of students, who carried the interest in philosophy into larger circles than strictly academic ones. Beginning in 1907, Caso assumed his first chair, and at the age of thirty was director of the School of Higher Studies of the National University. He did not retire from lecturing until two years before his death, and the memory of these years makes it possible to speak of an era of university life in Mexico, first in the Preparatory School, later in the School of Jurisprudence and that of Advanced Studies, and finally in the National College, of which Caso, like Vasconcelos, was a founding member. In addition he practiced journalism, and the newspapers of his time carry a great number of his articles and polemical writings on philosophical themes and problems of national interest.[66]

With his lectures, university courses, and articles for reviews Antonio Caso was preparing books that over the expanse of years would grow to constitute a considerable achievement. Without taking into account those which retain a heterogeneous character because they are mere compilations of articles, these books may be grouped in the following manner: studies in the history of philosophy and philosophical criticism, works on social and political philosophy, works on philosophy in a stricter sense. The following may be considered as belonging to the first group: *Filósofos y doctrinas morales* (1951); *La filosofía francesa contemporánea* (1917); *Historia y antología del pensamiento filosófico* (1926); *El acto ideatorio y la filosofía de Husserl* (first edition, 1934; second edition, 1946); *Meyerson y la física contemporánea* (1939); *Benito Díaz de Gamarra* (1940); *Positivismo, neopositivismo y fenomenología* (1941); *Filósofos y moralistas franceses* (1943); *Evocación de Aristóteles* (1946). In the second group there may be classified *Discursos a la nación mexicana* (1922); *México y la ideología nacional* (1924); *Sociología genética y sistemática* (first edition, 1927; second edition, 1962); *Nuevos discursos a la nación mexicana* (1934); *La filosofía de la cultura y el materialismo histórico* (1936); *La persona humana y el estado totalitorio* (1941); *El peligro del hombre* (1942); and *México, Ayuntamientos de cultura patria* (1943). In the third group may be placed *Problemas filosóficos* (1951); *Principios de estética* (first edition, 1925; second edition, 1944); *El concepto de la historio universal* (first edition, 1923; second edition, 1933); and *La existencia como economía, como desinterés y como caridad* (first edition, 1916; second edition, 1916; third edition, 1943).[67]

This simple list of titles and dates does not, of course, provide an adequate orientation among the themes with which Caso concerned himself. In addition to the fact that the anthologies repeatedly bring together essays composed at widely separated dates, one frequently finds these essays with additions and corrections which do not appear in the original. The same occurs in the books which were re-edited: each new edition increases the earlier and adds pages which had not existed before. This is particularly noticeable in those books which constitute Caso's basic concerns: the *Sociología* (Sociology) and, above all, *La existencia como economía, como destinterés y como caridad* (Existence as Economics, as Disinterestedness, and as Charity). This ceaseless renewal, a capacity which remained intact to the very last years of his life, has presented Caso's commentators with a multitude of problems concerning his intellectual evolution, over which we cannot linger here.[68]

The same teachers who were the guides of the Ateneo de la Juventud dominated the first periods of Caso's intellectual evolution: the great classics, Plato and Kant; in a place of preference, the pragmatism of James and the philosophy of Schopenhauer; and, of course, the contemporary French philosophers, principally Bergson and Boutroux.

However, beginning with the year 1933, Caso's books begin

to register successively the presence of the philosophy of the Baden school, the phenomenology of Husserl, the axiological derivations of Scheler and Hartmann, and the work of Heidegger. These new readings, however, did not redirect, but rather deepened, the original course of his thought, beginning with a fundamental nucleus, which is of chief interest here.

As in the case of the other members of his generation, Caso's thought is a reaction against positivism, an affirmation of liberty, of Christian roots, based on the conviction that man is a spiritual reality which constitutes the culmination of nature.

In this sense one speaks of a "new humanism," as Caso himself wrote in certain passages which Samuel Ramos later emphasized: this philosophy is a humanism

understood as an act essentially human in its origin, its development, and its term. If to philosophize is to explain (and this alone is what it should be), it is useless to explain human life by the world because ultimately for the philosopher, though not for the scientific investigator who must of necessity abstract his data from reality, the world is a psychological experience and is to be explained only by way of man. The fundamental truth of all philosophy is an anthropological truth, an intuition essentially identical with esthetic intuitions and differing from them only by reason of its universal, rather than individual, object.[69]

From this point of departure Caso projected an explanation of the world, literally, a "Christian cosmovision" which would be able to maintain itself without contradicting the philosophical and scientific conclusions of the culture of our time.

Caso decided to write that essay just after a three-months' course in the Popular Mexican University in the winter of 1915. The content of the course was the history of Christianity; in Caso's words,

a form of "cultus" to the heroes and the heroic, in the history of the most important fact in the evolution of humanity, the development of the Christian ideas and sentiments in the course of the centuries.[70]

The theme of the course does not seem to have been chosen

at random and even less so the theme of the essay. Still, if the latter may in part be explained as the consequence of a tradition, national and personal, and of an intimate conviction affirmed in opposition to the intellectual influence of positivism, the theme of the course, delivered before a popular audience, can not be understood without further taking into account a certain idea of the author's relative to his duty as an intellectual facing his circumstances. However, we shall return to this point further on.

Dr. José Gaos has insisted that in that opuscule which had become a whole book in its final form there is really implied an entire system of philosophy which Caso never succeeded in developing in all its detail.[71] In spite of the fact that he does not leave clearly established the relations between the different points of view of existence, in spite of the fact that many points remain at loose ends and that the essay lacks a certain formal and terminological precision, the exposition presents, in the first place, a conception of biological life as struggle, egoism, and appetite for domination that also extends to human life and the exercise of intelligence, including the science which is placed at its service. Not even play escapes the law of economy because it is a recollection of the struggle, a training for future action. The law of economy limits the function of science, from whose dominion the intuition of essences, esthetic contemplation, religion, and morality are free. In this conception there is effectively present the seed of a natural philosophy, a theory of knowledge and even a theory of objects.

In the second place, Caso studies existence as disinterestedness and shows how art breaks the law of the least effort. He further devotes two chapters to the study of the symbol, of form, and of esthetic values which constitute a fundamental part of the doctrine developed by the author in another book *Principios de estética* (Principles of Esthetics.) And finally, he treats of existence as charity, which in reality invests the economic formula of life and initiates the establishment of a morality based on the concept of sacrifice and love. All of which culminates in a chapter upon hope and another on faith, the remaining two theological virtues, which lead to a spiritualistic metaphysics of a strictly religious character.

Caso projects this religious and moral preoccupation into the political and social field and presents it as a solution of the problems of Mexico and of the world because he thinks, quite literally, that the social problem is a moral problem.[72] Such a theme really constitutes the nucleus of Caso's thought, the bond between his metaphysical and his sociological preoccupations; it is to be discovered in his first writings. It appears in 1915 in his course in the Popular University, which ought to be considered as a call to Christianity in the midst of the Mexican Revolution and the first World War. This theme is repeated in a small work of 1916, written immediately after the course but directed to a rather wide audience, the cultured Mexican middle class, to which he had to present Christianity without contradicting the philosophical and scientific conclusions of our time. It returns in the volume on Mexico which appeared in 1924, in which the author directly opposes to the concept of "Christ the King" of the Catholic Church the concept of "Christ the People" of sacrifice and of love of our neighbor.[73] And this theme is maintained up to the last books in which the notion of the person is purified and gains preference.

In Caso's thought there exist three levels of being: the thing, being without unity; the individual, being endowed with a life which cannot be divided; and the person, a spiritual reality which, as such, transcends itself in order to participate in the world of culture and to actualize itself as something singular and nonsubstitutible in human society.[74] The person knows his neighbor by axiological intuition, and this latter is the basis of society; however, the complete realization of the person is not achieved without a principle of solidarity, of participation in a moral association. It is at this point that individualism, an egoistic attitude of those who seek to dominate, is distinguished from personalism, which proclaims a society based on justice, solidarity, and the moral unity of men. The personalist seeks *to be more,* and this is possible only through participation in a true moral association for culture.[75] For the same reason the realization of the person is the only justification of society and culture.[76]

Caso also faces the question of socialism, which he considers true from many points of view. "Anyone who denies it without qualification is not a man of his time."[77] However, without denying it completely, the philosopher proposes to transcend at one stroke the points of view of both individualism and socialism. Both represent egotistic attitudes, for there is also an egoism of society which claims for itself the right to subordinate its members to itself unconditionally. The solution lies by way of ethics and juridical forms:

Neither the individual nor the community; rather, society based on justice. That is, the *moral unity of men,* respectful of values. The community which tyrannizes over man forgets that men are "persons," not "biological units," but spiritual centers of cultured action. The individual who opposes himself to the community as an absolute reality forgets that above the individual who feeds on his egotism there is human culture which is always a synthesis of values. Neither the individual nor the community develops values; rather, they are reflected by the historical continuity of the generations and the moral solidarity of peoples. Culture is, indissolubly, tradition and solidarity.[78]

There is no question, however, of·a purely irrational vindication, such as had been the error of classical liberalism; now the starting point is the idea that the individual and the state are two elements of human solidarity.

The liberty of conscience which denies any necessary principles is false, is not truly liberal, because it violates the laws of reason. Liberty can only be understood rationally.[79]

The same is true in the case of the principle of private property, which in classical liberalism is an immoral and absurd notion. Caso recognizes that

property is one of the props of human society if it is conceived as the prolongation, in the material order, of the right of personality, to be personal. It must be clearly understood that, given different persons, the limitations of the right to property is as essential as the right to property itself, because property is limited in virtue of the different personality of another subject who possesses a right, also a person. So the foundation of property is identical fundamentally with the basis of its limitation.[80]

The passages cited above constitute sufficient evidence of the way in which Caso faces social and political questions. Although he opposed "Maderoism" in 1910, although later he suffered privations as a consequence of the armed struggles, sometimes even threats, the philosopher knew how to penetrate very quickly to the meaning of Porfirism, and on the fall of Madero composed pages full of serenity on "The Internal Conflict of Our Democracy." In 1914 he wrote in condemnation of the dictatorship of Huerta, and the following year petitioned for a congress to reform the constitution of the republic. It is probable that after 1917, the year in which the new constitution was proclaimed, Caso's association with the revolutionary movement became definitive. In 1921 he served the Obregón government in the capacity of extraordinary ambassador in South America, and while it is true that his university lectures exhibit a strictly philosophical content, his interviews and official addresses were directed to making known the ethical and humanistic tone of the Mexican Revolution and to seeking solidarity with its government.[81] However, Caso wrote and published his interpretation of the history of Mexico up to 1924 in *El Problema de México y la ideología nacional* (The Problem of Mexico and the National Ideology).[82] In this little book the author presents the periods of the history of the country by means of its representative men; explains the destruction of positivism by the Revolution of 1910, initiated by the skepticism of Justo Sierra; wonders finally what might be the new constructive ideology; and replies by propounding the Christian religious attitude as the formula for solidarity. He considers that the most urgent problem is to gain "the conscience of the Mexican collectivity," to organize "the national conscience." [83] The historical reference which permits the master to take up the "liberal tradition" of Mexico and insert it into national trajectory, plus the need for solidarity born of the idea of Christian charity, condenses, as in a formula, the philosophy of Antonio Caso.

Like no other intellectual of his generation, Caso understood how to translate into clear ideas the ideals of the Mexican middle class, and his thought is testimony of the evolution of those ideas from the year 1910 on, his effort to free himself from philosophies learned by mere imitation, his quest for his own roots, his rejection of utopias, his transactions with reality. The apparent contradiction between the two terms of his philosophy, liberalism and charity, is only the expression on the ethicophilosophical plane of the compromise between the liberal past of Mexico and the demands of the peasants and workers who fought in the Revolution. In the same way, the marrow of the program of the Mexican Revolution found its juridical expression in the Constitution of 1917, which upheld, side by side with ethical and political liberalism, an interventionism in material and social matters that converted the state into the protector of the economically weaker classes.

The quest for unity and peace as the integration of the national consciousness, independent of the interests of individuals and groups, is based not only on adherence to political and social ideas which Caso considers to be rationally established on philosophical principles and sociological laws but also upon a national reality, on geographical, historical, and political conditions. These bases made it possible to eliminate the imitation of foreign experience and to discover one's own destiny in its true origins.

Some of the great polemics which Caso carried on in periodicals, in books, and from his university chair are to be explained in the light of the ideas which he defended after 1924 and which we have briefly expounded.

Against the Hispano-American utopias, Caso cited the imperious urgency of more proximate matters and pointed out that the fatherland has priority over race, since it is a reality, just

as race is an ideal, as is humanity.[84] Caso carried on very celebrated campaigns as a publicist, based on the spiritual value of
the person, in defense of the autonomy of the university and the
freedom of teaching. Against Catholicism and Marxism Caso
polemized on the basis of history and reason against what he
considered mystical attitudes.[85] Of his polemic with Marxism
there remained two books and a number of articles in which Caso
accumulated philosophical arguments highly questionable, given
his partial knowledge of the philosophy under discussion, though
this was in no way inferior to the knowledge possessed by his
opponent. But above all there prevailed after 1924 his argument
of national authenticity, presenting Mexican Marxism as an episode more of the imitation of the political ideologies of Europe
than as a doctrine arising from the depth of the fatherland.[86]

With this wide activity as a teacher, writer, and polemicist,
Caso spread and maintained the vitality of those ideas of the
Mexican middle class during the long period when he is the
most outstanding intellectual representative of Mexico. And
this, as Samuel Ramos has said, is what counts:

What matters above all is that the philosophy of Caso has made
history in Mexico. Now indeed the criterion for judging the historical
meaning of a philosophy among us is not the strict originality of its
ideas, but rather its power and its efficacy to work in the course of the
intellectual life of the country, giving impulse to its movement and
opening new avenues to it.[87]

SAMUEL RAMOS

In these ideas [of Antonio Caso] we can encounter, we who now
seek to continue the work of Mexican philosophy, the justification of
our own labors. Even more, in the pattern of Caso's philosophy there
are traced out the paths which we are following again in our reflection
(Samuel Ramos).[88]

Samuel Ramos was born in Zitácuaro on June 8, 1897. Later
he moved to Morelia, where he pursued studies at the National
College of San Nicolás de Hidalgo. There he made the acquaintance of philosophy through contact with a modest medical doctor,

a positivist, José Torres. A second move brought him to Mexico City, where he began the study of medicine, abandoning it, however, almost at once in order to devote himself to philosophy under the direction of Antonio Caso. In 1920 Vasconcelos selected him as a collaborator in the Secretariat of Education, and from that date until his death in 1959 he never left the work of education, either in administration or in the university.[89]

The teaching of Caso and the association with Vasconcelos constituted a decisive experience in the years of Ramos' youth, as he himself has written in the pages of his first book.[90] However, the first book already reveals certain readings, principally Ortega y Gasset and German philosophy as translated in the *Revista de Occidente,* which led him to separate himself from his teachers.

After 1925 there began to make its presence felt in Mexico a generation of intellectuals, those born about 1910, which had closely followed Vasconcelos in the Secretariat of Education and Caso in the university but which, nevertheless, manifested a different sensibility. With the passing of the violent stage of the Revolution, first under the protection of Vasconcelos and later on its own account, a group of young men wholeheartedly dedicated to literature, well acquainted with the European currents, and with a great sense of universality began to exercise its art. First they published *La Falange* (1922–1923); later *Ulises* (1927–1928), and still later, *Contemporáneos* (1928–1931), its most important review, which ended by giving its name to the group.[91] Although more circumspect and discreet than the teachers of the Ateneo, they began promptly enough to exhibit their differences. Samuel Ramos was the first to signal the independence of the group in an essay on Caso which is a settling of accounts with his teacher, not too judicious in tone, to which the latter responded in an essay of little better fortune.[92]

A short time later Ramos left the group, taken up into a larger, more heterogeneous group in which writers of different generations and intellectual disciplines gave themselves to the task of studying the Mexican "reality" under all its aspects. The

Revolution had disclosed a reality which the teachers of the Ateneo had not known at the beginning of their career. By contrast, the later generations had to accept it as their point of departure. We already know to what point Vasconcelos and Caso were no strangers to this movement; still, Ramos was able to see things clearly, to take seriously Caso's statement that the problem of Mexico was a moral problem and that it was urgent to achieve the integration of a national conscience, taking one's point of departure in the knowledge of the immediate reality. For this task he sought aid in the historicism and perspectivism of Ortega y Gasset.

Meanwhile, philosophy appears not to fall within the ideal framework of nationalism because it has always sought to take up as its position a universally human point of view, rebellious at the limitations of time and space. Ortega y Gasset, however, succeeded in resolving the problem by showing the historicity of philosophy in *El tema de nuestro tiempo*. Uniting these ideas with certain others which we had expressed in the *Meditaciones del Quijote,* that Mexican generation found the epistemological justification of a national philosophy.[93]

The passing of the culminating moments of the work of the thinkers of the Ateneo, of the years of greatest enthusiasm, and of the collaboration of the intellectuals with the revolutionary governments, and the shipwreck of the political venture, had left skepticism and bitterness on every hand. Moreover, the decade of the 1930's coincided with the period of the greatest radicalism in the Revolution; in the shadow of the "caudillos" there was accomplished a movement of social reconstruction, the meaning of which was still not clearly to be seen. This brought about the disillusionment of some of the most prominent initiators of the Revolution and occasioned the worst criticism from foreign observers. As a result, the climate of insecurity and depression in which the middle classes of the country lived became more turbid. Under these conditions Ramos had published in 1934 a book, *El perfil del hombre y la culture en México* (The Profile of Man and Culture in Mexico). The content of this book is very complex. It is offered as "an essay in characterology and in the philosophy of culture," and in its first part it compiles a series of historical and social facts and events which serve the author as a basis for pointing up certain notable features of the style of life of the Mexican and certain characteristics of his history which conclude with some notes for the philosophy of the history of Mexico. The central part of the book is a psychological study of the Mexican man. Applying Adler's theories, Ramos discovers an inferiority complex in the Mexican and makes systematic use of this idea to explain his character, both in private life as well as in the examination of certain of the great collective movements.[94] The investigation concludes by suggesting that this sentiment of inferiority has an historical origin which is to be sought in the conquest and colonization, even though it does not show itself until after Independence, when the country had to find its own national physiognomy.[95]

Beyond that sentiment, which serves Ramos in his systematic explanation of the Mexican character, his description discovers other traits equally negative. The justification of these results is to be sought not exclusively in the methods used, which of themselves contribute to the depreciation of the spiritual content of the facts studied, but also in that situation of insecurity and depression suffered by great portions of the population in those years, to which reference has been made above. However, what is of greatest interest is the last portion of the volume, in which Ramos traces the outline of Mexican culture without relying on established methods, but manipulating a series of new concepts suggested by the very complexity of the culture being studied.

The book ends with some notes on how our education and thought ought to be orientated, notes which are related to other writings of the author. In 1939 Ramos published a series of articles against the socialist orientation of education, which resulted in the awakening in Mexico of a vigorous movement of constitutional reform. The principal argument consists in affirming that the system of education which ought to prevail in a country cannot be imposed, since a people is not a plastic material upon which any form whatsoever can be impressed, but is only receptive to that form of culture which corresponds to the particular needs of its character and personality.[96] The basis of any educational reform must be the study of the culture of the man of Mexico, such as the book, to which reference has been made, presents it. However, on this basis education ought to correct vices and cultivate virtues in accord with an ideal orientation which a new philosophical anthropology ought to establish.[97] In seeking this ideal orientation, this integral sense of man, Ramos came into contact with the contradictions which have emerged from the Western tradition: the spiritual sense of life confronted by contemporary materialism. In quest of a "totalizing synthesis" he wrote *Hacia un nuevo humanismo. Programa de una antropología filosófica* (Toward a New Humanism: Program for a Philosophical Anthropology).[98]

Ramos concludes that "man is not exclusively a material being and even less a pure spirit." Spirit is consciousness, direction toward an end having value without, however, having a power of its own to realize that value. By contrast, the inferior endowments of man are the power which the spirit can elevate; every effective spiritual work is the fruit of cooperation between these two opposed elements whose unity of action precisely constitutes human life. According to Ramos the affirmation of the existence of spirit does not amount simply to the re-establishment of a traditional "spiritualism" because it recognizes, on the other hand, the value of vitality as first matter and as power.[99] On the social plane this doctrine returns his central place to man and establishes him as a creative power endowed with liberty in the midst of material conditions. As a consequence, the analogy which Ramos effectively recognizes

between culture and material conditions ("structure" and "super-structure" of Marxism) in a determinate moment of history, must be explained simply because the same spirit has created both.[100]

However, in addition to the program of "philosophical anthropology" Ramos in this book considers the concept of philosophy, the theory of objects, the objectivity of values, liberty and the human person—all of which constitute "a résumé of the philosophical convictions of the author" with the intention of taking part in the philosophical debate now going on in the contemporary world.[101]

The books to which we have referred, leaving aside the youthful essays, constitute the nucleus of the intellectual production of Ramos and sufficiently illustrate the content of his thought, which extends the movement begun by the teachers of the Ateneo de la Juventud, following its liberal, spiritualistic, and humanistic line begun as a reaction to positivism. Accentuating and deepening theories which Caso had only outlined, he raised to a national philosophy the conviction that the salvation of Mexico lay in education and the interest in culture. Approving the most modern European philosophy and acquiescing in the new conditions created by the success of the Mexican Revolution, Ramos undertook "to establish on positive data the ideals of the future life of Mexico." [102] In this he took a step beyond his teachers, who had taken their point of departure in myths or metaphysical and religious principles. By his efforts Ramos contributed to bringing to consciousness the aspirations of many Mexicans, among those who were to hold the decisive powers of the country after 1940, exactly when the reforms which had been accomplished in the previous decade began to show their effects.

CLOSING REMARKS

These notes about Mexican philosophers of the twentieth century constitute merely a contracted scheme in which an effort is made to distinguish, alongside of the well-known high points, a certain line of unity which links together all Mexican thought of the first half of the century. In order to establish this line, we have sought the relation of each author to the Mexican Revolution, the most relevant event in contemporary Mexican history. We have done this even at the risk of leaving out of the field of attention portions, more or less considerable, of its intellectual production and, above all, reducing to mere allusions the influences received from foreign philosophy.

Beyond the obvious limits of space, which impose a very brief exposition, the sketch suffers from other limitations much more essential; it is only a fragment of history that begins with the study of the generation of the Ateneo de la Juventud and stops before reaching the authors who are still living. This is to say that it prescinds from all the students of Antonio Caso, except Samuel Ramos, who for the most part began to publish after 1940; it also prescinds from the Spanish thinkers who were to come to Mexico after 1938 and to become definitely incorporated into its academic life, and from the most recent intellectual undertakings, moved by disciples of those two groups of teachers. By setting aside what is most actual in Mexican thought these lines of unity, which arise in the past and converge on the task of the present, are rendered more obscure. Further, the impossibility of making all the necessary references to other cultural activities, the necessity of leaving out of consideration secondary authors and writers not preoccupied with philosophical questions in the strict sense, leaves the picture incomplete and incurs the risk of making ideas seem original or arbitrary whose existence might be explicable in the light of certain antecedents.

Without doubt the three philosophers studied suffice to place in view two moments of Mexican thought of this century that embrace the activity of two generations. First, the activity of the Ateneo de la Juventud, whose achievement reached its peak about the year 1925; after those years Vasconcelos developed and repeated, with minor variations, the ideas expounded in his earlier works and composed his historical and autobiographical books. Caso remained open to new intellectual developments without, however, altering the essential nucleus of his thought. Next the generation of "Contemporaneos," represented by Ramos, whose work culminated about 1940. Beginning with this date, philosophy in Mexico will be characterized by such a great diversity of currents and movements, by such a richness of themes, that it will no longer be possible to reduce it in a short space to lines so simple, atlhough it will continue the life of reflection upon the Mexican and his culture.

Still the brief period we have studied shows the efforts of thought to make itself equal to a changing reality, and in this its greatest excellence resides. Without doubt, reality has permitted the maintenance of an enduring tendency culminating in a "new humanism" that presents itself to itself as an adequate reflection of the aspirations of the Mexican Revolution. The study of the man of Mexico and the educative efforts to correct his short-comings of character manifest the clear decision to go on to define a type of man more human and more worthy than that which it was possible to realize under "Porfirism," above all, a type of man who is not a fixed entity but rather a modifiable reality and one filled with possibilities which constitute a common responsibility.

NOTES

NOTES TO CHAPTER I
Pages 2–56

1. See Ángel Ma. Garibay K., *Historia de la literatura náhuatl,* 2 vols., Editorial Porrúa, Mexico, 1952–1953. About the beginning of the century Eduard Seler concerned himself with the theme of the authenticity of the texts of pre-Hispanic origin. See, principally, "Die religiösen Gesänge der Alten Mexikaner" in *Gesammelte Abhandlungen zur Amerikanischen Sprach und Altertums Kunde,* 5 vols., Verlag A. Asher and Co., Berlin, 1902–1923, vol. II, pp. 964–1107.

2. See Miguel León-Portilla, *La filosofía náhuatl, estudiada en sus fuentes,* first edition, 1956; second edition, Universidad Nacional Autónoma de México, 1959 (Russian edition, Moscow, 1961; English edition, *Aztec Thought and Culture,* University of Oklahoma Press, Norman, 1963).

3. Among the various studies and critical commentaries published about Nahuatl philosophy, see that of Dr. Francisco Larroyo, "Was there philosophy among the pre-Cortesian peoples?" in *Anuario de Filosofía,* Universidad de México, vol. I, Mexico, 1961, pp. 11–19. See also the comment, from a different point of view, of Patrick Romanell, with regard to the above mentioned work, "La filosofía nahuatl" in *Hispanic American Historical Review,* vol. XXXVII, no. 2, May 1957, pp. 235–236.

4. The theory of "historical invention" is expressed by Edmundo O'Gorman, with a specific application, in the work *La invención de América,* Fondo de Cultura Economica, Mexico, 1958.

5. Among the most important and recent works about the archeological discoveries of ancient Mexico, studied from an esthetic point of view, there may be consulted the following:

Salvador Toscano, *Arte precolumbiano de México y de la América Central,* second edition, Instituto de Investigaciones Estéticas, Mexico, 1952 (A new edition is in preparation).

Justino Fernández, *Arte mexicano, de sus orígenes a nuestros días,* Editorial Porrúa, Mexico, 1961.

Miguel Covarrubias, *Arte indígena de México y Centroamérica,* Universidad Nacional Autónoma de México, Mexico, 1960.

Raúl Flores Guerrero, *Arte mexicana, época prehispánica,* Editorial Hermes, Mexico, 1962.

6. See "Catálogo de los Códices Indígenas del México Antiguo" prepared by Miguel León-Portilla, and Salvador Mateos Higuera, supplement to the *Boletín Bibliográfico de la Secretaría de Hacienda,* no. iii, vol. III, Mexico, June 1957.

7. In the present article there are mentioned the principal manuscripts written in the native idiom.

8. See also the bibliography at the end of the present article.

9. See Manuel Gamio and others, *La población del valle de Teotihuacán,* 3 vols., Dirección de Talleres Gráficos de la Nación, Mexico, 1922. Also: Laurette Séjourné, *Un palacio en la ciudad de los dioses,* Instituto Nacional de Antropología e Historia, Mexico, 1959.

10. The *Historia tolteca-chichimeca* has been reproduced in facsimile in the *Corpus Codicum Americanorum Medii Aevi* (ed. Ernst Mengin), Copenhagen, 1942. There also exists a version of this text in German prepared by the same Ernst Mengin and Konrad Preuss, *Die Mexikanische Bilderhandschrift, Historia tolteca-chichimeca,* vols. I–II, in the Baessler Archiv, Berlin, 1937–1938. Finally, there is an incomplete version in Castilian of the German text, published in *Fuentes para la Historia de México,* Robredo, Mexico, 1947.

11. There exists a German version of this work prepared by Walter Lehmann, "Die Geschichte der Konigreiche von Colhuacan und Mexico" in *Quellenwerke,* Stuttgart, 1938. There is also a more recent Castilian version by Primo Feliciano Velázquez: *Códice Chimalpopoca* (Anales de Cuauhtitlán y Leyenda de los Soles), Instituto de Historia, Imprenta Universitaria, Mexico, 1945.

12. *Códices matritenses,* 3 vols. Facsimile reproduction prepared by Francisco del Pazo y Trenscose, Madrid, 1905–1907. Of the texts contained in the *Códices matritenses* there exist partial versions in German and Spanish. The more recent editions published by the Seminario de Cultura Náhuatl of the Universidad Nacional are supplied by Sahagún:

Ritos, sacerdotes y atavíos de los dioses, Fuentes Indígenas de la Cultura Náhuatl, 1, introduction, paleography, translation, and notes by Miguel León-Portilla, Seminario de Cultura Náhuatl, Instituto Historia, UNAM, Mexico, 1958.

Veinte himnes sacres de los nahuas, Fuentes Indígenas de la Cultura Náhuatl, 2, introduction, paleography, translation, and comments by Ángel Ma. Garibay K., Seminario de Cultura Náhuatl, Instituto de Historia, UNAM, Mexico, 1958.

Vida económica de Tenochtitlán (*I Pochtecáyetl*), paleography, translation, and notes by Ángel Ma. Garibay K., Seminario de Cultura Náhuatl, Instituto de Historia, UNAM, Mexico, 1960.

There exists a partial translation in English of the *Códice florentino:* Florentine Codex, Bks. I, II, III, IV, V, VII, VIII, IX, X, and XII; published by Charles E. Dibble and Arthur O. Anderson, Sante Fe, New Mexico, 1950–1960.

Book VI of the *Códice florentino* (unpublished) is in reality a collection of huehuetlatolli, or "discourses of the ancients" of the greatest importance for the study of the religious and moral thought inherited from Toltec times.

13. There is a facsimile reproduction of this manuscript published by Antonio Peñafiel, *Cantares Mexicanos,* photographic copy, Mexico, 1904.

Dr. Ángel Ma. Garibay K. has published versions of a good part of these texts, both in his *Historia de la literatura náhuatl,* 2 vols, Editorial Porrúa, Mexico, 1953–1954, as well as in other of his works mentioned in the bibliography at the end of these Notes. There is also a partial translation by Leonhard Schultze-Jena, "Alt-Aztekische Gesänge" in *Quellenwerke zur alten Geschichte Amerikas,* vol. VI, Stuttgart, 1957.

14. This is an unpublished manuscript of which some texts have been published by Dr. Garibay and the author.

15. The principal collections of huehuetlatolli are Book VI (unpublished) of the *Códice florentino,* cited above; those brought together by Fray Andres de Olmos, partially included in his *Arte para aprender la lengua mexicana,* Paris, 1875; those which Fray Juan Bautista in a very rare work entitled *Huehuetlatolli o plásticas de los viejos,* Mexico, 1600; as well as those which are preserved unpublished in the National Library of Mexico, in the Library of the University of California at Berkeley, and in the Library of Congress in Washington, D.C.

16. The present work may be considered, from the historiographic point of view, as a resumé of the more ample study published by the author: *La filosofía náhuatl estudiada en sus fuentes,* second edition, Universidad Nacional Autónoma de México, Mexico, 1959.

See also the author's *Tres formas de pensamiento náhuatl,* Seminario de Problemas Científicos y Filosóficos, Universidad Nacional Autónoma de México, Mexico, 1959.

17. When speaking of Quetzalcóatl, various meanings in the application of this term must be distinguished. On the one hand, it is the name of the priest, a cultural hero of Tula, born, it would seem, in the middle of the ninth century A.D. according to the correlation by Walter Lehmann, "Die Geschichte der Königreiche von Colhuacan und Mexico" in *Quellenwerke zur alten Geschichte Amerikas,* vol. I, Stuttgart, 1938. The title or name of Quetzalcóatl is also applied to the supreme dual god, venerated, probably, from Teotihuacanan times. Finally, the high priests of the Aztec religion also adopted this name.

There are two principal sources for the study of the life of Quetzalcóatl, the priest of Tula, in the Nahuatl tongue and further abundant references of a legendary character in the works of the chroniclers, both native and

Spanish, of the sixteenth century. The sources in the Nahuatl tongue are *Anales de Cuauhtitlán* in the *Códice Chimalpopoca*, phototype edition and translation by Primo F. Velázquez, Imprenta Universitaria, Mexico, 1945; and *Códice matritense de la Real Academia*, vol. VIII, facsimile edition of Paso y Troncoso, phototype of Hauser and Menet, Madrid, 1906.

18. The distribution of the world into its four dimensions, and the colors and symbols proper to them, can be principally studied in various codices, some of them of pre-Hispanic origin. See principally the *Códices Borgia and Vaticano B*. It should be added that in these and other codices the cosmic colors are not always the same. The variations probably reflect the symbolisms of what we have called the different schools of thought.

The symbolism of the colors of the various dimensions of the universe is frequent in the greater part of the cultures of ancient Mexico and of other countries of Asia and the Near East. See the recent comparative study by Carrol L. Riley, "Color-Direction Symbolism, an Example of Mexican-South-Western Contacts" in *América Indígena*, Instituto Indígenista Interamericano, vol. XXIII, no. 1, Mexico, January, 1963, pp. 49–60.

19. The very brief exposition which we have given here of the ancient myths which speak of the periodization of the world in ages or cycles is a theme which can be studied extensively in various codices, native texts, and chronicles of the sixteenth century. In the work already cited (*La filosofía náhuatl, estudiada en sus fuentes*, pp. 96–110), there is offered a much more extensive exposition, and there are also included references to eleven principal sources in which the doctrine of the ages or cycles may be studied directly.

20. *Anales de Cuauhtitlán* (*Códice Chimalpopoca*), fol. 4.

21. *Códice matritense de la Real Academia de la Historia*, fol. 176 r.

22. *Ibid.*, fol. 175 v.

23. *Ibid.*, fol. 175 r. and v.

24. *Anales de Cuauhtitlán* (*Códice Chimalpopoca*), fol. 5.

25. *Códice matritense de la Real Academia*, fol. 118 v.

26. *Ibid.*, fol. 109 v.

27. Ms. *Cantares mexicanos*, fol. 2 v.

28. See the Nahuan texts relevant to this possibility open to yóllotl in Miguel León-Portilla, *La filosofía náhuatl, estudiada en sus fuentes,* Universidad Nacional de México, Mexico 1959, pp. 258–271.

29. The texts in Nahuatl about the principle "in qualli, in yectli" may be seen in *La filosofía náhuatl*, cited above, pp. 230–242.

30. *Códice matritense de la Real Academia*, fol. 118 r.

31. Although there exist some works about Nezahualcóyotl as statesman and poet, there continues to be lacking a work which might give a complete idea, on firm historical bases, of his thought as a tlamatini. Unfortunately, there has been a great deal of imaginative thinking about Nezahualcóyotl, attributing to him compositions which, though they may reflect his thought, were not unquestionably his work. See in this regard what is indicated by Ángel Ma. Garibay K., *Historia de la literatura náhuatl*, vol. I, p. 256. Among the more important biographies of Nezahualcóyotl we will

mention only two: José María Vigil, *Nezahualcóyotl, el Rey Poeta,* revised edition, Biblioteca Mínima Mexicana, Ediciones de Andrea, Mexico, 1957. Francis Gillmer, *Flute of the Smoking Mirror* (A Portrait of Nezahualcóyotl), The University of New Mexico Press, 1949.

32. Ms. *Cantares mexicanos,* fol. 17 r.

33. *Ibid.,* fol. 2 v.

34. *Ibid.,* fol. 17 v.

35. *Ibid.,* fol. 70 r.

36. Ms. *Romances de los señores de la Nueva España* (unpublished, in Latin-American Collection of the Library of the University of Texas), fol. 19 v.

37. Ms. *Cantares mexicanos,* fol. 16 v.

38. Ms. *Romances de los señores de la Nueva España,* fol. 35 r.

39. Ms. *Cantares mexicanos,* fol. 13 v.

40. Ms. *Romances de los señores de la Nueva España,* fol. 19 v.–20 r.

41. *Ibid.,* fol. 4 v.–5 v.

42. *Ibid.,* fol. 34 r.

43. Fray Juan de Torquemada, *Monarquía indiana,* third edition (reproduction of the second edition, Madrid, 1723), Editorial Chávez Hayhos, Mexico, 1943, vol. I, p. 171. In this passage Torquemada expresses his doubt and states that he considers Tlacaélel "a fictitious and imaginary person." In contrast with this statement, however, when he treats of the numerous functions of the "cihuacóatl," or counselor of the king (an office which, according to the sources, Tlacaélel filled for the greater part of his life), he agrees that it was extraordinarily important, though he never mentions the name of Tlacaélel. See *ibid.,* vol. II, pp. 351–353.

44. See Fernando Alverado Tozozómoc, *Crónica mexicáyotl,* Nahuatl text and Castilian translation by Adrián León, Instituto de Historia, Universidad Nacional Autónoma de México, Mexico, 1949, especially pp. 96, 122–124.

45. Chimalpain Cuauhtlehuanitzin, Francisco Diego Muñón, *Sixième et septième relations* (1358–1612), published and translated by Remi Simeon, Paris, 1889, p. 85.

46. See "Anales Mexicanos, México-Azcapotzalco, 1426–1589" in *Anales del Museo,* Mexico, 1903, vol. I, 7, pp. 49–74.

Códice Ramírez, Relaciones de origen de los indios que habitan esta Nueva España según sus historias, Editorial Leyenda, Mexico, 1944.

Fray Diego de Durán, *Historia de las Indias de Nueva España y islas de tierra firme,* 2 vols. and atlas, José F. Ramírez, Mexico, 1867–1880.

Crónica mexicana, edited by J. M. Vigil, Editorial Leyenda, Mexico, 1944.

47. The *Códice Cozcatzin* is preserved unpublished in the Collection of Mexican Manuscripts of the National Library in Paris.

Códice Azcatitlan published by the Société des Américainistes de Paris, with commentary by R. H. Barlow, Paris, 1945.

Códice Xólotl, published by Charles E. Dibble, Instituto de Historia, Universidad Nacional de México, Mexico, 1951.

48. Henrico Martinez, *Reportorio de los tiempos e historia natural de Nueva España,* Secretaría de Educación Pública, Mexico, 1948, p. 129.

49. Fray Diego de Durán, *op. cit.*, vol. I, pp. 69–95.

50. *Ibid.*, vol. I, pp. 96–98.

51. Chimalpain, *op. cit.*, p. 106.

52. *Códice Ramírez*, p. 77.

53. *Códice matritense de la Real Academia*, fol. 192 v.

54. Fray Diego de Durán, *op. cit.*, vol. I, p. 95.

55. "Himno a Huitzilopochtli" in *Veinte himnes sacros de los náhuas,* translated by Ángel Ma. Garibay K., Fuentes Indígenas de la Cultura Náhuatl, Instituto de Historia, Universidad Nacional Autónoma de México, Mexico, 1958.

56. *Códice Ramírez*, p. 83.

57. Fray Diego de Durán, *op. cit.*, p. 326. It would seem beyond doubt that the words of Tlacaélel, stating that he had taken part in the government of the Aztec State for eighty or ninety years after the end of the war of Azcapotzalco, are a mere rhetorical exaggeration, since, according to the chronologies ordinarily accepted, Metecuhzoma Ilhuicamina died about 1469, having governed for 29 years. In any case, approximately 43 years had passed since the Tepanecas of Azcapotzalco had been conquered.

58. *Códice Ramírez*, p. 83.

59. Justino Fernández, *Coatlicue, estética del arte indígena antiguo,* second edition, Instituto de Investigaciones Estéticas, Mexico, 1959, pp. 268–269.

60. Ms. *Cantares mexicanos,* fol. 20 v.

61. *Ibid.*, fol. 18 r.

62. For the study of the biography of Tecayehuatzin, one may consult Diego Muñoz Camargo, *Historia de Tlaxcala,* Edición de Chavero, Mexico, 1892, p. 113; *Anales de Cuauhtitlán* in *op. cit.*, fol. 57, and Fray Juan de Torquemada, *Monarquía indiana,* third edition, facsimile reproduction of the second edition (Madrid, 1723, 3 vols.), Mexico, 1943, vol. I, p. 200.

63. Ms. *Cantares mexicanos,* Biblioteca Nacional de México, fol. 9 v. The whole dialogue, translated from Nahuatl into Castilian, has been published in Miguel León-Portilla, *Les antigues mexicanos, a través de sus crónicas y cantares,* Fondo de Cultura Económica, Mexico, 1961, pp 128–137.

64. *Ibid.*, fol. 14 v.

65. *Ibid.*, fol. 10 r.

66. *Ibid.*, fol. 10 v.

67. *Ibid.*, fol. 11 r.

68. *Ibid.*, fol. 11 v.

NOTES TO CHAPTER II
Pages 58–91

1. "What new transpires (in America) is nothing more than the echo of the old world and the reflection of a foreign life." Hegel, *Lectures on the*

Philosophy of Universal History (quoted by the author from the Spanish translation of José Gaos, *Revista de Occidente,* Madrid, 1928, vol. I, p. 186).

2. For example, Frederick Jackson Turner, *The Frontier in American Life,* 1920, a thesis taken up again by Walter Prescott Webb in *The Great Frontier,* 1952. Also the thought-provoking ideas about the "mestizo" of Latin-America as the new historical man of Vicente Riva Palacie, *México a través los siglos,* vol. II, 1884–1889, collected by Justo Sierra and others.

3. Edmundo O'Gorman, *La idea del descubrimiento de América,* Mexico, 1951; *La invención de América,* Mexico, 1958; and the corrected and augmented English edition, *The Invention of America,* Bloomington, Indiana, 1961.

4. We are not unaware of the existence of a small, dissident group of historians of the school of Vignaud that holds that Columbus affirmed that he had the purpose of going to Asia only after he had returned from his first voyage. Apart from the fact that this discrepancy affects our criticism in no way, it has been established that it is without convincing historical basis.

5. Edmundo O'Gorman, *La idea del descubrimiento de América.*

6. See above, note 4.

7. For a discussion about this way of understanding the meaning of the legend of the nameless pilot see Marcel Bataillon and Edmundo O'Gorman, *Dos concepciones de la tarea histórica,* Imprenta Universitaria, Mexico, 1955.

8. This statement appeared for the first time in Gonzalo Fernández de Oviedo y Valdéz, *Sumario de la natural historia de las Indias,* Toledo, 1526.

9. Reference is to the thesis of Oviedo, who identified America with the Hesperides, and of Francisco López de Gomara, who accepted as certain the intervention of the nameless pilot. For an exposition of these theses see O'Gorman, *La idea del descubrimiento de América,* pp. 53–89.

10. This solution was formulated by the bastard son of Christopher Columbus, Don Fernando Colon, in his *Vida del almirante,* first edition in Italian, Venice, 1571. See also O'Gorman, *La idea del descubrimiento de América,* pp. 93–127.

11. This solution was formulated at great length by Baron Alexander von Humboldt, *Cosmos,* 1845–1859; see O'Gorman, *La idea del descubrimiento de América,* pp. 266–302.

12. Thus, for example, in the most recent and authoritative history of Columbus: Samuel Eliot Morison, *Admiral of the Ocean Sea,* Boston, 1942, vol. I, p. 77.

13. This supposition that it was America herself that revealed her being to being perceived involuntarily shows through the images employed by the historians when they describe the moment at which, in their view, the discovery of America took place. Morison, for example, writes: "Never again may mortal men hope to recapture the amazement, the wonder, the delight of those October days in 1492 when the New World gracefully yielded her virginity to the conquering Castilians." *Admiral of the Ocean Sea,* vol. I, p. 308.

14. In a more complete exposition one would have to give an account of two relatively accidental, but important questions: (1) of the process itself of the interpretation of Columbus' act as a discovery, and (2) how the absurdity to which this process reduces itself has passed unnoticed. Here we shall be content with the most pertinent observations. The problem implied in the first question is to explain how the interpretation arose and why it maintained itself after the first, but above all, after the second failure. For one who wishes to understand, the answer is obvious: the essentialist idea conditions the entire process, and if one asks why it acquired such a powerful influence, the answer must be that it is only a particular instance of the influence which for centuries of thought was possessed by the classical substantialist idea, which sees in the being of things an essence immanent to them. The second question clarifies itself by the equivocation which the formulation of the casual discovery of America contains. As a matter of fact, the "casual" act is, strictly speaking, the sighting of the island and not the "discovery"; however, as it is supposed that to show the existence of a thing is equivalent to the revelation of its being, the casualness of the one is transferred to the other. Thus, when they tell us that Columbus casually discovered America when he came upon that island, what is really being said is that when Columbus chanced upon it, America revealed itself in the form of an occult quality or essence which is already possessed at that moment.

15. O'Gorman, *La invención de América* and its revised and enlarged edition. See above, note 3.

16. O'Gorman, *The Invention of America*, pp. 79–88.

17. For these details, see *ibid.*, pp. 88–122.

18. Thus I translate the word "invenio," which usually is translated by the verb "to discover" (descubrir). For a justification of my procedure, see O'Gorman, *The Invention of America*, note 117, on pp. 167–168.

19. It has been insisted from the first and with many conspicuous repetitions that the name "America" involves an injustice to Columbus. This would certainly be the case if the thesis about discovery was correct or certain, though even then the fault would in no way fall on Vespucci. Roberto Levillier has answered to the point in his fine and important book *América la bien llamada*, Buenos Aires, 1948. We gladly acknowledge the debt we owe to the distinguished Argentine historian, although we differ in respect to the scope of Vespucci's intervention. See O'Gorman, *The Invention of America*, p. 122.

20. Before this great geographical revolution, a transatlantic voyage was a venture into cosmic space in the same sense that the imminent interplanetary voyages are. The great difference, however, is that the former was rigorously and literally "to leave the world," while now, since the invention of America, such a tremendous experience is no longer possible, strictly speaking, because the world has no limits in principle.

21. Francisco López de Gamora, *Historia general de las Indias*, Zaragoza, 1522–1533. In the dedicatory "Epistle" to the emperor he says that the

natural features of America are very different from those of the Old World and adds that this "is no small consideration of the Creator, since the elements are the same, there as here." On the general meaning of Joseph de Acoata *Historia natural y moral de las Indias,* Seville, 1590, see my preface to the Mexican edition, Fonde de Cultura Económica, 1962.

22. It is evident that in the case of the essentialist idea that was held traditionally about America, it is not possible to understand the concept of this entity as a "New World" according to the explanation we have given. In fact, it is impossible to think how America could be a "new world" if it is believed that it had existed forever. This lack of comprehension is already to be observed in those writers of the sixteenth century who do not know the reason why America was conceived in this fashion. Francisco López de Gomara, in the work and passages cited above, offers four different reasons which alone show the reigning confusion on these matters. The expression "new world" and other similar terms such as "new orb" and "other world" were employed by Padre Mártir, Colón, and Vespucci. However, their meaning is different from that which we have made clear because they imply an unacceptable duality of worlds. For this reason Vespucci abandoned their use. See O'Gorman, *The Invention of America,* in the passages indicated under the entry "World" in the index.

23. The idea of cultural Europocentrism found new and vigorous affirmation in Herder, whose ideas had so much influence on the great German idealist thinkers and through them on many contemporary thinkers.

24. We should make clear that there is no question of a fatalistic predetermination because the goal is not postulated as the objective of a metahistorical intention as in the divine designs of providence or the intentions of nature in idealism.

25. This would be the moment to explain the manner in which the ancient cultures of the original inhabitants of the lands known by the Europeans as American were understood. Rigorously, they represented an obstacle to the effort to transpose the old Europe. Thus, no proper historical meaning is assigned them. If he accepted them as expressions of the form of life proper to "natural man"—that is, man simply as the apex of the hierarchy of living beings—the most he conceded was to interpret them as the results of a divine design that prepared the advent of the Gospel, so that their meaning depended on an external factor, which was nothing else, it is clear, than European history extended to become universal history.

26. Justice demands that we recognize the profoundly modern understanding shown by Ferdinand the Catholic of the entire American problem. The regrettable thing was that on the death of Isabelle his influence in these matters was practically eliminated.

27. Edmundo O'Gorman, "Precedentes y sentido de la Revolutión de Ayutla" in *Plan de Ayutla: Commemoración de su primer centenario,* Imprenta Universitaria, Mexico, 1954. In other studies we have outlined some of the ideas contained in this essay. See O'Gorman, "La historiografía" in *México: cincuenta años de revolución,* Fonde de Cultura Económico, Mex-

ico, 1960–1962, vol. IV, pp. 191–203; and my preface to the English edition of the *Evolución política del pueblo mexicano* of Justo Sierra soon to be published by the University of Texas.

NOTES TO CHAPTER IV
Pages 130–183

1. In addition to the texts themselves, the article by F. López Cámara, "El cartesianismo en Sor Juana y Sigüenza y Góngora," has been of inestimable help in the preparation of this work; but above all, I owe a debt to the study by Doctor José Gaos, "El sueño de un sueño," whose conclusions have been made use of to a great extent here.

2. The nun herself assigns greater importance, in the *Respuesta a Sor Filotea*, pp. 470–471, to the *Primero sueño;* "I have never written anything by my own will . . . ; so that I do not recall having written anything entirely to my own taste, except the short work called the *Dream*."

3. José Gaos, *op. cit.,* p. 68.

4. *Ibid.,* p. 69: "Though imagined, created, or poetic, it does not prove precisely false, but, quite the contrary, supremely true, with the truth that comes from transposing and expounding as a dream the concept of the whole of life as a dream and the experience of the desire for knowledge as a dream." However, Sor Juana herself was careful to point out in the *Respuesta a Sor Filotea*, p. 460, the philosophical truth-value of what she discoursed upon while dreaming. She says that not even the dream freed the imaginative faculty from thinking: "indeed it could work in it (the dream) more freely and unimpededly, confirming with greater clarity and tranquillity the impressions which it had preserved from the day, arguing, composing verses, of which you could make a very great catalogue and of certain reasonings and nuances of thought which I have achieved better asleep than awake."

5. The entire *Primero sueño* indicates this universal desire for knowledge. The *Respuesta a Sor Filotea* tells how, from the time she was a girl, this restlessness for knowledge guided her steps. There was no knowledge that she considered foreign to her; her understanding never rested, not even when her superioress or the doctors took away her books.

6. Sor Juana, *Primero sueño*, p. 346, where we find: "the quick vision freely sweeps what lies before the eyes, without fearing distance, or being afraid of any opaque obstacle or interposed object, and freely moves through all the realm of creation."

7. Sor Juana, *Respuesta a Sor Filotea*, pp. 463–464: "Oh, if all of us— and I, who am ignorant, the first—would take the measure of our talent before studying . . . With ambitious covetousness to equal or even to surpass others, how little courage would remain with us and from how many errors we would spare ourselves and how many twisted intelligences that move about everywhere would not do so."

8. See José Gaos, *op. cit.,* p. 61: "The attested astronomical knowledge

remains within the old and mediaeval system of the world, still dominant, even among the cultivated ... who knew about the Copernican system. However, if the physiological knowledge exceeds such knowledge. ... The description of sleeping and waking ... indicates a reading of medical books or conversation on medical material."

9. Sor Juana, "Loa para San Ermenegildo," *Obras completas,* vol. III, pp. 98–99: "I pray you, wait awhile and do not, so incensed in your opinion and obstinate, give utterance to words, thinking the force of the argument is there; it is not a question of words, but a contest of concepts, and with reason as judge, he who disputes most subtly and not he who shouts the loudest will win."

10. See Sor Juana, *Respuesta a Sor Filotea,* pp. 468–469.

11. José Gaos, *op. cit.,* p. 37, describes the meaning of the poem in this way: "the *Dream* is the poem of the dream of the desire for knowledge as a dream. ... The poetess creates a fiction, a fable, pretending to dream which she has experienced when quite awake: that the desire for knowledge is a dream, a chimera. ... Further, the *Respuesta a Sor Filotea* is fundamentally a statement justifying this desire."

12. Sor Juana, *Primero sueño,* pp. 353–354.

13. *Ibid.,* p. 349: "permitting it hardly to draw, from a confused concept, the embryonic report which, not properly formed, showed an unordered chaos, full of confused impressions put together in complete disorder and separated in the same manner, impressions which, the more they are combined, the more disunited and full of diversity they appear."

14. *Ibid.,* pp. 349–352.

15. *Ibid.,* p. 350.

16. José Gaos, *op. cit.,* p. 65, says: "Neither of the two methods come to the poetess from Cartesianism. Between the *Discourse on Method* of Descartes and the method of which the poem speaks there is no relation but the word "method."

17. Sor Juana, *Primero sueño,* pp. 353–354.

18. *Ibid.,* p. 355.

19. An important factor in the flux of indecision is the fear of going beyond truths imposed either by education or by the will of men. In the *Respuesta a Sor Filotea,* pp. 443–444, she says with regard to sacred themes: "I confess that many times this fear has taken the pen from my hand and has pushed things back to the same understanding from which they would like to originate. ... What understanding, what study, what materials, what preparations for it do I have except four superficial generalities? Leave these matters for one who understands them because I do not want trouble with the Holy Office, because I am ignorant and tremble to utter any proposition which does not sound right or to twist a meaning in any place."

20. Sor Juana, *Primero sueño,* p. 356.

21. See José Gaos, *op. cit.,* p. 65: "the 'if' intuition and discourse are the methods of the entire intellectual tradition because they are the only methods possible for all intellectual activity, the dream of the failure of

both methods becomes nothing less than the dream of the failure of all the methods of human knowledge and the entire intellectual tradition."

22. *Ibid.*, p. 67.

23. Sor Juana, *Respuesta a Sor Filotea*, pp. 447–448: "always directing the steps of my study to the height of Sacred Theology; for it seemed necessary to me that in order to reach that place, I had to climb by the steps of the human sciences and arts; for how was one to understand the style of the Queen of the Sciences if one did not understand that of the handmaidens? How, without logic, could one know the general and special methods with which Sacred Scripture is written? How, without Physics, could one know so many cultural questions of the natures of the animals, of the sacrifices where so many things once declared are symbolized and many others that exist?"

24. José Gaos, *op. cit.*, p. 70.

25. *Ibid.*, p. 71.

26. All the references of the *Libra* will be placed in the text, indicating the paragraphs to which they correspond. I acknowledge, in justice, that I owe a great deal of what is here stated to my teacher, Dr. José Gaos, whose *Preface* to the *Libra* not only has provided me with definitive criteria but also with dates, judgments, and interpretations which are too numerous to enumerate.

27. He distinguishes, of course, between astronomy and astrology; he denies the common opinions about the sublunary changes caused by the stars; he refutes the opinion that the comets were announcements of calamities and were formed of the "exhalations of dead bodies" and of human sweat; he shows how all these errors were based on a false science, superstition, and false fears.

28. The fact that Don Carlos opposes the free exercise of reason to authority does not mean that he accords little importance to the classic writers. On the contrary, custom and necessity made it necessary for him to quote about two hundred of them, among which are "biblical, Greek, Latin, scientific, and literary" writers. The criterion varies. Sometimes it is the modern against the traditional; at other times, the traditional confronting the traditional. In expounding a mathematical explanation, he likes to point out that this is the way it is found in the books; or sometimes, when doubting some observations, he asks in what books they are to be found or to which writers they are to be referred. And, if indeed he affirms that authority is valid in matters of fact, but not in scientific matters, he uncritically mixes authors of different standing and different times, and his preferences are not based on modern reasons. See José Gaos, *Libra astronómica y filosófica*, Presentación, pp. xvi–xvii.

29. *Ibid.*, p. xv.

30. *Ibid.*, p. xviii.

31. *Ibid.*, p. xi.

32. See Germán Posada Mejía, *Literatura histórica en el México del siglo XVIII.*

33, See Bernabé Navarro, *La introducción de la filosofía moderna en México*, Chap. II.

34. José Miranda in his book *Humboldt y México* makes the first classification of the period of the Mexican Illumination. With numerous data and good judgment he has made clear the events necessary for understanding the progress of ideas. Nevertheless, he attributes to the movement a greater slowness than it actually had and, above all, insists on indicating as its principal cause the influence of Spain, almost forgetting the impulse given by the Neo-Hispanic writers themselves. Thus he assigns the definitive triumph of the Illumination to enlightened despotism, which, beginning in 1775, sent true scientists and created institutions destined for the study of science. But by this time our Illumination was aready established both in philosophy and science. The works and documents show that the professors arrived from Spain did not bring new ideas with them but, on the contrary, took advantage of the modern climate created by the Creoles.

35. Monelisa Lina Pérez-Marchand, *Des etapas ideológicas del siglo XVIII en México a través de los papeles de la Inquisición.*

36. See Pablo González Casanova, *El misoneísmo y la modernidad cristiana en el siglo XVIII.*

37. Samuel Ramos, *Historia de la filosofía en México,* p. 86.

38. In this regard, José Gaos says in his preface to the *Tratados* of Gamarra, p. xxv: "The tenuousness of the vein of philosophy *in the strict sense* in the Spanish speaking countries compared with the peoples who are the protagonists of modern western philosophy, has had the effect of moving the writers of the *History of Philosophy* in our countries to include something more than philosophemes and philosophers, at least the teaching of philosophy and what is implied in it or related to it, teaching centers, teaching publications or to approach the true history of philosophy."

39. Space forbids us to consider the ideas of Gamarra, Alzate, Bartolache, and Hidalgo. Those interested may consult the works of the present author: "Alzate y la filosofía de la ilustración," *Filosofía y Letras,* no. 37, for Alzate; "Descartes en la filosofía de la ilustración mexicana," *Filosofía y Letras,* no. 39, for Bartolache; "Teología ilustrada de Hidalgo," *Historia Mexicana,* no. 9, for Hidalgo. On Gamarra the following writings may be consulted: Victoria Junco Posadas, *Algunas aportaciones al estudio de Gamarra o el eclecticismo en México* (thesis), Mexico, 1944; Juan Benito Díaz de Gamarra, *Tratados,* edited and preface by José Gaos, UNAM, 1947; *ibid.,* *Elementos de filosofía moderna,* vol. I, preface and notes by Bernabé Navarro, UNAM, 1963.

40. These facts, which culminate in the person of Clavijero, have occasioned a very thought-provoking study by José Miranda, "Clavijero en la ilustración mexicana," *Cuadernos Americanos,* July–August 1946, p. 180 sqq.

41. Following the idea of Pedro Henríquez Ureña, as well as the theses of Gabriel Méndez Plancarte, Navarro investigated the sources of the Jesuit movement in his work *La introducción de la filosofía moderna en México.* Here we do nothing else but make use of the documents to which he makes reference; in some instances we also follow his interpretations. However, we are in disagreement with his opinion that the Jesuits restored scholasticism and were not moderns. The very same documents lead us to

an opinion contrary to his. Neither can we accept the importance assigned
to the Jesuits in comparison to the other orders, the diocesan clergy, and
the university.

42. *Ibid.*, p. 155.

43. *Ibid.*, p. 229.

44. Clavijero, *Historia antigua de México,* vol. I, p. 47.

45. B. Navarro, *op. cit.*, p. 131.

46. *Ibid.*, p. 176.

47. J. L. Maneiro and M. Fabri, *Vidas de mexicanos ilustres del siglo
XVIII*, p. 16.

48. *Ibid.*, p. 123.

49. J. L. Maneiro and M. Fabri, *op. cit.*, p. 23.

50. B. Navarro, *op. cit.*, p. 129.

51. *Ibid.*, pp. 193–194.

52. *Ibid.*, p. 181.

53. *Ibid.*, p. 184.

54. In some places they show, as earlier in Singüenza y Góngora and
later in Gamarra, the limits of their knowledge. For example, Clavijero
affirms nothing about the substance of the heavens, the ether, since "as
philosophers we say nothing because it is a matter far removed from the
human mind." *Ibid.*, p. 187. See also pp. 191–192.

55. Bernabé Navarro studied the Jesuits from two points of view: that
they are purely and simply scholastics, that their modernity is an inclination, residing in an extrinsic method and not in their doctrines. He was thus
able to maintain that their task consisted in renewing the tradition and that
their physical science did not destroy metaphysics, the more so because
they distinguished between the phenomenal and the noumenal orders. But
all this goes contrary to the texts adduced to prove it.

56. B. Navarro, *op. cit.*, p. 115.

57. *Ibid.*, p. 145.

58. *Ibid.*, p. 180.

59. Abad exemplifies this attitude: "I have also tried in teaching you,"
he writes at the end of his metaphysics, "to treat not only the peripatetic
doctrines but also the more recent philosophers, in such wise that you may
understand them yourselves." *Ibid.*, p. 174.

60. For more information see Chapter IV-1 of B. Navarro, *op. cit.*

61. B. Navarro, *op. cit.*, p. 149.

62. *Ibid.*, p. 155.

63. *Ibid.*, p. 165.

64. *Ibid.*, p. 161.

65. *Ibid.*, p. 162.

66. *Ibid.*, p. 187. Navarro by contrast thinks (p. 188) that the atoms
are accepted as elements in the purely physical order and that matter and
form remain as principles of the metaphysical order.

67. Alegre says in this regard: "in special physics I treated first of the
heavens . . . remaining in what appeared to me the system of Tycho Brahe."
B. Navarro, *op. cit.*, p. 147.

68. For this whole question see pages 183–186 of the work cited.
69. B. Navarro, *op. cit.*, p. 147.
70. J. J. de Eguiara y Eguren, *Anteloquia,* p. 30, says: "The philosophy of Gassendi and Descartes and that which outside Spain is studied by cultured men not only pleased them a great deal, but they have drunk of it and have made it known in their writings as occasion offered without, however, departing from our predecessors and from the peripatetic philosophy."
71. B. Navarro, *op. cit.*, p. 193.
72. *Ibid.*, p. 184.
73. *Ibid.*, p. 177.
74. See *Humanistas del siglo XVIII,* edited with an introduction by Gabriel Méndez Plancarte.

Notes to Chapter V
Pages 184–219

1. Gabriel Méndez Plancarte, *Humanistas del siglo XVIII,* UNAM, 1941, pp. 47, 49.
2. See Monelina Lina Pérez Marchand, *Dos etapas ideológicas del siglo XVIII en México a través de los papeles de la inquisición,* Colegio de México, 1945.
3. See José Miranda, "El influjo político de Rousseau en la Independencia mexicana" (The Political Influence of Rousseau on Mexican Independence) in *Presencia de Rousseau,* UNAM, 1962, p. 262.
4. Resolution of the Ayuntamiento of Mexico City, session of July 19, 1808, in Genaro García, *Documentos históricos mexicanos,* Museo Nacional, Mexico, 1910, vol. II, doc. 3.
5. "Memoria póstuma del licenciado Verdad" (Posthumous Memorial of the Advocate Verdad) under date of September 12, 1808, in G. García, *op. cit.*, vol. II, doc. 53.
6. Vote on the proposition presented by Villaurrutia, in G. García, *op. cit.*, vol. II, doc. 46.
7. "Memoria póstuma del licenciado Verdad" in G. García, *op. cit.*, vol. II, doc. 53.
8. Vote on the proposition presented by Villaurrutia, in G. García, *op. cit.*, vol. II, doc. 46.
9. "Congreso Nacional de las Colonias" in G. García, *op. cit.*, vol. VII.
10. Quoted by Servando Teresa de Mier, *Historia de la revolución de Nueva España, antiguamente Anáhuac,* by José Guerra (pseudonym of de Mier), London, 1813, vol. I, p. 90.
11. "Acta del Ayuntamiento de México," July 19, 1808, in G. García, *op. cit.*, vol. II, doc. 3.
12. "Representación Nacional de las Colonias" and deposition in its process, in G. García, *op. cit.*, vol. II, p. 40.
13. The following opinion of Jesús Reyes Heroles summarizes the situation well: "The contractual explanation of the origin of civil society . . .

neither necessarily nor exclusively found its inspiration in Rousseau. In some cases it is pre-Rousseauan, finding support in what we might call the traditional Spanish idea, centering about the estates and conceiving liberties as privileges, duly modified and semimodernized by Spanish authors like Martínez Marina and Jovellanos, a line of thought which provided the basis of the effort toward Independence in Mexico in 1808; or perhaps in authors who, situated in the rationalist and modern current of thought, are also earlier than Rousseau, as is the case of Grotius, Hobbes, or Locke," in "Rousseau y el liberalismo mexicano" (Rousseau and Mexican Liberalism) in *Presencia de Rousseau,* UNAM, 1962, pp. 301–302.

14. José Miranda, *Las ideas a instituciones políticas mexicanas; primera parte, 1521–1820,* Instituto de Derecho Comparado, UNAM, 1952, pp. 277, 280.

15. Exposition of August 31, 1808, in G. García, *op. cit.,* vol. II, doc. 55.

16. "Memoria póstuma del licenciado Verdad" in G. García, *op. cit.,* vol. II, doc. 53.

17. See José Miranda, *Las ideas a instituciones políticos mexicanas; primera parte, 1521–1820,* pp. 127 sqq., 135 sqq.

18. Vote on the proposition presented by Villaurrutia, in G. García, *op. cit.,* vol. II, doc. 46.

19. "Memoria póstuma del licenciado Verdad" in G. García, *op. cit.,* vol. II, doc. 53.

20. Report on the junta of August 9, 1808, reviewed by the "Real Acuerdo," in G. García, *op. cit.,* vol. II, doc. 51.

21. "Manifesto contra el edicto de la Inquisición" (Manifesto Against the Edict of the Inquisition).

22. Letter to Calleja of April 22, 1811, in Carlos María Bustamante, *Cuadro histórico de la Revolución Mexicana,* second edition, M. Lara, Mexico, 1843–1946, vol. I, p. 208.

23. *Semanario Patriótico Americano,* n. 7, and *El Ilustrador Americano,* n. 5.

24. *Semanario Patriótico Americano,* n. 4, and *Quinto Juguetillo,* Mexico, 1812.

25. See Mier (Guerra), *Historia de la revolución de Nueva España, antiguamente Anáhuac,* London, 1813.

26. A certain parallelism can be noted between these ideas of Mier about America and other similar ideas of Jovellanos on Spain. Jovellanos, too, sought for a Spanish "constitution" which had been "lost" and to which a return should be made (Letter to Dr. Prado, cited by Jean Sarraulh, *La España ilustrada de la segunda mitad del siglo XVIII,* Fondo de Cultura Económica, Mexico, 1957, p. 574). Nevertheless, the idea does not seem to have performed a central function in the Spanish author nor did it have the same consequences, as in the corresponding reflection of Mier.

27. "Manifesto contra el edicto de la Inquisición" (Manifesto Against the Edict of the Inquisition).

28. "Causa contre Allende, ampliación a la pregunta 63" (Process

Against Allende, Elaboration Relative to Question 63) in G. García, *op. cit.*, vol. VI.

29. *Semanario Patriótico Americano*, nos. 24 and 25.

30. José Miranda thought that he saw in this expression a Rousseauan echo ("El influjo político de Rousseau en la Independencia mexicana," *op. cit.*, p. 275). Nevertheless, it seems to me that "voz commún de la nación" would sound equally familiar to any hearer who did not know Rousseau if he were at all familiar with the juridical current which took its source in Suárez. It proves, as a matter of fact, impossible to determine the exact origin of expressions of this type if one takes them in isolation from the real context, for in them modern and traditional ideas coincide. The general ideological context and the political use made of them should decide their meaning.

31. Issue of November 17, 1810, and "Desengaño a los americanos . . ." in *Morelos, documentos inéditos y poco conocidos,* Museo Nacional, SEP, 1927, vol. I, issue of March 23, 1813; in Alfonso Teja Zabre, *Morelos,* Espasa Calpe, Buenos Aires, 1946, p. 145.

32. "Sentimientos a la Nación" in *Morelos, documentos inéditos y poco conocides,* vol. II.

33. Hernández y Dávalos, *Colección de documentos para la guerra de Independencia de México de 1808 a 1821,* Mexico, 1877, vol. I, doc. 287.

34. Hernández y Dávalos, *op. cit.,* vol. III, doc. 95.

35. Letter to Riaño from Celaya, September 21, 1810, in *Documentos de la guerra de Independencia,* SEP, Mexico, 1945, p. 11.

36. *Semanario Patriótico Americano,* n. 7.

37. "Desengaños de los americanos . . ." in *Morelos, documentos inéditos poco conocides,* vol. I.

38. *El Despertador Americano,* n. 9.

39. Mier (Guerra), *op. cit.,* vol. I, p. 272.

40. Mier, "Situación de las castas en América" in *Escritos inéditos,* El Colegio de México, Mexico, 1944, p. 335.

41. Proclamation of September 10, 1811, in Lucas Alamán, *Historia de Méjico,* Editorial Jus, Mexico, 1942, vol. II, p. 592.

42. Speech before the Congress of Chilpancingo, in *Morelos, documentos inéditos y poco conocides,* vol. I, p. 180.

43. *El Pensador Mexicano,* n. 3.

44. In *La Revolución de Independencia,* p. 102, he maintained that the principal source of inspiration had been that of the Constitution of Cádiz, based on a statement of Morelos himself. However, the analysis of the Constitution of Apatzingán made by Morelos shows that little was taken from the Spanish Constitution directly; the similarity between the two constitutions is to be traced, much more probably, to the common sources which they shared (see J. Miranda, *Las ideas . . . ,* pp. 362–363).

45. "Puede ser libre la Nueva España?" (Can New Spain Be Free?) in *Escritos inéditos,* El Colegio de México, Mexico, 1944, p. 215.

46. *Ibid.*

47. *El Ilustrador Americano,* n. 21.
48. Proclamation of Iturbide in Iguala on February 24, 1821, in *Documentos de la guerra de Independencia,* SEP, Mexico, 1945.
49. *Ibid.*
50. Carlos Navarro y Rodrigo, *Vida y memorias de Agustín de Iturbide,* A. Pola, Mexico, 1906, p. 342.
51. Letter of José Ma. Tornel to Santa Anna, December 16, 1822, in *Gaceta Imperial de México,* n. 146.
52. Carlos Navarro y Rodrigo, *op. cit.,* p. 342.
53. See J. Miranda, "El influjo político de Rousseau en la Independencia mexicana," *op. cit.,* pp. 267–276.
54. Speech of Iturbide on the occasion of the installation of the "Junta Nacional Instituyente" in *Gaceta Imperial de México,* n. 132.

NOTES TO CHAPTER VII
Pages 246–287

1. Pedro Henríquez Ureña, "Horas de estudio" (Hours of Study) (1910) in *Obra crítica,* edited by E. S. Speratti Piñero, Fondo de Cultura Económica, Mexico, 1960, p. 52.
2. Justo Sierra, "Discurso pronunciado en la velada que tuvo lugar en el Teatro Arbeu, la noche del 22 de marzo de 1908, en honor del maestro don Gabino Barreda" (Discourse Pronounced at the Soirée Which Took Place at the Arbeu Theatre, the Evening of March 22, 1908, in Honor of Maestro Don Gabino Barreda) in *Discursos* (Discourses), vol. V of *Obras Completas,* Universidad Nacional de México, Mexico, 1948, pp. 387–396.
Concerning the intellectual evolution of Justo Sierra see Agustín Yáñez, *Don Justo Sierra, su vida, sus ideas y su obra* (Don Justo Sierra: His Life, His Ideas, and His Work), second edition, UNAM, Mexico, 1962. See especially Chapter VIII.
3. The following also formed part of the group, or worked with it, in one field or another: Jesús T. Acevedo, Alfonso Gravioto, Ricardo Gómez Robelo, Manuel de la Parra, Luis Castillo Ledón, Nemesio García Naranjo, Roberto Argüelles Bringas, Edwardo Colín, Genaro Fernández MacGregor, Isidro Fabela, Julio Torri, Martín Luis Guzmán, Rafael López, Roberto Montenegro, Diego Rivera, Carlos González Peña, Manuel Ponce, Mariano Silva y Acévez, Federico Mariscal, and others. Special attention is merited by the Dominican Pedro Henríquez Ureña, who came to Mexico in those years and with his enthusiasm and spirit of work brought about the spiritual community of the group.
4. The chronicle of these events may be found in Alfonso Reyes, *Pasado inmediato y otros ensayos* (The Immediate Past and Other Essays), El Colegio de México, Mexico, 1941; in Pedro Henríquez Ureña, "Horas de estudio" (Hours of Study), *op. cit.,* and *ibid.,* "La influencia de la revolución en la cultura intelectual de México" (The Influence of the

Revolution on the Intellectual Life of Mexico) and "La Cultura de las humanidades" (The Culture of the Humanities) in *Obra crítica*.

5. This series was under the patronage of Justo Sierra and Ezequiel A. Chávez, Secretary and Undersecretary, respectively, of Public Instruction and Beaux Arts, who also presided over some of the sessions. The publication of the lectures was under the patronage of Pablo Macedo, director of the School of Jurisprudence, and these appeared under the title *Conferencias del Ateneo de la Juventud* (Lectures of the Ateneo de la Juventud), Imprenta Lecaud, Mexico, 1910. In 1962 the University of Mexico reprinted the volume with a preface by Juan Hernández Luna, who also added as appendices some texts by Pedro Henríquez Ureña, José Vasconcelos, Alfonso Reyes, and Vicente Lombardo Toledano.

6. Henríquez Ureña, "Horas de estudio" (Hours of Study) (1910) in *Obra crítica*, p. 72.

7. Criticism has not directed its attention to this point; nevertheless it is indubitable that Christianity is not absent from the work of any of the members of the Ateneo, but constituted an essential element in the philosophical thought of the most important of them, some of whom developed in the direction of an orthodox Catholicism; and in a group of young liberals so alert to the intellectual movement of their time, family education does not seem to offer an adequate explanation of this fact. On the other hand, Antonio Caso makes reference to "religious modernism" when he enumerates the philosophical schools then vigent in his polemic of 1922 with the "renegade" positivist Francisco Bulnes. Cited by Juan Hernández Luna, who summarized the polemic in *Antonio Caso: embajador extraordinario de México* (Antonio Caso: Ambassador Extraordinary of Mexico), SALM, Mexico, 1963.

8. Henríquez Ureña, "Horas de estudio" (Hours of Study) in *Obra crítica*, pp. 52 ff.

9. José Vasconcelos, "Don Gabino Barreda y las ideas contemporáneas" in *Obras completas*, Libreros Mexicanos Unidos, Mexico, 1957, pp. 37 ff. The law of the three stages has also been discussed by Caso in his lectures of 1909 on the history of positivism and by Pedro Henríquez Ureña in his comments on these essays in "Horas de estudio."

10. Vicente Lombardo Toledano called attention to this since 1930 in *El sentido humanista de la Revolución Mexicana*, vol. I, no. 2, of the *Revista Universidad de México*, reprinted by Hernández Luna in the volume *Conferencias del Ateneo de la Juventud*, UNAM, Mexico, 1962. More recently, Emilio Uranga in "El pensamiento filosófico" in *Mexico: 50 años de revolución* (Mexico: 50 Years of Revolution), Fondo de Cultura Económica, Mexico, 1962, vol. IV, pp. 541–544.

11. Vicente Lombardo Toledano, *op. cit.*, in *Conferencias del Ateneo de la Juventud*, p. 173.

12. The phrase is that of Antonio Caso in an interview given in 1921, quoted by Juan Hernández Luna in *Antonio Caso: embajador extraordinario de México*, p. 54. On the political significance of positivism in these years consult section five of the study by Leopoldo Zea, *Apogeo y decadencia*

del positivismo en México (Apogee and Decadence of Positivism in Mexico), El Colégio de México, Mexico, 1944.

13. The observation is that of José Gaos, *Filosofía mexicana de nuestros días* (Mexican Philosophy in Our Times), Imprenta Universitaria, Mexico, 1954, p. 73.

14. In the year 1920, 23.7 per cent of the population was engaged in agriculture and only 3.7 in industry, while the services of the bureaucracy, traditional refuge of the middle classes, represented 2.4 per cent. Data from A. González Cosío, "Clases y estratos sociales" (Social Classes and Strata) in *México: 50 años de revolución,* vol. II, p. 54. Madero refers to the middle class as to the discontent of the "poor intellectuals" in his *La sucesión presidencial,* quoted by Victor Alba in *Las ideas sociales contemporáneas en México* (Contemporary Social Ideas in Mexico), Fondo de Cultura Económica, Mexico, 1960, p. 148.

15. Statement of P. Romanell, *La formación de la mentalidad mexicana. Panorama actual de la filosofía en México,* El Colégio de México, Mexico, 1954, p. 75. In the same sense Victor Alba refers to the "preparers of the Revolution" in *Las ideas sociales contemporáneas en México,* p. 119.

16. To these precursors—Wistano Luis Orozco, Molina Enríquez, the brothers Flores Magón, and others—we cannot give attention here; the reader may, however, find sufficient information in the study by Lombardo Toledano, *op. cit.;* in the book by Victor Alba; in the books of Silva Herzog: *Un ensayo sobre la Revolución Mexicana* (An Essay on the Mexican Revolution), Mexico, 1946; *El mexicano y su morada* (The Mexican and His Abode), Mexico, 1960; and in the first volume of *Breve historia de la Revolución Mexicana* (Short History of the Mexican Revolution), Fondo de Cultura Económica, Mexico, 1960; in the volume of Luis Cabrera, *Viente años después* (Twenty Years After), Botas, Mexico, 1938; in the book by M. González Ramírez, *La revolución social de Mexico. Las ideas. La violencia* (The Social Revolution in Mexico. The Ideas. The Violence), Fondo de Cultura Económica, Mexico, 1960; in the essay of J. Hernández Luna, "Los precursores intelectuales de la Revolución Mexicana" **(The Intellectual Precursors of the Mexican Revolution)** in *Filosofía y Letras,* edited by the University of Mexico, no. 57–59 (1955), pp. 270–317; and in Moisés González Navarro, "La ideología de la Revolución Mexicana" (The Ideology of the Mexican Revolution) in *Historia Mexicana,* vol. X, no. 4, pp. 628–636.

17. Lombardo Toledano, *op. cit.,* and, later, Alfonso Reyes in *Pasado inmediato y otros ensayos,* p. 8, call these facts concomitants of the revolutionary movement. Emilio Uranga, *op. cit.,* vol. IV, pp. 543–544, speaks of "essential correspondence" and of "coetaneous phenomena." The decisive point is to eliminate any expression which might, even metaphorically, suggest a relation of causality.

18. Henríquez Ureña was to say in an essay of 1924 (*Obra crítica,* p. 613): The activities of our group were not bound (save for the participation of one or another of its members) to those of political groups; it had not entered our plans to assault the policy-making positions in public educa-

tion, for which we did not feel that we had reached sufficient maturity; we had given thought, up to that time, only to the renewal of ideas. . . .

It is fitting to recall that Antonio Caso belonged to the "Club Reeleccionista" of Mexico City and had sometimes acted as a speaker in the National Convention of April 1909; in addition, he was director of the organ of the above-mentioned club, *La Reelección, Semanario Político*. Alfonso Reyes, for filial reasons, adhered to the cause of his father, General Bernardo Reyes. Vasconcelos, on the other hand, was secretary of the "Centro Antirreeleccionista de México," from the beginning of its activities in May 1909, and director of *El Antirreeleccionista*, the periodical organ of Madero's party.

19. José Vasconcelos, "La juventud intelectual mexicana y el actual momento histórico de nuestro país," a toast at the banquet given in his honor by the Ateneo de la Juventud, June 17, 1911. Published in the *Revista de Revistas*, June 25, 1911; not included in the edition of the *Obras completas* which we have cited, but to be found in the volume of Hernández Luna, *Conferencias del Ateneo de la Juventud*, pp. 134–137. On page 138 Vasconcelos adds: "And it should be well understood that we do not pretend to maintain intact the educational regimen in which we were formed, but that we advocate reforms so well tested that they will prove durable, so that there may be progress along the path we have begun to follow, instead of departing from it. . . ."

20. Vasconcelos, in Luna, *Conferencias del Ateneo de la Juventud*, p. 138.

21. See Alfonso Reyes, *op. cit.*, p. 7.

22. E. García Máynez, "Elogio de Vasconcelos" (Eulogy of Vasconcelos) in *Memoria del Colegio Nacional*, vol. IV, no. 3, Mexico, 1960, p. 115.

23. Herminio Ahumada, *José Vasconcelos*, Ediciones Botas, Mexico, 1937.

24. A. Castro Leal has traced the response of the succeeding generations of intellectuals, beginning with his own, in the prologue of his *Páginas escogidas de Vasconcelos* (Selected Pages from Vasconcelos), Ediciones Botas, Mexico, 1940, pp. 31–33.

25. The publishing house México Joven completed its printing in June 1929 in the Talleres de la Editorial Cultura.

26. José Vasconcelos, "Tratado de metafísica" in *Obras completas* (Complete Works), vol. III, p. 394.

27. *Ibid.*, p. 620.

28. *Ibid.*, pp. 627–628.

29. If we omit the periodical articles which never were collected into volumes, what Vasconcelos published before 1929 was considerable; it did not seem, however, to have a very extensive diffusion.

"Teoría dinámica del derecho" (Dynamic Theory of Law) (1907); his law thesis, which has been printed in the *Revisita Positiva* by Don Agustín Aragón.

The lecture on "Gabino Barreda y las ideas contemporáneas" (Gabino Barreda and Contemporary Ideas) (1910) included in the volume *Conferencias del Ateneo de la Juventud*.

Four philosophical essays, important as foreshadowings of his thought: "Pitágoras, una teoría del ritmo" (Pythagoras, a Theory of Rhythm) (1916), first published in Cuba and again, four years later, in Mexico; "El monismo estético" (Esthetic monism) (1917); "Estudios indostánicos" (Hindustani Studies) (1920); "La revulsión de la energía" (The Transformation of Energy) (1924); a literary text, "Prometeo vencedor" (Prometheus Victorious) (1920); five essays which were not reprinted later in the *Obras completas* (Complete Works): "La caída de Carranza" (The Fall of Carranza) (1920); "Divagaciones literaries" (Literary Meanderings) (1922); "Los últimos 50 años" (The Last 50 Years) (1924); "Ideario de acción" (Ideology of Action) (1924); "Teoría de los cinco estados" (Theory of the Five Estates) (1924).

La raza cósmica (The Cosmic Race) (1925) and *Indología* (Indology) (1927), two works of real importance for their content, both printed in Spain.

30. *La raza cósmica* (The Cosmic Race) in *Obras completas* (Complete Works), vol. II, pp. 905–906.

31. *Ibid.*, p. 919.

32. *Ibid.*, p. 942.

33. *Indología* (Indology) in *Obras completas* (Complete Works), vol. II, p. 1128.

34. Nationalist attitudes are rejected as exaggerated regionalisms in *La raza cósmica* in *Obras completas* (Complete Works), vol. II, p. 912, and in *Indología* in *Obras completas* (Complete Works), vol. II, p. 1191.

35. The author, on the other hand, is aware of the fragileness of his theses and recognizes that he uses them as weapons of combat; see *Indología* in *Obras completas* (Complete Works), vol. II, p. 1085.

36. *La raza cósmica* in *Obras completas* (Complete Works), vol. II, pp. 928–930; the law is expounded again in *Indología* in *Obras completas* (Complete Works), vol. II, p. 1284; however, there is further announced in the following pages a sublaw of five stages: the stage of the soldier, of the lawyer, of the economist, of the engineer, and of the philosopher.

37. *Ibid.*, pp. 935–936.

38. *Indología* in *Obras completas* (Complete Works), vol. II, pp. 1205, 1206, and 1228. This is the point at which Vasconcelos' ideas on history and his social prophecies enter into contact with his metaphysical system.

39. *Ibid.*, pp. 1272 and 1301. We must not forget that 1917–1925 are the dates which "mark the golden period of Marxism in Mexico" according to H. Bernstein, "El marxismo en México 1917–1925" (Marxism in Mexico: 1917–1925) in *Historia Mexicana*, vol. VII, no. 4, April–June 1958. On the other hand, Vasconcelos himself, some years later, has given this deliberately anti-Marxian interpretation of his theory of race in the article "Consciencia de raza" (Consciousness of Race) reprinted in *¿Qué es la Revolución?* (What Is the Revolution?), Ediciones Botas, Mexico, 1937; not included in the *Obras completas* (Complete Works).

40. The most detailed and direct information about this undertaking is to be found in the writings of Vasconcelos; the most objective, perhaps, in

the small book of Samuel Ramos, *Veinte años de educación en México* (Twenty Years of Education in Mexico), Imprenta Universitaria, Mexico, 1941.

41. The allegory of the Maecenas which is told relative to "Mexican Painting" and which alludes to these years of work in the Ministry of Education expounds the divine mission of the philosopher-coordinators to give complete expression to the epochs, the races, and the world: see *Pesimismo alegre* (Happy Pessimism) in *Obras completas* (Complete Works), vol. I, pp. 222–226.

42. During those years the following men were active in the field of education: Moisés Sáenz, Ezequiel A. Chávez, Manuel Gamio, and Rafael Ramírez; Antonio Caso occupied the rectorship of the university.

43. Vasconcelos brought together in a book various documents, letters, and addresses dating from these years in the Ministry of Education. They may be seen in Volume II of the *Obras completas* (Complete Works), pp. 771 ff.

44. The leading groups of "Vasconcelosism" were made up of young intellectuals and, above all, students who had followed, since preparatory school or from the university, the work of the Minister of Education. However, these were also joined by groups of dissatisfied soldiers, who gave support to the candidacy of General Villarreal. To these must be added the "Christ-defenders" who maintained numerous groups under arms in various states of the Republic; old followers of Madero who had fought in the "Partida Antirreeleccionista"; anarchists of the period of "Flores Magón"; and owners of estates, followers of Porfirio Díaz dispossesed by the Revolution who lent aid in the hope of recouping their loss. President Portes Gil conducted himself adroitly; the partisans of Villarreal rebelled, and the government crushed the rebellion; the attitude of the "Christ-defenders" was neutralized by an understanding with the Church; concession of autonomy to the university helped to calm the students.

45. Vasconcelos has recounted his political campaign in *El proconsolado* in *Obras completas* (Complete Works), vol. II. Mauricio Magdaleno, one of his young partisans, has written a chronicle of unusual interest, *Las palabras perdidas* (The Lost Words), Fonda de Cultura Económica, Mexico, 1956. Portes Gil has presented the government's point of view in *Quince años de política mexicana* (Fifteen Years of Mexican Politics), Botas, Mexico, pp. 171 ff.

46. Examples of these literary efforts are to be found in *Pesimismo alegre* (Happy Pessimism) (1931), reprinted in *Obras completas* (Complete Works), vol. I; *Cuentos* (Tales) (1933); *Bolivarismo y monroísmo* (Bolivarism and Monroeism) (1934); *Notas de viaje* (Travel Notes), *Los robachicos* (The Robbers) (1946); reprinted in *Obras completas* (Complete Works), vol. II; *La mancornadora* (The Mancornadora) (1936) and *¿Qué es la Revolución?* (What Is the Revolution?) (1937), not reprinted in the *Obras completas* (Complete Works). On this aspect of Vasconcelos' work may be consulted, in addition to the essay of Catro Leal cited above, that of José Luis Martínez, "La obra literaria de José Vasconcelos" in

Filosofía y Letras, no. 26, April–June 1947, Universidad Nacional Autónoma de México.

47. *¿Qués es la Revolución?* (What Is the Revolution?), p. 154.

48. The following works may be considered biographical: *Simón Bolívar* (*interpretación*), (Simón Bolívar: An Interpretation) (1939) in *Obras completas* (Complete Works), vol. II; *Hernán Cortés, creador de la nacionalidad* (Hernán Cortés, Creator of Nationality), Ediciones Xóchitl, Mexico, 1941; and *Don Evaristo Madero* (1958). These last two works are not included in the edition cited or the *Obras completas* (Complete Works). The following fill out the work on the Hispano-American theme: *Bolivarismo y monroísmo* (1934) in *Obras completas* (Complete Works), vol. II; *La idea franciscana de la conquista de América* (The Franciscan Idea of the Conquest of America) (1943), not reprinted in the *Obras completas* (Complete Works). The following may be considered autobiographical: *Ulises criollo* (The Creole Ulysses) (1935); *La tormenta* (Torment) (1936); *El desastre* (Disaster) (1937); *El proconsulado* (The Proconsulate) (1939), all included in the edition of the *Obras completas* (Complete Works) cited. Further, *La flama. Las de arriba en la revolución* (The Flame. Those Who Are at the Head of the Revolution) (1959), not included in the *Obras completas* (Complete Works). The following may be considered as belonging to the history of Philosophy: *Historia del pensamiento filosófico* (The History of Philosophical Thought) (1937) and the *Manual de filosofía* (Manual of Philosophy) (1940), both to be found in vol. IV of the *Obras completas* (Complete Works). On this aspect of Vasconcelos' work one should consult José Bravo Ugarte, "Historia y odisea vasconceliana" (The History and Odyssey of Vasconcelos) in *Historia Mexicana,* vol. X, no. 4, April–June 1961.

49. Vasconcelos, *De Robinson a Odisea* (From Robinson to Odysseus) in *Obras completas* (Complete Works), vol. II, p. 1714.

50. "*The* book about Vasconcelos has not yet been published," García Máynez lamented in 1960, and his statement remains valid even today, even though there do exist some acute studies of great interest, for the most part, short. García Máynez himself has contributed *Elogio de Vasconcelos* (Eulogy of Vasconcelos) already cited; Castro Leal the introduction to *Páginas escogidas,* also cited; Oswaldo Robles has written "José Vasconcelos, el filósofo de la emoción creadora" (José Vasconcelos, The Philosopher of Creative Emotion) in *Filosofía y Letras,* April–June 1947; Fernández Mac-Gregor the introduction to *Vasconcelos,* a publication of the Secretaría de Educación, Mexico, 1942; José Sánchez Villaseñor, *El sistema filosófico de José Vasconcelos* (The Philosophical System of José Vasconcelos), Editorial Polis, Mexico, 1939; two articles by José Gaos reprinted in the following volumes respectively: *Pensamiento de lengua española* (Thought in the Spanish Language), Editorial Stylo, Mexico, 1945; and *Filosofía mexicana de nuestras días* (Mexican Thought in Our Day), Imprenta Universitaria, Mexico, 1954. Basave Fernández del Valle, *la filosofía de José Vasconcelos,* Ediciones Cultura Hispánica, Madrid, 1958; the chapter dedicated to Vasconcelos by Patrick Romanell in his book *La formación de la mentalidad*

mexicana (The Making of the Mexican Mind), El Colegio de México, Mexico, 1954; and the chapter by Abelardo Villegas in his book, *La filosofía de le mexicano* (The Philosophy of the Mexican), Fonda de Cultura Económica, Mexico, 1960.

51. Vasconcelos, *Todología* in *Obras completas* (Complete Works), vol. IV, p. 818.

52. *Ibid.*, pp. 833–836.

53. *Ibid.*, p. 857.

54. *Ibid.*, p. 864. The modes of esthetic knowledge are, in addition, forms of enjoyment and achieve their highest expression in the liturgy. The latter is the form in which beings (things) begin to partake of the divine.

55. *Ibid.*, pp. 879–880 and 885.

56. *Ibid.*, p. 868. In that science of destiny which is ethics neither abstract postulates nor repeated observations carry weight; the point of reference is the end to be reached, the great end which becomes the norm. Religion is the philosophy of the ethical. As a consequence, ethics derives its norms from the type of faith its accepts.

57. All these distinctions are made by taking as a base the chapter which is entitled "El ser en sí" (Being in Itself), which suppresses entire sections of chapters of the first and only earlier edition prior to the one we have cited; (compare the edition of Botas, Mexico, 1952). As an example of those ontological distinctions, we may cite the classification of "seres fugaces" (ephemeral beings) and "seres perennes' (enduring beings) which is retained in both editions and which places, on the one hand, the anelids, organisms which, because they do not reproduce themselves sexually do not die as individuals, alongside the angels, spiritual and also asexual persons and, on the other hand, the ephemeral being which has its origin in sexual combination and according to physical atomic laws. *Ibid.*, pp. 917–918.

58. Compare the chapter "Filosofía y teología" (Philosophy and Theology), p. 836, with the chapter "El ser y sus categoríes" (Being and Its Categories), p. 919, in *Obras completas*, vol. IV.

59. *Ibid.*, p. 843.

60. Vasconcelos, *De Robinson a Odiseo* in *Obras completas* (Complete Works), vol. II, p. 1587.

61. See Vasconcelos, "El problema del poder" in *Memoria de el Colegio Nacional de 1951*, vol. VI, no. 16, p. 37; and "La clase media" (The Middle Class) in *Memoria de 1954*, vol. III, no. 9, p. 27.

62. Alfonso Reyes, "En memoria de Antonio Caso" (In Memory of Antonio Caso) in *Cuadernos Americanos*, May–June 1946, p. 121.

63. See note 18 above.

64. Caso was first sectional officer of the Secretariat of Public Instruction; secretary-general of the National University; legal counsel to the Postmaster's Office; secretary of the Ayuntamiento of Mexico City; director of the National School of Advanced Studies; director of the National Preparatory School; president of the University Delegation to the celebration in Spain of the discovery of America; Extraordinary Ambassador of Mexico in 1921; Rector of the National University of Mexico.

65. Mexico's international situation was difficult in 1921. Neither the
United States nor the European powers had recognized the Obregón government but had tried, rather, by pressures and solicitation to secure a
commercial treaty to protect their financial interests which would guarantee
their works in Mexico on the same conditions which obtained prior to 1910.
A detailed account of Caso's voyage, its purpose and results, may be found
in the book by Juan Hernández Luna, *Antonio Caso, embajador extraordinario de México* (Antonio Caso, Extraordinary Ambassador of Mexico),
SALM, Mexico, 1963.

66. Consult the book by Rosa Krauze de Kolteniuk, *La filosofía de
Antonio Caso* (The Philosophy of Antonio Caso), Universidad Nacional
Autónoma de México, Mexico, 1961. See also J. Hernández Luna, "Las
polémicas filosóficas de Caso" (The Philosophical Polemics of Caso) in
Homenaje a Antonio Caso (In Homage to Antonio Caso), Editorial Stylo,
Mexico, 1947.

67. The volumes of articles, alluded to before, remain outside of this
classification: *Ensayos críticos y polémicos* (Critical and Polemical Essays)
(1922); *Doctrinas y ideas* (Doctrines and Ideas) (1924); and *Discursos
heterogéneos* (Heterogeneous Essays) (1925). Further, two polemical writings: *Ramos y yo* (Ramos and I) (1927) and a book in collaboration with
Guillermo Héctor Rodríguez, *Ensayos polémicos sobre la escuela filosófica
de Marburgo* (Polemical Essays on the Philosophical School of Marburg)
(1945). In addition, two books of poems: *Crisopeya* (1941) and *El
políptico de los días del mar* (1935).

68. José Gaos, for example, in a lecture in 1946 indicated five periods;
in an essay written the following year he lays stress on only three: that
of a beginning and two later periods, the line of division being the year
1933, when Caso, revising one of his books, for the first time utilized the
currents of contemporary German philosophy. The two essays of Gaos are
to be found in *Filosofía mexicana de nuestras días* (Mexican Philosophy in
Our Times), cited above, pp. 92 and 97. Rosa Krauze (*op. cit.*, p. 57)
makes reference to only two periods, citing the same dividing date as Gaos.
Patrick Romanell distinguished three stages: anti-intellectualism, pragmatism, and dualism. See Romanell, *La formación de la mentalidad mexicana*
(The Making of the Mexican Mind), p. 83.

69. Caso's words are to be found in *Problemas filosóficas* (Philosophical
Problems), Editorial Porrúa, Mexico, 1915, p. 225; Ramos has recalled
them in "La filosofía de Antonio Caso" (The Philosophy of Antonio Caso)
in *Caudernos Americanos*, May–June 1946, p. 131.

70. Caso, *La existencia como economía, como desinterés y como caridad*
(Existence as Economy, as Disinterestedness, and as Charity), Secretaría de
Educación, Mexico, 1943, p. 13.

71. See Gaos, "El sistema de Caso" (The System of Caso) in *Filosofía
mexicana de nuestras días* (Mexican Philosophy in Our Times), p. 105.

72. In 1924 Caso published a small volume which he himself dated
December 1923, entitled *El problema de México y la ideología nacional*

(The Problem of Mexico and the National Ideology). We cite the second edition published by Libro-Mexicano, Mexico, 1955, p. 66. In 1943 Caso reproduced the greater part of the chapters of this book, adding a few others, in a new volume entitled *Mexico: apuntamientos de cultura patria* (Mexico: Notes on the National Culture), Imprenta Universitaria, Mexico.

73. Caso, *El problema de México y la ideología nacional* (The Problem of Mexico and the National Ideology), p. 66 of the edition cited.

74. Caso, *La persona humana y el estado totalitario* (The Human Person and the Totalitarian State), Universidad Nacional, Mexico, 1941, pp. 187–190.

75. *Ibid.*, pp. 100 and 189.

76. Caso, *El peligro del hombre* (Man's Peril), Editorial Stylo, Mexico, 1942, pp. 53–55. The book is actually the second part of *La persona humana y el estado totalitario*.

77. Caso, *La persona humana y el estado totalitario*, p. 59.

78. *Ibid.*, p. 192.

79. *Ibid.*, p. 141.

80. *Ibid.*, p. 142.

81. J. Hernández Luna in his book *Antonio Caso, embajador extraordinario de México* (Antonio Caso, Ambassador Extraordinary of Mexico) quotes various interviews in the newspapers of Montevideo and Buenos Aires in which Caso presents the contemporary history of Mexico as a step from "existence as economy" (Porfirism) to "existence as distinterestedness" (Maderoism) and, finally, to "existence as charity" (the social revolution in Mexico).

82. A forerunner of this study is the essay "Catolicismo, Jacobinismo y Positivismo" (Catholicism, Jacobinism, and Positivism) reprinted in *Discursos a la nación mexicana* (Addresses to the Mexican Nation), Librería Porrúa, Mexico, 1922.

83. Caso, *El problema de México y la ideología nacional*, pp. 80 and 82 of the edition cited.

84. Caso, "La patria mexicana y la raza hispanoamericana" (The Mexican Nation and the Hispano-American Race) in *Excelsior*, April 19, 1924; cited by L. Zea, "Caso y la mexicanidad" (Caso and Mexicanism) in *Homenaje a Antonio Caso* (In Honor of Antonio Caso), Centro de Estudios filosóficos, Editorial Stylo, Mexico, 1947.

85. "Catholicism is the past," Caso wrote in *Excelsior* for August 30, 1924; "socialism is perhaps the future, Mexico is the present. May she never fail to be so!" But later he added the following on the mission of the Mexican Revolution: "to destroy the 'caciques' (cliques) in the first place and to oppose to them the psychological and moral reality of the Mexican race, as an emblem of victory in the crusade of the times, where fatal blows are aimed at both mysticisms." Quoted by J. Hernández Luna, *Antonio Caso, embajador extraordinario de México*, p. 81.

86. Caso, *El problema de México y la ideología nacional*, p. 29. The two books referring to Marxism are *Nuevos discursos a la nación mexicana* (New

Addresses to the Mexican Nation), Librería Robredo, Mexico, 1934; and *La filosofía de la cultura y el materialismo histórico* (The Philosophy of Culture and Historical Materialism), Ediciones Alba, Mexico, 1936.

87. Ramos, "Discurso" on assuming membership in the Colegio Nacional, in *Memoria de el Colegio Nacional,* vol. VII, no. 7, 1952, p. 229.

88. *Ibid.*

89. In the Secretariat of Education Ramos was head of the University Extension, senior officer and head of Intellectual Cooperation. In the University of Mexico, Ramos taught at the National Preparatory School and in the Faculty of Philosophy and Letters. Later he was director of his faculty and coordinator of humanities. From 1952 he was a member of the National College. Further information may be found in the book by Juan Hernández Luna, *Samuel Ramos: su filosofar sobre lo mexicano* (Samuel Ramos: His philosophical Reflections on the Mexican), UNAM, Mexico, 1956.

90. Ramos, *Hipótesis,* Ediciones Ulises, Mexico, 1928. In the essay entitled "El irracionalismo" (Irrationalism) Ramos relates his "return to reason" and discovers the hidden springs of a doctrine which "offers itself as a constructive and renovating method, while it conceals in its hidden depths a destructive and regressive passion" (p. 112). In the essay "Mi experiencia pragmatista" (My Experience with Pragmatism) he explains his "escape from pragmatism," his first enthusiasm for, and later alienation from, Antonio Caso (pages 115 ff.).

91. The group—one of the most distinguished in our literary history— was really homogeneous and was composed for the most part of artists and writers dedicated to literary creation. However, they also wrote philosophical and social essays. They include Jaime Torres Bodet, Jorge Cuesta, and, of course, those who later dedicated themselves to philosophy: José Romano Muñoz, Adolfo Menéndez Samará, and Samuel Ramos.

92. The essay appeared in the review *Ulises* and later in the volume *Hipótesis,* cited above, pp. 87–99. Antonio Caso replied in a pamphlet entitled *Ramos y yo (un ensayo de valoración personal)* (Ramos and I: An Essay in Personal Valuation), Editorial Cultura, Mexico, 1927.

93. Ramos, *Historia de la filosofía en México* (History of Philosophy in Mexico), Imprenta Universitaria, 1943, p. 149.

94. Ramos, *El perfil del hombre y la cultura en México,* third edition, Espasa-Calpe, Buenos Aires, 1951, pp. 51–53.

95. *Ibid.,* p. 15.

96. These essays were brought together in a volume *Veinte años de educación en México* (Twenty Years of Education in Mexico), Imprenta Universitaria, Mexico, 1941. The argument here noted is found on pp. 10–11.

97. *Ibid.,* pp. 80–81. We read: "The true educative reform, that which reaches to the very foundation of the problem of national culture, has yet to be accomplished. It would be that reform which, taking its point of departure in a profound knowledge of the Mexican spirit, will undertake to correct its vices and cultivate its virtues, aspiring to the creation of a human

type superior to that existing; the system of education which is sought is that which would seek to render to the Mexican race its highest fruits. Such an education could not be entirely spiritual, however, even less could it be entirely material. It could not be orientated solely toward the meaning of technic, or toward the culture of the mind. Much rather would it be directed toward forming *men* in the integral sense of the word. The moment has arrived to rise above all partial points of view and to fuse them into a totalizing synthesis."

98. Ramos, *Hacia un nuevo humanismo: Programa de una antropología filosófica* (Toward a New Humanism: Program for a Philosophical Anthropology), Casa de la España in Mexico, 1940. The relation of this book with *Veinte años de educación en México* (Twenty Years of Education in Mexico) and *El perfil del hombre y la cultura en México* (The Profile of Man and Culture in Mexico) is sufficiently clear. Further, Ramos has expressly pointed out this relationship in the preface to the third edition of this latter book (p. 17 of the edition cited). The relation to *Historia de la filosofía en México* (History of Philosophy in Mexico) (1943) leaps to view. Before 1934 Ramos had published *El caso Strawinsky* (The Strawinsky Case) (1929); in 1935 he published a study on *Diego Rivera*, and in 1938 *Más allá de la moral de Kant* (Beyond the Moral Doctrine of Kant). After his publications about 1940 there appeared only one book of his, *Filosofía de la vida artística* (Philosophy of the Artistic Life), Espasa-Calpe, Buenos Aires, 1950, in which he collects the lectures on esthetics given his university courses, reflecting a very broad experience as a reader and a spectator on artistic questions. However, he always returned to his preferred themes: in various articles he concerned himself with the culture and the man of Mexico, and at his death he was planning a new version of his *Historia de la filosofía en México* and up updated edition of his *Hacia un nuevo humanismo*.

99. *Hacia un nuevo humanismo* (Toward a New Humanism), pp. 150–153.

100. *Ibid.*, p. 147.

101. *Ibid.*, p. 32.

102. *Historia de la filosofía en México* (History of Philosophy in Mexico), p. 153.

BIBLIOGRAPHY

CHAPTER I

Caso, Alfonso, *El pueblo del sol,* Fondo de Cultura Económica, Mexico, 1953; second edition, 1962.

Durán, Fray Diego, *Historia de las Indias de Nueva España y islas de tierra firme,* 2 vols., Mexico, 1867–1880.

Fernández, Justino, *Coatlicue, estética del arte indígena antiguo,* Mexico, 1954; second edition, 1959.

————, *Arte mexicano, de sus orígenes a nuestros días,* Editorial Porrúa, Mexico, 1958; second edition, 1961.

García Icazbalceta, Joaquín, *Nueva colección de documentos para la historia de México,* 5 vols., Mexico, 1886–1892.

Garibay K. Angel Ma., *Poesía indígena de la altiplanicie,* Biblioteca del Estudiante Universitario, no. 11, Mexico, 1940; third edition, 1962.

————, *Épica náhuatl,* Biblioteca del Estudiante Universitario, no. 51, Mexico, 1945.

————, *Historia de la literatura náhuatl,* 2 vols., Editorial Porrúa, Mexico, 1953–1954.

Ixtlilxóchitl, Fernando de Alva, *Obras históricas,* 2 vols., *Mexico,* 1891–1892.

León-Portilla, Miguel, *La filosofía náhuatl, estudiada en sus fuentes,* second edition, Universidad Nacional Autónoma de México, 1959.

————, *Tres formas de pensamiento náhuatl,* Seminario de Problemas Científicos y Filosóficos, Universidad Nacional Autónoma de México, 1959.

Motolinia, Fray Toribio de Benavente, *Memoriales,* Paris, 1903.

Orozco y Berra, Manuel, *Historia antigua y de la conquista de México,* 4 vols., Mexico, 1880. Second edition prepared by **Angel Ma. Garibay K.,** Editorial Porrúa, Mexico, 1960.

Paso y Troncoso, Francisco del, *Leyenda de los soles,* Florence, 1903.

Sahagún, Fray Bernardino de, *Historia general de las cosas de Nueva España,* edition prepared by Ángel Ma. Garibay K., 4 vols., Editorial Porrúa, Mexico, 1956.

Van Zantwijk, Rudolf, A. M., "Aztec Hymns as the Expression of the Mexican Philosophy of Life," in *Internationales Archiv für Etnographie,* vol. XLVIII, no. 1, pp. 67–118, Leiden, 1957.

CHAPTER IV

Clavijero, Francisco Javier, *Historia antigua de México,* vol. I, Colección de Escritores Mexicanos, Editorial Porrúa, S. A., Mexica, 1945.

Díaz de Gamarra, Juan Benito, *Tratados,* Biblioteca del Estudiante Universitario, Ediciones de la Universidad Nacional Autónoma de México, Mexico, 1947.

Gaos, José, *Un sueño de un sueño* in *Historia mexicana,* vol. X, El Colegio de México, Mexico, 1960.

González Casanova, Pablo, *El misoneísmo y la modernidad cristiana en el siglo XVIII,* El Colegio de México, 1948.

Humanistas del siglo XVIII, Biblioteca del Estudiante Universitario, Universidad Nacional Autónoma de México, Mexico, 1962.

López Cámara, Francisco, "El cartesianismo en Sor Juana y Sigüenza y Góngora," in *Filosofía y Letras,* no. 39, Universidad Nacional Autónoma de México, Imprenta Universitaria, Mexico, 1950.

Maneiro, J. L. and Fabri, M., *Vidas de mexicanos ilustres del siglo XVIII,* Biblioteca del Estudiante Universitario, Universidad Nacional Autónoma de México, Mexico, 1956.

Miranda, José, "Clavijero en la ilustración mexicana" in *Cuadernos Americanos,* vol. XXVIII, Fondo de Cultura Económica, Mexico, 1946.

Humboldt y México, Instituto de Historia, Universidad Nacional Autónoma de México, Mexico, 1962.

Navarro, Bernabé, *La introducción de la filosofía moderna en México,* El Colegio de México, Mexico, 1948.

O'Gorman, Edmundo, "La filosofía en la Nueva España" in *Boletín del Archivo General de la Nación,* vol. XIII, no. 3.

Pérez Marchand, Monelisa Lina, *Dos etapas ideológicas del siglo XVIII a través de los papeles de la Inquisición,* El Colegio de México, Mexico, 1945.

Posada Mejía, Germán, *Nuestra América, notas de historia cultural,* Publicaciones del Instituto Caro y Cuervo, Bogotá, 1959.

Ramos, Samuel, *Historia de la filosofía en México,* Universidad Nacional Autónoma de México, Mexico, 1943.

Sigüenza y Góngora, Carlos de, *Libra astronómica filosófica,* Nueva Biblioteca Mexicana, Universidad Nacional Autónoma de México, Mexico, 1959.

Sor Juana Inés de la Cruz, *Primero sueño,* in *Obras completas,* vol. I, Fondo de Cultura Económica, Mexico, 1951.

————, *Respuesta de la poetisa a la muy ilustre Sor Filotea de la Cruz,* in *Obras completas,* vol. IV, Fondo de Cultura Económica, Mexico, 1957.

CHAPTER V
Documents

Documentos de la Independencia, Museo Nacional de Arquelogía y Etnografía, SEP, Mexico, 1928.

Morelos, documentos inéditos y poco conocidos, Museo Nacional de Arquelogía y Etnografía, SEP, 1927.

Cuevas, Mariano, *El Libertador, documentos selectos de don Agustín de Iturbide,* Editorial Patria, Mexico, 1947.

García, Genaro, *Documentos históricos mexicanos,* Museo Nacional, Mexico, 1910.

Hernández y Dávalos, J. E., *Colección de documentos para la guerra de Independencia de México, de 1808 a 1821,* Mexico, 1877.

Miguel i Vergés, J. M., *La Independencia mexicana y la prensa insurgente,* El Colegio de México, 1941.

Histories of the Period of Independence

Alamán, Lucas, *Historia de Méjico,* new edition, Editorial Jus, Mexico, 1942.

Bustamante, Carlos Ma., *Cuadro histórico de la Revolución Mexicana,* second edition corrected, J. Marciano Lara, Mexico, 1943.

Guerra, José (pseudonym of Servando Teresa de Mier), *Historia de la revolución de Nueva España, antiguamente Anáhuac,* London, 1813.

Mora, J. M. L., *México y sus revoluciones,* L. de la Rosa, Paris, 1845.

Zárate, Julio, *Méjico a través de los siglos,* vol. III, Mexico, 1910.

Studies on the Thought of the Independence Movement

López Cámara, Francisco, *La génesis de la conciencia liberal en México,* El Colegio de México, 1954.

Miranda, José, *Las ideas e instituciones políticas mexicanas; primera parte: 1521–1820,* Instituto de Derecho Comparado, UNAM, 1952.

Reyes Heroles, Jesús, *El liberalismo mexicano. Los Origens,* vol. I, Facultad de Derecho, UNAM, 1957.

Villoro, Luis, *La revolución de Independencia,* UNAM, 1953.

CHAPTER VI

Barreda, Gabino, *Estudios,* Imprenta Universitaria, Mexico, 1941.

Ramos, Samuel, *Historia de la filosofía en México,* Imprenta Universitaria, Mexico, 1943.

Zea, Leopoldo, *El positivismo en México,* El Colegio de México, Mexico, 1943.

———, *Apogee y decadencia del positivismo en México,* El Colegio de México, Mexico, 1944.

———, *Dos etapas del pensamiento en Hispanoamerica,* El Colegio de México, Mexico, 1949.

———, *The Latin American Mind,* University of Oklahoma Press, Norman, Oklahoma, 1963.

CHAPTER VII
General

Ahumada, Herminio. *José Vasconcelos,* Botas, Mexico, 1937.

Alba, Víctor. *Las ideas sociales contemporáneas en México,* Fondo de Cultura Económica, Mexico, 1960.

Basave Fernández del Valle, Agustín. *La filosofía de José Vasconcelos,* Cultura Hispánica, Madrid, 1958.

Bravo Ugarte, José. "Historia y odisea vasconceliana" in *Historia mexicana,* vol. X, no. 4, April–June, 1961.

Castro Leal, Antonio. "Introduction" to *Páginas escogidas de José Vasconcelos,* Botas, Mexico, 1940.

Fernández Macgregor, Genaro. "Introduction" to *Vasconcelos,* Secretaría de Educación, Mexico, 1942.

Fernández, Justino. "El pensamiento estético de Samuel Ramos" in *Diánoia,* Mexico, 1960.

Gaos, José. *Filosofía mexicana de nuestros días,* Imprenta Universitaria, Mexico, 1954.

———. *Pensamiento de la lengua española,* Stylo, Mexico, 1945.

Guy, Alain. "Samuel Ramos y el humanismo filosófico de México" in *Diánoia,* Mexico, 1960.

González Navarro, Moisés. "La ideología de la Revolución Mexicana" in *Historia mexicana,* vol. X, no. 4.

Henríquez Ureña, Pedro. *Obra crítica,* Fondo de Cultura Económica, Mexico, 1960.

Hernández Luna, Juan. *Antonio Caso, embajador extraordinario de México,* SALM, Mexico, 1963.

———. "Los precursores intelectuales de la Revolución Mexicana," *Filosofía y Letras,* nos. 57–59, UNAM, Mexico, 1955.

———. "La filosofía contemporánea en México," *Filosofía y Letras,* no. 27, UNAM, 1947.

———. *Samuel Ramos, su filosofar sobre lo mexicano,* UNAM, Mexico, 1956.

Krauze de Kolteniuk, Rosa. *La filosofía de Antonio Caso,* UNAM, Mexico, 1961.

Reyes, Alfonso. *Pasado inmediato y otros ensayos,* El Colegio de México, Mexico, 1941.

Romanell, Patrick. *La formación de la mentalidad mexicana. Panorama actual de la filosofía en México,* El Colegio de México, 1954.
————. "Ortega en México: Tributo a Samuel Ramos" in *Diánoia,* 1960.
Sánchez Villaseñor, José. *El sistema filosófico de Vasconcelos,* Polis, Mexico, 1939.
Uranga, Emilio. *El pensamiento filosófico,* "México, 50 años de revolución," Fondo de Cultura Económica, Mexico, 1962.
Villegas, Abelardo. *La filosofía de lo mexicano,* Fondo de Cultura Económica, Mexico, 1960.
Zea, Leopoldo. "Vasconcelos y Ramos en la Filosofía mexicana" in *Diánoia,* 1960.

Homenaje a Caso, Centro de Estudios Filosóficos, Stylo, 1947:
Gaos, José, "Las mocedades de Caso."
García Máynez, Eduardo, "Antonio Caso, pensador y moralista."
Robles, Oswaldo, "Antonio Caso y el heroísmo filosófico."
Patrick, Romanell, "Don Antonio Caso y las ideas contemporáneas en México."
Zea, Leopoldo, "Antonio Caso y la mexicanidad."
Moreno, Rafael, "Caso, su concepto de la filosofía."
Hernández Luna, Juan, "Las polémicas filosóficas de Antonio Caso."
Gaos, José, "La biblioteca de Caso."
Brightam, Sheffield, "Antonio Caso visto desde la Universidad de Boston."
García Bacca, David, "La filosofía de las ciencias según Antonio Caso."
Uranga, Emilio, "Antonio Caso y Emile Meyerson."
Ramos, Samuel, "La estética de Antonio Caso."
Terán, Juan Manuel, "La filosofía de la historia en Antonio Caso."
Recaséns Siches, Luis, "La filosofía social de Antonio Caso."

Conferencias del Ateneo de la Juventud, second edition prepared by Juan Hernández Luna, UNAM, Mexico, 1962.

Works of José Vasconcelos

Obras completas, Libreros Mexicanos Unidos, Mexico, 1957–1961 (4 vols.).
La flama, Editora Continental, fourth edition, Mexico, 1960.
Qué es la Revolución, Botas, Mexico, 1937.
Hernán Cortés, creador de la nacionalidad, Xóchitl, Mexico, 1941.
Qué es el comunismo, Botas, Mexico, 1936.

Works of Antonio Caso

Filósofos y doctrinas morales, Porrúa, Mexico, 1915.
Historia y antología del pensamiento filosófico, Secretaría de Educación Pública y Librería Franco-Americana, Mexico, 1926.
El acto ideatorio y la filosofía de Husserl, Porrúa, Mexico, 1936.

Meyerson y la física moderna, La Casa de España in Mexico, 1939.
Positivismo, neopositivismo y fenomenología, Centro de Estudios Filosóficos, Mexico, 1941.
Filósofos y moralistas franceses, Stylo, Mexico, 1943.
Evocación de Aristóteles, Biblioteca Enciclopédica Popular, Mexico, 1946.
Nuevos discursos a la nación mexicana, Robredo, 1934.
Sociología, Polis, 1939.
La filosofía de la cultura y el materialismo histórico, Alba, Mexico, 1936.
La persona humana y el Estado totalitario, UNAM, Mexico, 1941.
El peligro del hombre, Stylo, Mexico, 1942.
México (*apuntamientos de cultura patria*), Imprenta Universitaria, 1943.
Los problemas filosóficos, Porrúa, Mexico, 1915.
Principios de estética, second edition, Porrúa, Mexico, 1944.
El concepto de la historia universal y la filosofía de los valores, Botas, Mexico, 1933.
La existencia como economía, como desinterés y como caridad, Secretaría de Educación Pública, Mexico, 1943.
Doctrinas e ideas, Botas, Mexico, 1924.
Discursos heterogéneos, Herrero, Mexico, 1925.
Ramos y yo, Cultura, Mexico, 1927.
El problema de México y la ideología nacional, second edition, Libro-Mex, Mexico, 1955.

Works of Samuel Ramos

Hipótesis, Ulises, 1958.
Historia de la filosofía en México, Imprenta Universitaria, Mexico, 1943.
El perfil del hombre y la cultura en México, third edition, Espasa-Calpe, Buenos Aires, 1951.
Veinte años de educación en México, Imprenta Universitaria, Mexico, 1941.
El caso Strawinsky, Contemporáneos, Mexico, 1959.
Diego Rivera, second edition, UNAM, Mexico, 1938.
Más allá de la moral de Kant, Cuadernos de México Nuevo, 1938.
Filosofía de la vida artística, Espasa-Calpe, Buenos Aires, 1950.
Hacia un nuevo humanismo, La Casa de España in Mexico, 1940.

INDEX

DATE DUE

PRINTED IN U.S.A.